Contents

ERRATA LIST - SECOND PRINTING
Mortality Table Construction
by Robert W. Batten

Page 7 Line 12 - $(0 \leq t \leq 1)$ should read $(0 < t \leq 1)$

Page 147 Denominator of next to last fraction - The internal) after the 4700 should be removed.

Page 153 Line 5 - The term F_t^{z+1} should be F_t^{z-1}.

Page 164 Mathematical Expressions - The dividing lines for both fractions were omitted.

Page 238 Answer to Exercise 15 - First term should be $_{1/3}E'_{x-1/3}$.

Page 244 Answer to Exercise 7(b) - $_\delta D_{51}^z$ should be $_\delta D_{50}^z$; Parenthesis should be closed at end of line.

Page 245 Answer to Exercise 10, line 3, last term - $\frac{3}{12} \cdot P_{30}^z$ should be $\frac{3}{12} \cdot P_{30}^{z+1}$.

Page 245 Next to last line - Should read as follows:

$$+ {}_\alpha m_x + \frac{3}{4} \cdot {}_\alpha m_{x+1}$$

Page 246 Answer to Exercise 13a, lines 3 and 4 - Should read as follows:

$${}_\alpha m_x{:}x = CYM - CYB \text{ (Assumed on Nov. 1)}$$

$${}_\delta m_x{:}x = CYM - CYB \text{ (Assumed on May 1)}$$

Page 246 Answer to Exercise 13(b) - $\displaystyle\sum_{z=1976}^{1977}$ should be $\displaystyle\sum_{z=1977}^{1978}$

Page 246 Answer to Exercise 16a - Entire answer should read as follows:

$$E_t\Big]_t^{t+1} = \sum_{z=1976}^{1977} \left[\frac{5}{12} \cdot E_t^z + \frac{5}{12} \cdot P_t^{z+1} + \frac{1}{6} \cdot E_{t+1}^{z+1} + \frac{7}{12} \cdot {}_\alpha D_t^z \right.$$
$$\left. + \frac{1}{6} \cdot {}_\delta D_t^{z+1} \right]$$

Page 246 Answer to Exercise 16b - The dividing line for the fraction $\dfrac{28}{2650\frac{1}{6}}$ was omitted.

APPENDIX

Instructions for Annual Study of Mortality Under Standard Ordinary Issues Experience Between 1975 and 1976 Anniversaries   227

Answers   234

Preface
for the Society
of Actuaries

There can be few subjects in the actuarial syllabus that are equal in importance to the measurement of mortality. All actuarial work associated with the pricing of life insurance and pension products, and with the valuation of life insurance and pension reserves, depends upon a proper analysis of observed mortality data. The subject of exposure formulas can be a difficult one, and it is particularly important that textbooks on this subject be able to make the required concepts clear to the student. Perhaps it is for this reason that the Education and Examination Committee has often used textbooks developed by people who have actually taught this subject to actuarial students.

The current textbook continues this tradition. The author is Professor Robert W. Batten, who teaches various courses in actuarial science at Georgia State University while heading its program of actuarial education. His teaching experience will be a key ingredient in making this textbook a useful one, expecially for students who are studying the material on their own. The Board of Governors and the Education and Examination Committee of the Society of Actuaries are deeply grateful to Professor Batten for the effort he has devoted to this work, which will be a valuable contribution to the education of future generations of actuaries.

ROBERT T. JACKSON
President
Society of Actuaries

J. ALAN LAUER
General Chairman
Education and Examination
Committee

JOHN A. FIBIGER
Chairman
Advisory Committee on
Education and Examinations

Preface

This book is designed to aid the student of actuarial science in comprehending the development and construction of mortality tables, traditionally among the primary tools of the actuary. The principles outlined in this text are applicable to the derivation of many types of decrement tables which are founded upon relatively elementary probability theory. Primary attention, however, is accorded the process of determining rates of death among persons who have met the standards of insurability of a life insurance company and who have subsequently entered into a contract of insurance with that company.

The preponderance of men and women who have aspired to actuarial careers have followed the traditional route of self-study subsequent to completion of academic degree programs in fields such as mathematics, economics, or finance. For this reason, any textbook to be used in such an environment must be self-contained and, as nearly as possible, self-explanatory. It is the belief of the author that a dedicated student will be able to master the subject matter of this text with a thorough reading of each chapter, followed by a careful analysis and detailed solution of each of that chapter's exercises before proceeding further.

The mathematical skills required of an actuary have too often been exaggerated. No amount of formal mathematical education can serve the actuary as well as an understanding and a true enjoyment of basic algebra and calculus combined with a penchant for a logical, reasoned approach to problem solving. In this text, only Chapter One has significant mathematical content; prior knowledge of only the most elementary life contingencies relationships is required of the reader. Few of the exercises require mathematical skills. Instead, heavy emphasis is placed upon exercises which are designed to illustrate the basic principles of each chapter and which test the student's insights rather than the ability to solve problems mechanically with a battery of formulas.

No text should ever be written in the area of mortality measurement without recognizing the contributions of the late Harry Gershenson, felt by many to be the most innovative teacher ever to instruct actuarial students. Although not primarily a teacher, this outstanding actuary will surely be best remembered for his brilliant classroom presentations sponsored by the Actuaries Club of New York. The single most significant contribution by Mr. Gershenson was probably his 1961 textbook *Measurement of Mortality*, which at once revolutionized and simplified what had previously been a somewhat complex and mystifying subject area. A generation of actuarial students has marveled at the utter simplicity of the analogy between a toll road and the age continuum of human life. The author is deeply indebted to Mr. Gershenson not only for his pioneering in the field of mortality measurement but for a demonstration of classroom teaching techniques which could and should serve as a model for a college professor in any discipline.

The author is deeply indebted to many persons at Georgia State University whose advice and encouragement were indispensable. Dr. Kenneth Black, Jr., Dean of the College of Business Administration, and Dr. John W. Hall, Chairman of the Department of Insurance, should be singled out in this regard. Others at the university who carefully reviewed the manuscript and made many valuable suggestions include Dr. Eli A. Zubay and Dr. John E. Brown. In addition, special thanks go to graduate students Marc L. Preminger, A.S.A., and Phillip B. Funk, A.S.A., who painstakingly reviewed the entire text and whose comments resulted in numerous adjustments in the final draft. Perhaps more than to any single person, however, the author is indebted to those students whose inquisitive search for a true understanding of mortality measurement during the past decade led to many of the techniques and explanations which appear in this text.

Special thanks go to the Society of Actuaries, which encouraged the undertaking of this project from its inception. Many individual members of the Society were especially instrumental in the development of the text, notably Joseph R. Lawrence, F.S.A., Edward A. Lew, F.S.A., and members of the Education and Examination Committee. In addition, the Society graciously agreed to the inclusion of a few of their recent examination questions as well as a few selected questions from the Gershenson text. The author is grateful to the Society for its decision to adopt this text as a part of the Course of Reading for its examination series.

Finally, the dedicated and enthusiastic typing and editing efforts of Mrs. Eileen Guynes were instrumental throughout the entire process of producing the manuscript. Of course, no persons who assisted in this effort bear any responsibilities for errors which may remain; these are the sole responsibility of the author.

A textbook which is primarily concerned with death may seem to present depressing, somber prospects to both the writer and the reader. It is the sincere hope of the author that such prospects will be dispelled by students who agree with him that the underlying theory is elegant in its simplicity and therefore is to be enjoyed rather than merely tolerated.

RWB

Mathematical Foundations

INTRODUCTION

The modern actuary is a complex individual working in a complex environment. Actuarial responsibilities vary widely according to type of employment as well as the actuary's educational and experiential background. Yet, those relatively few members of the general public who are conversant with the term *actuary* almost invariably associate it with a person whose occupation involves the calculation of premium rates from a model known as a mortality table. This narrow image attributed to practitioners of actuarial science is widespread, and it seems unlikely to disappear either with the passage of time or with the relentless trend of the actuarial profession toward broader and more varied fields of activity. Yet, an actuary could hardly deny the absolute necessity of mortality tables (and tables measuring other decrements) to most, if not all, actuarial work.

Most elementary textbooks on life insurance mathematics treat the mortality table as if it were handed down by some omniscient seer. It is often presented as fact and then used in a multitude of numerical examples, permitting the student to infer that the table utilized in the textbook illustrations is somehow uniquely capable of providing optimum results. Generally, very little space is accorded the principles underlying the table's construction or its characteristics which distinguish it from other tables which could have served the purposes of the text equally well.

In reality, a major task of the actuary is the selection of the table, from a myriad of existing tables, which is most appropriate for the purpose immediately at hand. A grasp of the concepts of demography as well as of the features and characteristics of these existing tables is indispensable to the reaching of a judicious decision. However, the actuary is often compelled to choose or even construct a table which reflects the recent experience of a particular company or of several companies with similar underwriting philosophies. In such cases, a knowledge of the methods used in the construction of such tables is necessary. Therefore, although much of this text deals with techniques applicable to the construction of tables of a general nature, the reader will find that many of the specifics will deal with the construction of mortality tables from records compiled from life insurance company experience.

Before proceeding further, it is necessary to offer a definition of a term whose usage is basic to all that follows. The use of the word *exposure* in the context of table construction refers to the number of annual units of human life which are subject to death, disability, or some other decrement, within a defined period of observation. In a rather loose manner, this exposure value becomes the denominator of a mortality rate or rate of decrement due to some other cause. The determination of the corresponding numerator is relatively routine, being merely the observed number of deaths or the number of lives which leave a defined group due to the cause being measured.* It is therefore the exposure calculation which encompasses most of the theory to be developed in this text.

The mathematical theory underlying the construction of tables is not at all complex. In fact, it will be presented in its entirety in this introductory chapter. Only an elementary knowledge of life contingencies is required. The student will find that his most powerful tool will be a thorough understanding of the various mortality assumptions and their implications regarding the treatment of exposure.

MORTALITY ASSUMPTIONS

Most mathematical symbols which are unique to actuaries are annualized measures or denotations of risk. For example,

d_x = the number of persons, according to a given mortality table, who are expected to die in a *one-year* interval between ages x and $x + 1$;

q_x = the probability, according to a given mortality table, that a life aged x will not survive to age $x + 1$;

μ_x = the *annualized* force of mortality operative at age x.

However, in the construction of life tables, it is necessary to consider certain probabilities which are not annualized. For example, a life may come under observation in a mortality study at age $32\frac{1}{3}$. The amount of exposure to be attributed to such a life in the unit interval from 32 to 33 is, as we shall see, dependent on our assumption as to the pattern of mortality in an interval of time less than a year. Each of the approximately 100 intervals of

---

* For the sake of convenience, the implication will be made throughout the text that the measurement of *mortality* is the task with which we are concerned. The reader should be cognizant that essentially all of the theory to be developed could be applied to construction of tables measuring decrements other than that of death.

age within the typical mortality table possesses a pattern of mortality, or distribution of deaths, within its unit length. Discovery of this pattern, or, more realistically, reasonably accurate prediction of this pattern for each such interval, is essential if the resulting table is to be a satisfactory representation of the observed experience. Quantities such as $_t q_x$ and $_{1-t} q_{x+t}, 0 \leq t \leq 1$, will play a major role in theory development. Fortunately, we shall discover that various assumptions, each of which is inherently reasonable, will lead to numerical values for probabilities which, though different, will nonetheless be arithmetically quite similar. Therefore, selection of a specific assumption may be based upon considerations of convenience rather than considerations of accuracy.

Uniform Distribution of Deaths

In one of the first attempts to describe algebraically the mortality experience of human lives, Abraham de Moivre proposed, early in the eighteenth century, that the survivorship curve (l_x) of a mortality table could be represented by a single straight line. His hypothesis, that from an arbitrary number of births equal numbers would die each year until the entire cohort had expired, has of course been found unrealistic. Yet, a spin-off from this hypothesis is in wide use today, that is, the assumption that between any two ages which are one unit apart, deaths tend to occur uniformly.

A mathematical statement of the "uniform distribution of deaths" hypothesis is that the function $f(t) = {}_t q_x{}^*$ is linear over the interval $0 \leq t \leq 1$. Under this assumption,

$$_t q_x = a + bt \qquad (0 \leq t \leq 1).$$

Clearly,

$$_1 q_x = a + b = q_x,$$

and

$$_0 q_x = a = 0.$$

Solving,

$$a = 0, \qquad b = q_x,$$

and thus

$$_t q_x = t \cdot q_x \qquad (0 \leq t \leq 1).$$

Thus, rather than considering the entire survivorship curve as a single straight line, the assumption in question merely considers it to be a connected series of straight lines, each with its own slope, generally unique. This simple assumption merely states that the probability of the death of a person aged x within a quarter of a year, for example, is one-fourth as great as the rate which would apply over the full one-year interval. Or, given that n

---

* Although the age represented by x in this and subsequent mortality assumptions is often an integer, there is no requirement that this be so. In many instances, the *unit age interval* will not run from one integer to the next.

deaths occur in a year between two ages which are separated by a single year, this assumption is equivalent to treating their distribution such that one death is allocated to each nth equal part of the year of age.

Easily obtainable from this initial assumption are the following results, each of which the student should verify:

1. $\mu_{x+t} = \dfrac{q_x}{1 - t \cdot q_x}$ $\qquad$ $(0 \le t \le 1)$.

2. $\mu_x = q_x$.

3. $\mu_{x+1} = \dfrac{q_x}{1 - q_x} > q_x$.

4. $l_{x+t} = l_x - t \cdot d_x$ $\qquad$ $(0 \le t \le 1)$.

5. $_{1-s}q_{x+t} = \dfrac{(1 - s)q_x}{1 - t \cdot q_x}$

$\qquad = (1 - s)\mu_{x+t}$ $\qquad$ $(0 \le t \le s \le 1)$.

6. $_t p_x \mu_{x+t} = q_x$ $\qquad$ $(0 \le t \le 1)$.

The student will realize that the last of these results indicates that the negative derivative (with respect to t) of $_t p_x$, $_t p_x \mu_{x+t}$, is constant. Thus it follows directly that $_t p_x$, and hence $_t q_x$, is linear. Therefore,

$$_t p_x \mu_{x+t} = q_x$$

if and only if $_t q_x$ is linear.

Especially notable among these results is the fact that μ_{x+t} is an increasing function of t and, more specifically, is an increasing hyperbola. The increasing nature of this function should not be surprising, as the student is well indoctrinated to the fact that the force of mortality is relentless in its attack on human life. Of course, exceptions to this generalization may be found at certain points on the mortality curve, notably at the very young ages or in the early adult years. Such exceptions should warn us that even the most reasonable of assumptions may in some instances be found defective.

The student should also notice that the overall μ_x function, created by the uniform distribution assumption, is discontinuous. This is seen by noting that

$$\mu_{x+1} = \frac{q_x}{p_x}$$

when the interval from x to $x + 1$ is being considered and that

$$\mu_{x+1} = q_{x+1}$$

when the interval from $x + 1$ to $x + 2$ is being considered. These two expressions are not necessarily equal, as $q_x = p_x \cdot q_{x+1}$ only in a very special case. Not surprisingly, this special case is that of the assumption of uniform deaths throughout the *two-year* interval from x to $x + 2$.

The Balducci Hypothesis

A second pattern of mortality, often used as an estimate of the distribution of deaths over a unit age interval, was suggested by the Italian actuary Gaetano Balducci in 1920. Although the Balducci hypothesis does not lend itself to a simple verbal description, unlike the uniform distribution assumption, it has nonetheless proven to be a quite reasonable indicator of the shape of the survivorship curve in many instances.

Balducci assumed that the function $f(t) = {}_{1-t}q_{x+t}$ is linear over the interval $0 \leq t \leq 1$. Under this assumption,

$$_{1-t}q_{x+t} = a + bt \qquad (0 \leq t \leq 1).$$

Clearly,

$$_1q_x = a = q_x,$$

and

$$_0q_{x+1} = a + b = 0.$$

Solving,

$$a = q_x, \qquad b = -q_x,$$

and thus

$$_{1-t}q_{x+t} = (1 - t)q_x \qquad (0 \leq t \leq 1).$$

The student should verify that each of the following is a direct result of the Balducci hypothesis:

1. $\mu_{x+t} = \dfrac{q_x}{1 - (1 - t)q_x} \qquad (0 \leq t \leq 1).$

2. $\mu_x = \dfrac{q_x}{1 - q_x} > q_x .$

3. $\mu_{x+1} = q_x .$

4. $l_{x+t} = \dfrac{l_x \cdot l_{x+1}}{l_{x+1} + t \cdot d_x} \qquad (0 \leq t \leq 1).$

5. $_{1-s}q_{x+t} = \dfrac{(1 - s)q_x}{1 - (s - t)q_x} \qquad (0 \leq t \leq s \leq 1).$

6. $_tq_x = \dfrac{t \cdot q_x}{1 - (1 - t)q_x}$ $(0 \le t \le 1)$.

7. $_{1-t}p_{x+t}\,\mu_{x+t} = q_x$ $(0 \le t \le 1)$.

The last of these results substantiates that $_{1-t}p_{x+t}$ is linear, because its derivative with respect to t, $_{1-t}p_{x+t}\,\mu_{x+t}$, is found to be the constant q_x under the Balducci hypothesis. Thus,

$$_{1-t}p_{x+t}\,\mu_{x+t} = q_x$$

if and only if $_{1-t}q_{x+t}$ is linear.

Under the Balducci hypothesis, the survivorship function l_{x+t} is represented graphically by the reciprocal of a straight line, i.e., a hyperbola, rather than by the straight line produced under the earlier assumption. Such a result makes the discovery of a simple physical interpretation under Balducci much less likely than under the assumption of uniform deaths.

The student will note that the pattern of the force of mortality under the Balducci hypothesis is opposite to that encountered under the assumption of a uniform distribution of deaths. Under Balducci, the μ_{x+t} curve is a *decreasing* hyperbola over the unit interval $0 \le t \le 1$. This is a somewhat disconcerting result, but the student must be ever-conscious of the fact that its decreasing nature is evident only over single-unit age intervals. Although mathematically easy to show, it should be clear from general observation that the μ_{x+t} curve is discontinuous at end points of the unit intervals. Were the curve to be continuous, a *decreasing* force of mortality over the entire span of life would be the implausible result.

Constant Force of Mortality

A third mortality assumption, which is in a very real sense intermediate to the two already considered, is that of a constant force of mortality over a given unit age interval. The discontinuity of the resulting force of mortality curve is again evident.

Under the assumption

$$\mu_{x+t} = \mu \qquad (0 \le t \le 1),$$

the following results are obtained, each of which the student should verify:

1. $_tq_x = 1 - e^{-\mu t}$ $(0 \le t \le 1)$.

2. $_{1-t}q_{x+t} = 1 - e^{-\mu(1-t)}$ $(0 \le t \le 1)$.

3. $\ln\,_tp_x$ is linear $(0 \le t \le 1)$.

4. $l_{x+t} = l_x \cdot e^{-\mu t}$ $(0 \le t \le 1)$.

A characteristic feature of this assumption is that, within any unit age interval, the probability of survival is a function only of duration. Age is irrelevant with the *caveat* that both the beginning and ending age of the interval defined by the probability under consideration be within the closed unit interval over which the assumption is effective. That is,

$$_{1/4}q_x = {}_{1/4}q_{x+(1/4)} = {}_{1/4}q_{x+(1/3)} = {}_{1/4}q_{x+(1/2)},$$

and so on, but no information is available with respect to $_{1/4}q_{x+(7/8)}$. It is interesting to note that this is the only assumption yet considered under which

$$_{1/2}q_x = {}_{1/2}q_{x+(1/2)},$$

a result which, at most ages, would seem to be well within the realm of reason.

An outgrowth of the above observation is the result

$$p_x = (_tp_x)^{1/t} \qquad (0 \le t \le 1).$$

Thus, for example, if $p_x = .729$, it follows that

$$_{1/3}p_x = .9 = {}_{1/3}p_{x+(1/3)},$$

and

$$_{2/3}p_{x+(1/4)} = .81.$$

Note that $_{2/3}p_{x+t} = .81$ is valid only for $0 \le t \le \frac{1}{3}$.

Other Assumptions

Although accorded very little importance in actuarial literature, an unlimited number of alternatives theoretically exist for describing mortality patterns within the unit age interval. For example, any function of the form

$$f(t) = {}_tq_x \qquad (0 \le t \le 1)$$

is mathematically sound as long as

$$f(0) = 0 \quad \text{and} \quad f(1) = q_x.$$

Or, one might suggest

$$f(t) = {}_{1-t}q_{x+t} \qquad (0 \le t \le 1),$$

where

$$f(0) = q_x \quad \text{and} \quad f(1) = 0.$$

As examples of these two forms, we might have

$$f(t) = {}_tq_x = (\tfrac{1}{3}t + \tfrac{2}{3}t^2)q_x$$

or

$$f(t) = {}_{1-t}q_{x+t} = (1 - t^2)q_x.$$

Such functions are of little practical interest. It is generally conceded that whatever the unknown "true" pattern of mortality from one age to the next, it should be assumed to be relatively simple. Most practitioners have agreed that, in most cases, one of the three specific assumptions considered in this chapter is suitable. The student must remain aware, however, that any one assumption is surely inadequate and must be modified when conditions warrant. Yet, as we shall observe in Chapter Two, a specific one of these assumptions is almost invariably applied in mortality table construction. The justification for the ultimate choice is based upon practical considerations. We should have no clue to its identity at this stage, having considered only the underlying mathematical theory.

COMPARISON OF THE ASSUMPTIONS

A comparison of the assumptions developed in the preceding section will be concerned only with the three primary assumptions. The comparisons will be simplified by the use of the letters A, B, and C to represent uniform distribution of deaths, the Balducci hypothesis, and the assumption of a constant force of mortality, respectively, each being operative over the unit age interval from x to $x + 1$.

Force of Mortality

It has already been made evident that the force of mortality over any unit age interval increases under A, decreases under B, and is constant under C. The resulting patterns are represented in Figure 1-1. It should be observed that the slopes of the curves A and B in Figure 1-1 have been somewhat distorted in order to facilitate illustration of distinctions among the three assumptions. At most ages, the μ_{x+t} curves tend to be much more nearly horizontal than indicated in the figure. A similar observation may be made with respect to Figures 1-2 and 1-3, which appear later in this section.

The "mirror image" nature of the forces of mortality produced by assumptions A and B is verified by the fact that

$$\mu_{x+t}^A = \mu_{x+1-t}^B \qquad (0 \le t \le 1).$$

It is easily seen from this equality that these two curves intersect at $t = \frac{1}{2}$. The fact that μ_{x+t}^C falls above the level of $\mu_{x+(1/2)}^A$ and $\mu_{x+(1/2)}^B$ is not quite so obvious. However, the nature of the concavity of μ_{x+t}^A and μ_{x+t}^B provides a valuable clue. Formal demonstration of this result is left to the student as an exercise.

The comparative magnitude of certain probabilities based upon assumptions A and B is especially easy to determine from Figure 1-1, as illustrated in the following example.

FIGURE 1-1

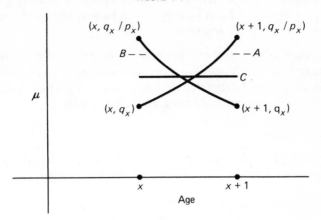

EXAMPLE 1-1   Compare $_{1/4}q^A_{x+(1/3)}$ with $_{1/4}q^B_{x+(1/3)}$.

SOLUTION   From the formulas

$$_{1/4}q^A_{x+(1/3)} = \frac{\frac{1}{4} \cdot q_x}{1 - \frac{1}{3} \cdot q_x} \quad \text{and} \quad _{1/4}q^B_{x+(1/3)} = \frac{\frac{1}{4} \cdot q_x}{1 - \frac{5}{12} \cdot q_x},$$

clearly $_{1/4}q^B_{x+(1/3)}$ is the larger. This is evident not only from a comparison of the denominators of the formulas but also from the fact that the interval in question, $[x + \frac{1}{3}, x + \frac{7}{12}]$, lies predominantly in the left-hand half of the unit age interval. From Figure 1-1, one can see that the left-hand half of the interval is that half over which assumption B produces heavier mortality than assumption A. From a mathematical standpoint, it can also be observed that the area under the μ curve from $x + \frac{1}{3}$ to $x + \frac{7}{12}$ is greater under assumption B than assumption A. Thus,

$$\int_{1/3}^{7/12} \mu^B_{x+t}\, dt > \int_{1/3}^{7/12} \mu^A_{x+t}\, dt,$$

implying that

$$\exp\left(-\int_{1/3}^{7/12} \mu^A_{x+t}\, dt\right) > \exp\left(-\int_{1/3}^{7/12} \mu^B_{x+t}\, dt\right)$$

Finally,

$$_{1/4}p^A_{x+(1/3)} > {}_{1/4}p^B_{x+(1/3)} \Rightarrow {}_{1/4}q^B_{x+(1/3)} > {}_{1/4}q^A_{x+(1/3)}.$$

EXAMPLE 1-2   If $_{5/12}q^A_{x+(1/4)} = {}_{5/12}q^B_{x+k}$, find k.

SOLUTION   By appealing to formulas already derived, to considerations of symmetry and Figure 1-1, or to mathematical derivation, it is easily shown that $k = \frac{1}{3}$. Symmetric considerations provide the ideal approach. In this way the problem can be solved with little effort by observing that the intervals $\left[x + \frac{3}{12}, x + \frac{8}{12}\right]$ and $\left[x + \frac{4}{12}, x + \frac{9}{12}\right]$ are symmetric to each other with respect to $x + \frac{1}{2}$, the center of the interval.

Comparisons of such probabilities under assumptions A and B with those under assumption C are somewhat more tedious mathematically but provide no serious difficulties. Fortunately, assumption C is by far the least popular of the three, and such comparisons are rarely required.

Survivorship Function

The pattern of the function l_{x+t}, $0 \le t \le 1$, for the three assumptions is easily uncovered. Clearly, l^A_{x+t} is linear. As observed earlier,

$$l^B_{x+t} = \frac{l_x \cdot l_{x+1}}{l_{x+1} + t \cdot d_x} \qquad (0 \le t \le 1).$$

It can then be demonstrated that

$$\frac{d}{dt} l^B_{x+t} < 0 \quad \text{and} \quad \frac{d^2}{dt^2} l^B_{x+t} > 0.$$

Thus we see that l^B_{x+t} is a decreasing hyperbola which is concave upward. Since the values of l_x and l_{x+1} are independent of any mortality assumption, l^A_{x+t} and l^B_{x+t} can be compared graphically as in Figure 1-2.

FIGURE 1-2

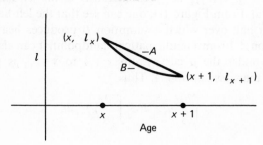

The position which l^C_{x+t} should occupy in Figure 1-2 is seen by first noting the following result from a consideration of Figure 1-1:

$$\int_0^z \mu^A_{x+t}\, dt < \int_0^z \mu^C_{x+t}\, dt < \int_0^z \mu^B_{x+t}\, dt \qquad (0 < z < 1).$$

Therefore,

$$\exp\left(-\int_0^z \mu^B_{x+t}\, dt\right) < \exp\left(-\int_0^z \mu^C_{x+t}\, dt\right) < \exp\left(-\int_0^z \mu^A_{x+t}\, dt\right) \qquad (0 < z < 1).$$

It follows that since

$$_zp_x^B < {}_zp_x^C < {}_zp_x^A \qquad (0 < z < 1),$$

we have the desired result

$$l_{x+z}^B < l_{x+z}^C < l_{x+z}^A \qquad (0 < z < 1).$$

Figure 1-3 illustrates the relative magnitudes of the survivorship function

FIGURE 1-3

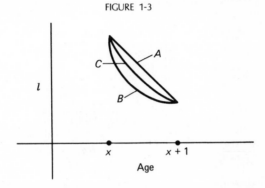

over the unit age interval. Even though it is difficult to determine from mere observation of Figure 1-3, it should be understood that l_{x+t}^B is hyperbolic in nature, whereas l_{x+t}^C is exponential.

EXAMPLE 1-3   Compare the number of anticipated deaths in the first half of a given year of age with those of the second half, using the three major assumptions.

SOLUTION   The result is immediate from a consideration of Figure 1-3. At any interior point of the unit interval, $l_{x+t}^A > l_{x+t}^C > l_{x+t}^B$. The uniform distribution of deaths assumption, by its very definition, anticipates equal numbers of deaths in the two halves of the year. Therefore, the other two assumptions anticipate more deaths in the first half of the year than the second. Further examination of Figure 1-3 suggests that a greater differential is produced by assumption B than by assumption C.

The following comprehensive example should be helpful in the application of the mathematical foundations which have been laid in Chapter One.

EXAMPLE 1-4   If $q_x = .271$, find $_{1/3}q_{x+(1/2)}$ under each of assumptions A, B, and C. Account logically for the relative magnitude of the results.

SOLUTION   Assumption A:

$$_{1/3}q_{x+(1/2)} = \frac{\frac{1}{3} \cdot q_x}{1 - \frac{1}{2} \cdot q_x} = \frac{2 \cdot q_x}{6 - 3 \cdot q_x} = \frac{542}{5187}.$$

FIGURE 1-4

	"A" $_tq_x = t \cdot q_x\,, 0 \le t \le 1$	"B" $_{1-t}q_{x+t} = (1-t)\,q_x\,, 0 \le t \le 1$	"C" $\mu_{x+t} = \mu\,, 0 \le t \le 1$
μ_{x+t}	$\dfrac{q_x}{1 - t \cdot q_x}$	$\dfrac{q_x}{1 - (1-t)\,q_x}$	μ
μ_x	q_x	q_x / p_x	μ
μ_{x+1}	q_x / p_x	q_x	μ
$_tq_x$	$t \cdot q_x$	$\dfrac{t \cdot q_x}{1 - (1-t)\,q_x}$	$1 - e^{-\mu t}$
$_{1-t}q_{x+t}$	$\dfrac{(1-t)\,q_x}{1 - t \cdot q_x}$	$(1-t)\,q_x$	$1 - e^{-\mu(1-t)}$
$_{1-s}q_{x+t}$	$\dfrac{(1-s)\,q_x}{1 - t \cdot q_x}$	$\dfrac{(1-s)\,q_x}{1 - (s-t)\,q_x}$	$1 - e^{-\mu(1-s)}$
l_{x+t}	$l_x - t \cdot d_x$	$\dfrac{l_x \cdot l_{x+1}}{l_{x+1} + t \cdot d_x}$	$l_x \cdot e^{-\mu t}$

Form of μ_{x+t}	Increasing Hyperbola	Decreasing Hyperbola	Constant
Form of l_{x+t}	Linear	Decreasing Hyperbola	Decreasing Exponential

$$l_{x+t}^A > l_{x+t}^C > l_{x+t}^B$$

$$L_x^A > L_x^C > L_x^B$$

$$\mu_{x+t}^A = \mu_{x+1-t}^B$$

$$\int_0^1 \mu_{x+t}^A\, dt = \int_0^1 \mu_{x+t}^B\, dt = \int_0^1 \mu_{x+t}^C\, dt$$

Assumption B:

$$_{1/3}q_{x+(1/2)} = \frac{\frac{1}{3} \cdot q_x}{1 - \frac{1}{6} \cdot q_x} = \frac{2 \cdot q_x}{6 - q_x} = \frac{542}{5729}.$$

Assumption C:

$$_{1/3}q_{x+(1/2)} = 1 - {}_{1/3}p_{x+(1/2)} = 1 - {}_{1/3}p_x = 1 - \sqrt[3]{p_x}$$
$$= 1 - \sqrt[3]{.729} = 1 - .9 = .1.$$

The interval of age in question, from $x + \frac{1}{2}$ to $x + \frac{5}{6}$, is totally in the right-hand half of the unit age interval. In the right-hand half of any unit interval, assumption A produces relatively high mortality, while that produced under assumption B is relatively low. As assumption C is intermediate to the other two, it could have easily been predicted in advance that

$$_{1/3}q^{B}_{x+(1/2)} < {}_{1/3}q^{C}_{x+(1/2)} < {}_{1/3}q^{A}_{x+(1/2)}.$$

SUMMARY

Figure 1-4 provides a recapitulation of the important characteristics of the three basic mortality assumptions.

The mathematical results which have been developed form the theoretical basis upon which we may now build. Whereas only passing reference has been made thus far to the application of this theory to mortality table construction, the student should rest assured that the connection will be developed in detail in Chapter Two. At this stage, an intimate understanding of the mechanical results of the various mortality assumptions is essential. Only after giving careful consideration to each exercise should the student feel prepared to proceed to Chapter Two and its treatment of the effect of the assumptions on the determination of exposure values and, subsequently, rates of mortality.

EXERCISES

1. If $_{1-t}q_{x+t} = (1 - t)q_x$, $0 \leq t \leq 1$, and $_{1/3}q_{x+(1/2)} = .03$, find q_x.
2. Find $_{1/4}q_x$ if $_{1-t}p_{x+t}\mu_{x+t} = .04$, $0 \leq t \leq 1$.
3. Find $_{1/2}q_{28\frac{1}{4}}$ if $\mu_{28\frac{1}{4}+t} = 1/(10 - t)$, $0 \leq t \leq 1$.
4. Under which of the "popular" mortality assumptions does the following result hold?

$$\frac{\mu_{x+1}}{l_{x+1}} = \frac{\mu_x}{l_x}.$$

5. Derive each of the following:
   (a) $_{1-s}q_{x+t} = (1-s)\mu_{x+t}$, $0 \le t \le s \le 1$, given that

$$_tq_x = t \cdot q_x, \qquad 0 \le t \le 1.$$

   (b) $_{1-s}q_{x+t} = (1-s)\mu_{x+t+1-s}$, $0 \le t \le s \le 1$, given that

$$_{1-t}q_{x+t} = (1-t)q_x, \qquad 0 \le t \le 1.$$

6. If $q_x = \mu_{x+t}/(1 + t \cdot \mu_{x+t})$, $0 \le t \le 1$, and $q_{40} = .01$, find $_{3/4}q_{40\frac{1}{4}}$.
7. If $\mu_{x+t} = a/(1 + a \cdot t)$, $0 \le t \le 1$, express a in terms of q_x.
8. Under the Balducci hypothesis, it is known that

$$_{1/2}q_{50\frac{3}{4}} = \tfrac{2}{3} \cdot {}_{3/4}q_{50\frac{1}{4}}.$$

   If $q_{50} = .04$, find q_{51}, assuming that the unit age interval runs from integer to integer.
9. If $l_{x+t} = a/(3+t)$, $0 \le t \le 1$, $l_{x+(1/2)} = 800$, and $l_{x+1} = 700$, evaluate $l_{x+(3/4)}$ without finding a.
10. Assuming the Balducci pattern of mortality, express the following probability verbally:

$$\frac{\tfrac{1}{2} \cdot p_x \cdot q_x}{1 - \tfrac{1}{2} \cdot q_x}.$$

11. If $\mu_{x+t} = k$, $0 \le t \le 1$, and $_{1/4}q_x = .6 \cdot {}_{1/2}q_x$, evaluate $_{3/4}q_{x+(1/8)}$.
12. If $\ln {}_{1-t}p_{x+t} = .004(t-1)$, $0 \le t \le 1$, evaluate
   (a) q_x.
   (b) $_{1/4}q_{x+(3/4)}$.
   (c) $_{1/8}q_{x+(1/8)}$.
13. If μ_{x+t} is linear, $0 \le t \le 1$, $p_x = e^{-.25}$, and $_{1/4}p_x = \sqrt[9]{_{3/4}p_x}$, find $\mu_{x+(3/4)}$.
14. If $_{1/3}q_x = \tfrac{1}{10}$ and $_{(1/3)-t}q_{x+t}$ is linear, $0 \le t \le \tfrac{1}{3}$, find $_{1/6}q_x$.
15. If $_{(3/4)-t}q_{x+t}$ is linear, $0 \le t \le \tfrac{3}{4}$, and $_{1/4}q_{x+(1/2)} = .01$, find $_{1/4}q_x$.
16. If $f(t) = {}_tq_{30\frac{1}{3}}$ is linear, $0 \le t \le \tfrac{2}{3}$, and $_{2/3}q_{30\frac{1}{3}} = .02$, find
   (a) $_{1/2}q_{30\frac{1}{3}}$.
   (b) $_{1/2}q_{30\frac{1}{4}}$.
   (c) $\mu_{30\frac{2}{3}}$.
17. If $_{1-t}q_{x-(3/4)+t} = .004(1-t)$, $0 \le t \le 1$, find $_{1/8}q_x$.
18. If $_tq_x = kt$, $0 \le t \le 5$, find μ_{x+4} in terms of k.
19. There are 1000 persons now aged 40, of whom 32 are expected to die before age 41. How many will die between $40\tfrac{3}{8}$ and $40\tfrac{3}{4}$ if

   (a) $_{1-t}q_{40+t} = \dfrac{(1-t)q_{40}}{1 - t \cdot q_{40}}$, $\qquad 0 \le t \le 1$?

   (b) $_{1-t}q_{40+t} = (1-t)q_{40}$, $\qquad 0 \le t \le 1$?
20. If $_{1/4}q_x = .01$, find the value of $_{1/2}q_{x+(3/8)}$ when
   (a) $_tq_x = t \cdot q_x$, $0 \le t \le 1$.

(b) $_{1-t}q_{x+t} = (1-t)q_x, 0 \le t \le 1.$
(c) μ_{x+t} is constant, $0 \le t \le 1.$

21. Assume that $_{1/2}q_x = .04.$
    (a) Explain whether the value of q_x would be greater under the assumption of uniform deaths or the Balducci hypothesis, each operating over the unit age interval from x to $x+1$.
    (b) Verify your result by direct calculation.
    (c) For what unit age interval $[k, k+1]$ is the value of q_k independent of the use of assumption A or B?

22. Find the probability that a person aged $30\frac{1}{6}$ on April 1, 1978 will die in the second half of 1978 given that $q_{30} = .12$ and
    (a) $_tq_{30} = t \cdot q_{30}, 0 \le t \le 1.$
    (b) $_{1-t}q_{30+t} = (1-t)q_{30}, 0 \le t \le 1.$

23. Assume that $_tq_{35\frac{1}{4}} = .04t, 0 \le t \le 1,$ and that $_{1-t}q_{36\frac{1}{4}+t} = .04(1-t),$ $0 \le t \le 1.$
    (a) Find $_{1/4}q_{36}$ and $q_{35\frac{1}{4}}.$
    (b) Explain logically why $q_{35\frac{1}{4}}$ is greater than .04.
    (c) Arrange the following in increasing numerical order:

    $$_{1/4}q_{35\frac{1}{4}}, \quad _{1/4}q_{36}, \quad _{1/4}q_{36\frac{1}{4}}, \quad _{1/4}q_{36\frac{1}{2}}.$$

24. Given that $q_{30} = .060$ and $q_{30\frac{1}{2}} = .063,$ find the value of $_{1/3}p_{30\frac{1}{2}}$ under each of the following assumptions for which x is limited to integral values only:
    (a) $_{1-t}q_{x+t} = (1-t)q_x, 0 \le t \le 1.$
    (b) $_tq_x = t \cdot q_x, 0 \le t \le 1.$
    (c) $_{1-t}q_{x+(1/2)+t} = (1-t)q_{x+(1/2)}, 0 \le t \le 1.$
    (d) $_tq_{x+(1/2)} = t \cdot q_{x+(1/2)}, 0 \le t \le 1.$

25. Assume that $l_x = 27,720$ and that $l_{x+1} = 20,790.$
    (a) How many deaths are anticipated between ages $x+\frac{1}{3}$ and $x+1$ if $_tq_x = t \cdot q_x, 0 \le t \le 1$?
    (b) How many deaths are anticipated between ages x and $x+\frac{2}{3}$ if $_{1-t}q_{x+t} = (1-t)q_x, 0 \le t \le 1$?
    (c) Explain why the answers to (a) and (b) are different.

26. If $q_x = \frac{3}{4}$ and $l_{x+1} = 25,$ find the duration $t, 0 \le t \le 1,$ such that the difference between l^A_{x+t} and l^B_{x+t} is maximized.

27. For a fixed value of q_x over the unit interval $[x, x+1]$, prove mathematically that $\mu^A_{x+(1/2)} = \mu^B_{x+(1/2)} < \mu^C_{x+(1/2)}.$ Approximate the excess of $\mu^C_{x+(1/2)}$ over $\mu^A_{x+(1/2)}$ or $\mu^B_{x+(1/2)}$ in terms of $q_x.$

CHAPTER TWO

The Concept

of Exposure Determination

INTRODUCTION

As indicated in the preceding chapter, the three mortality assumptions which have been investigated are, for practical purposes, quite reasonable. Probabilities such as $_{1/2}q_{x+(1/3)}$ are found to show very little variation when calculated under each of the assumptions. For example, if $q_x = .006$, it can be shown that assumptions A, B, and C produce six-place numerical values for $_{1/2}q_{x+(1/3)}$ of .003006, .003003, and .003005, respectively. It seems clear, then, at least for ages at which q_x is relatively small, that the variability in probabilities produced by the three assumptions is negligible. Thus, in actual practice, the choice of a mortality assumption may be based upon practical and computational considerations rather than upon an investigation of the degree of accuracy produced.

Our basic objective in this chapter is to choose a mortality assumption with which we shall hereafter be content in all but rare cases. Once this mortality assumption is selected, the theoretical foundation will have been completely laid for the development of mortality rates from various sources of data. We may then proceed to the actual calculation of exposure values, and then of mortality rates, by seemingly dissimilar but, in fact, virtually equivalent techniques.

PRACTICALITY OF ASSUMPTIONS

We begin our search for the optimum mortality assumption for table construction by noting that most practical problems may be analyzed with a diagram such as that shown in Figure 2-1. This simple diagram indicates that A lives were under observation at exact age x, that n lives (to be referred to as *new entrants*) entered the mortality study at age $x + r$, that w lives (to be referred to as *withdrawals*) withdrew from observation at age $x + s$, and

FIGURE 2-1

that B lives remained at age $x + 1$. Further, D deaths were observed among persons actually under observation. An obvious relationship among these quantities is

$$A + n - w - D = B.$$

A person who withdrew at age $x + s$ and who then died prior to age $x + 1$ would *not* be counted as a death.

The question which we face is a relatively simple one; that is, what rate of mortality was observed over the unit age interval from age x to age $x + 1$? More concisely, we wish to determine the value of q_x. The solution to the problem, in its initial form, is available from a basic application of the theory of life contingencies:

$$A \cdot q_x + n \cdot {}_{1-r}q_{x+r} - w \cdot {}_{1-s}q_{x+s} = D. \qquad (2\text{-}1)$$

Assumptions A, B, and C, respectively, now lead to the following three simplifications of the basic equation:

$$A \cdot q_x + n \cdot \frac{(1 - r)q_x}{1 - r \cdot q_x} - w \cdot \frac{(1 - s)q_x}{1 - s \cdot q_x} = D,$$

$$A \cdot q_x + n \cdot (1 - r)q_x - w \cdot (1 - s)q_x = D,$$

and

$$A \cdot q_x + n[1 - (1 - q_x)^{1-r}] - w[1 - (1 - q_x)^{1-s}] = D.$$

The mathematical complexities of solving for q_x under assumption A or C are evident. On the contrary, assumption B easily produces

$$q_x = \frac{D}{A + n(1 - r) - w(1 - s)}, \qquad (2\text{-}2)$$

a formula whose reduction to a numerical value is trivial upon the determination of the necessary values of A, n, w, D, r, and s, each of which will be either known or assumed in any practical application.

Not only is Equation (2-2) easy to obtain, but it should also be noted that its denominator has a logical interpretation which further simplifies its derivation. This is most easily seen by referring back to Figure 2-1. Clearly, the A lives are subject to the risk of death for the full year of age, and the n lives are exposed for the fractional part, $1 - r$, of the year. Whereas this exposure is slightly overstated because of the exit of the w lives, compensation for this overstatement is accomplished by eliminating the exposure of the w lives for the fraction of a year, $1 - s$, during which they are not technically subject to the risk of death.

For example, if $A = 1000$, $n = 50$, $w = 40$, $r = \frac{1}{3}$, and $s = \frac{3}{4}$, the denominator of (2-2) is immediately found to be

$$1000 + 50(\tfrac{2}{3}) - 40(\tfrac{1}{4}) = 1023\tfrac{1}{3}.$$

The logic of considering the exposure of each of the A, n, and w groups to be the time remaining from their entry (or exit) until age $x + 1$ is satisfying.* Its simplicity is magnified when one contemplates the arithmetical nightmare produced by the solution for q_x based upon assumption A or C.

EXAMPLE 2-1 Suppose $A = 1000$, $n = 50$, $w = 40$, $r = \frac{1}{3}$, $s = \frac{3}{4}$, and $B = 998$. Calculate q_x, to six decimals, under assumptions A, B, and C.

SOLUTION Assumption A:

$$1000q_x + \frac{\tfrac{2}{3} \cdot q_x}{1 - \tfrac{1}{3} \cdot q_x} \cdot 50 - \frac{\tfrac{1}{4} \cdot q_x}{1 - \tfrac{3}{4} \cdot q_x} \cdot 40 = 12.$$

By iterative techniques, an answer of .011726 is obtained.

Assumption B:

$$1000q_x + 50(\tfrac{2}{3} \cdot q_x) - 40(\tfrac{1}{4} \cdot q_x) = 12.$$

Thus, $q_x = .011726$.

Assumption C:

$$1000q_x + 50[1 - (1 - q_x)^{2/3}] - 40[1 - (1 - q_x)^{1/4}] = 12.$$

By applying the binomial theorem, and ignoring all terms involving q_x raised to a power higher than 2, we obtain

$$q_x = .011714.$$

Note that assumption C produces a result identical to that of assumption B if only the first power of q_x is retained.

The near-identity of the three answers in Example 2-1 is obvious. Yet great effort was expended to apply assumptions A and C, while assumption B produced a rapid, effortless answer. Probably no single argument could be more forcefully made for the choice of the Balducci hypothesis for the determination of mortality rates from observed data.

The student should note that Example 2-1 is based upon a single point, $x + r$, at which new entrants are assumed and a different single point, $x + s$, at which withdrawals occur. If it may be assumed that all new entrants

---

* The fact that reduction of exposure for deaths which occur prior to $x + 1$ is not effected in the same way as for withdrawals is a crucially important one which will be discussed later in this chapter.

and withdrawals are placed at a common point, the complexity of the computations under assumptions A and C is somewhat reduced. However, if several points of entry and withdrawal are established, the calculation of q_x under these assumptions becomes increasingly tedious. Under assumption B, the effort involved is essentially independent of the number of entry and withdrawal points, a fact which further enhances the attractiveness of the Balducci hypothesis.

A final argument suggesting the ultimate choice of the Balducci hypothesis involves the calculation of the force of mortality μ_{x+t} from observed data similar to those given in Example 2-1. Under assumption B, we know that

$$\mu_{x+t} = \frac{q_x}{1 - (1 - t)q_x}$$

and that

$$q_x = \frac{D}{A + n(1 - r) - w(1 - s)} = \frac{D}{E},$$

where D represents the observed deaths between ages x and $x + 1$ and E represents the corresponding exposure in the calculation of q_x. Therefore,

$$\mu_{x+t} = \frac{D/E}{1 - (1 - t)(D/E)} = \frac{D}{E - (1 - t)D}. \tag{2-3}$$

The result, then, is that the denominator of the expression for μ_{x+t} is the exposure calculated in the determination of q_x reduced by the appropriate fraction of deaths expected prior to age $x + 1$. For example,

$$\mu_{x+(1/3)} = \frac{D}{E - \frac{2}{3} \cdot D}.$$

Figure 2-1 may now be refined for the case in which μ_{x+t} is required. Rather than placing D at the end of the interval, as in Figure 2-1, we now place D at age $x + t$ and proceed to treat these deaths in exactly the same way that withdrawals were treated earlier. Such an analysis is clearly consistent with Equation (2-3). The student must realize that the placing of D at age $x + t$ in Figure 2-2 does not indicate that all deaths occur at that

FIGURE 2-2

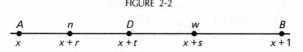

specific age. Rather, it is merely a physical representation of Equation (2-3) and is not logically explainable. It is sufficient to say that it is a direct mechanical result of the choice of assumption B.

A similar diagrammatic device for the calculation of μ_{x+t} under either assumption A or C does not exist. It must be granted, however, that considerations regarding the calculation of the force of mortality are not of sufficient importance to justify our choice of the Balducci hypothesis. Under *any* assumption, μ_{x+t} is rather easy to compute, once the value of q_x is determined. The advantage of placing the deaths at the appropriate point on a diagram is largely esthetic in nature. The decision to use the Balducci hypothesis throughout the text is primarily based upon the ease of finding the q_x values and in reality was reached due to the fact that $_{1-t}q_{x+t}$ is a probability encountered in mortality table construction to a far greater extent than the probability $_tq_x$. The student should assume in all subsequent work that, unless specifically stated otherwise, the Balducci hypothesis should be applied to any problem encountered in the construction of tables.

Two important definitions must be introduced before proceeding. Under the Balducci hypothesis, we have found that

$$q_x = \frac{D}{E}$$

and that

$$\mu_{x+t} = \frac{D}{E - (1-t)D} \qquad (0 \le t \le 1).$$

The quantity E will be referred to as *the exposure associated with* q_x. The quantity $E - (1-t)D$, which we shall label as $_tE'_x$, is referred to as *the exposure associated with* μ_{x+t}.

EXAMPLE 2-2   Assume that 500 lives are under observation at age 30, that 50 lives come under observation at age $30\frac{1}{2}$, that 20 lives withdraw at age $30\frac{1}{4}$, and that 40 lives withdraw at age $30\frac{4}{5}$. Six deaths are observed. Calculate, using the Balducci hypothesis,
   (a) The exposure associated with q_{30};
   (b) The exposure associated with $\mu_{30\frac{1}{3}}$;
   (c) The value of t, $0 \le t \le 1$, which maximizes the value of μ_{x+t}.

FIGURE 2-3

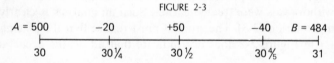

SOLUTION   Figure 2-3 simplifies the solution.
   (a) $E_{30} = 500 - 20(\frac{3}{4}) + 50(\frac{1}{2}) - 40(\frac{1}{5}) = 502.$
   (b) $_{\frac{1}{3}}E'_{30} = E_{30} - \frac{2}{3}(6) = 498$, by visualizing the six deaths at age $30\frac{1}{3}$ on the diagram.
   (c) Since $_tE'_{30} = E_{30} - (1-t)D$, this denominator of μ_{x+t} is minimized when t equals 0. Thus, μ assumes its largest value at the left-hand extreme of the unit interval. It is important to note that this result is consistent with the decreasing nature of the μ_{x+t} curve under the Balducci hypothesis.

TREATMENT OF DEATHS

Probably no single result is as crucial to the development of exposure formulas as that dealing with the treatment of deaths under the Balducci hypothesis. Specifically, we need to determine the point at which deaths are assumed to cease their contribution of exposure. The obvious answer to this question may seem to be that upon death no further exposure may be contributed. However, this seemingly logical result will be shown to be incorrect.

Consider the situation, discussed earlier, in which A lives are under observation at age x, n new entrants come under study at age $x + r$, w withdrawals leave the study at age $x + s$, and D deaths occur between ages x and $x + 1$. We have determined, under the Balducci hypothesis, that

$$q_x = \frac{D}{A + n(1 - r) - w(1 - s)}.$$

If this formula is "correct" under the stated assumptions, its denominator must verify the amount of exposure contributed by any given individual. To illustrate such verifications, we shall designate each individual by an ordered pair (a, b), where a represents the means whereby he originally entered the study and b represents the means whereby he exited from the observed group. To any such ordered pair must be allocated the identical amount of exposure from each of two standpoints, that is, from the formula itself and from an analysis of the assumptions underlying the exposure formula.

The ordered pairs which are relevant in the present discussion are

$$(A, w), \quad (A, D), \quad (A, B), \quad (n, w), \quad (n, D), \quad \text{and} \quad (n, B).$$

A reference to Figure 2-1 will show that no other possibilities exist for a meaningful ordered pair.

Let us first consider the ordered pair (A, w). The assumptions underlying this discussion suggest that this life is exposed from age x to age $x + s$, or a total of s years. The denominator of the expression for q_x substantiates this result, crediting one unit because of the first element of the ordered pair and subtracting $1 - s$ units because of its second element. Since

$$1 - (1 - s) = s,$$

the formula has indeed produced the correct amount of exposure for (A, w).

Next, let us consider the ordered pair (A, D). Determination of the appropriate exposure from the assumptions is troublesome because, up to this point, we have intentionally avoided a discussion of where to place D on the exposure diagram used to determine q_x. Therefore, let us first note from the exposure formula that (A, D) is credited exactly one unit of exposure, receiving one unit from the A term and none from either the n term or the w term. This uncovers a key result: *The deaths D must be placed at the end of the unit age interval for purposes of calculating exposure.* Otherwise, the exposure formula would produce a conflict with the exposure obtained by reading from left to right on an exposure diagram used as a model to perform calculations under the Balducci hypothesis.

An alternative, but quite similar, rationalization for the above conclusion is simply that the exposure associated with q_x under the Balducci hypothesis does not contain a subtractive term for the deaths. The physical interpretation resulting from the Balducci hypothesis is somewhat hard to accept initially, as it leads to the conclusion that lives which have expired continue to contribute exposure beyond the date of their death. In fact, a death occurring just after age x could contribute exposure for nearly a full year after death. Perhaps more implausible is the fact that, as we shall see shortly, a person may contribute exposure to a study not only after his death but even beyond the terminal date of the period of observation.

The student should not be concerned with a search for a logical interpretation of the result which has just been stated. This result follows from the imposition of the Balducci hypothesis. The tendency of students to think of the result as illogical must be tempered with the realization that it is merely an automatic mathematical consequence of an assumption as to the pattern of mortality.

The other ordered pairs, (A, B), (n, w), (n, D), and (n, B), should be subjected to an analysis similar to that performed on (A, w) and (A, D). The student should verify that exposures of 1, $s - r$, $1 - r$, and $1 - r$, respectively, are obtainable both from the basic assumptions and from the exposure formula.

The Balducci treatment of deaths in an exposure formula is sometimes carelessly described as "deaths are credited with a full year of exposure in the year of death." Such a statement is obviously not always true, as evidenced by a life who is a new entrant and then a death in the same unit age interval. Such a life would contribute exposure only from the point of entry to the end of the unit age interval, an amount which is clearly less than one unit.

One further point of caution is advisable. The result that deaths contribute exposure to the end of the unit age interval in which death occurs is applicable only to the computation of the exposure associated with q_x. Computation of $_tE'_x$, the exposure associated with μ_{x+t}, illustrates that, in some instances, reduction in exposure is in fact made because of the deaths. As observed earlier, the denominator of the expression for μ_{x+t} may be obtained by subtracting exposure for the deaths from the point at which the force of mortality is required until the end of the unit age interval. Thus, there is a reduction for the lives which terminate due to death in much the same way as for withdrawn lives. The fact that the amount of such reduction is the length $1 - t$ is another which is not intuitively apparent but rather a mathematical outgrowth of the Balducci hypothesis. The placing of the deaths D at time t on our diagram, rather than at time 1, has been referred to as the *shuttling* of the deaths. Shuttling, then, is merely a technique through which the exposure associated with μ_{x+t} can be easily computed directly from a diagram.

The treatment of deaths under other mortality assumptions does not lend itself to the simple analysis made possible under Balducci.* This fact further supports our choice of the Balducci hypothesis as the ideal representation of intra-age mortality for the construction of tables.

Finally, it should be recognized that there is no distinctive characteristic of deaths which specifically requires that they be accorded the special treatment of being considered to contribute exposure until the end of the unit age interval. Such treatment is generally accorded to deaths simply because mortality is the decrement under investigation. However, if a study is implemented to determine lapse rates, then the lapsing policies are the ones exposed to the end of the unit interval, and deaths are treated as if they were withdrawals in a mortality study. Similarly, if death rates due to a specific cause, say cancer, are under investigation, deaths due to all other causes are treated as if they were withdrawals, with only the cancer-related deaths being credited with exposure beyond the actual date of death. In any case, only those lives removed from the study by operation of the specific decrement being measured are accorded the treatment generally associated with deaths in a mortality investigation.

POTENTIAL AND CANCELLED EXPOSURE

Although the introduction of the concepts of potential and cancelled exposure does not add any new substance to the theory already developed, these terms are quite helpful in easing the terminology burden and in illustrating the overall exposure concepts. Simply stated, when any individual life first enters a mortality study, he is accorded a certain amount of *potential* exposure for the age interval in which he enters and for all subsequent age intervals. Upon his exit from the observed group, a similar negative adjustment is made, with this reduction being classified as *cancelled* exposure. This cancellation is even effected for deaths, but only for those age intervals subsequent to the one in which death actually occurs. The difference between the amounts of potential and cancelled exposure is referred to as the total exposure contributed by the life to a particular interval of age.

In considering the amounts of potential and cancelled exposure to be assigned to any life, heavy reliance is placed upon the treatment of deaths

---

* Chapter 6 of *Measurement of Mortality*, by Harry Gershenson, analyzes in depth the treatment of deaths under various assumptions other than Balducci.

arising from the Balducci hypothesis. For this reason, it must be made clear that a discussion of potential and cancelled exposure is only meaningful in the presence of the assumption that the Balducci hypothesis is valid. As stated earlier, only this mortality assumption permits a simplified treatment through which the exposure contributed by an individual life may be readily determined from a simple diagram.

Before the assignment of potential and cancelled exposure may begin, a unit age interval consistent with the desired form of the final rates of mortality must be defined. For purposes of simplicity, let us assume that we want to obtain values of q_x for integral values of x. Therefore, we shall divide the entire age continuum into one-year segments whose end points coincide with the integral ages. More complex illustrations in later chapters will vary from this one, in that the unit age intervals may, for example, run from $20\frac{1}{3}$ to $21\frac{1}{3}$, $21\frac{1}{3}$ to $22\frac{1}{3}$, and so on.

Consider a person who comes under observation at age $30\frac{1}{3}$ on August 1, 1976. Clearly, it is not then known on what date he will leave the study. However, he has the potential to remain under observation until the end of the unit age interval running from age 30 to age 31 and is therefore credited with $\frac{2}{3}$ of a unit of potential exposure for this interval on his date of entry. Suppose, then, that he withdraws from the observed group on November 1, 1976, at which time his age is $30\frac{7}{12}$. In this case, he can no longer satisfy the original potential of $\frac{2}{3}$ of a year, as he withdrew before age 31 was attained. An adjustment is required, and this is effected by subtracting, or cancelling, the $\frac{5}{12}$ of a year remaining until his 31st birthday. The net result,

$$\tfrac{2}{3} - \tfrac{5}{12} = \tfrac{1}{4},$$

indicates this person's total contribution of exposure to the year of age from 30 to 31. This final value of $\frac{1}{4}$ of a year is correct, as the person was actually under observation for exactly three months.

Suppose, however, that our sample life had died, while under observation, on November 1, 1976. The Balducci treatment of deaths may now be restated, in light of our new terminology, to say that there is no cancellation for deaths in the unit age interval in which death occurs. Thus, exposure contribution continues, after death, until the date upon which age 31 would have been reached. The potential exposure remains $\frac{2}{3}$ of a year, and the lack of cancellation produces

$$\tfrac{2}{3} - 0 = \tfrac{2}{3},$$

resulting in a contribution of $\frac{2}{3}$ of a year.

Now let us suppose that our sample life remained under observation until December 31, 1978, on which date the period of observation defining the study ended. The exposure between ages 30 and 31 is $\frac{2}{3}$ of a year, as no cancellation is required in this case. Then, upon attainment of age 31 on April 1, 1977, a full unit of potential exposure begins to be realized for the age interval from age 31 to 32. On April 1, 1978, the life is still under observation, meaning that there is no cancellation for the preceding interval and that an additional potential of one unit begins for the unit interval between ages 32 and 33, even though it is known that the observation period will terminate before the full year's exposure can be realized. However, during this interval, the ending date of the observation period intervenes, requiring cancellation. Since the life is aged $32\frac{3}{4}$ on this date, the remaining $\frac{1}{4}$ of a year must be cancelled, producing

$$1 - \tfrac{1}{4} = \tfrac{3}{4}$$

as the exposure for this final interval.

The three cases may be considered diagrammatically as follows, keeping in mind that the ending date in Cases 1 and 2 is not a factor, falling subsequent to the attainment of age 31.

CASE 1. Entered at age $30\frac{1}{3}$; withdrew at age $30\frac{7}{12}$. See Figure 2-4.

FIGURE 2-4

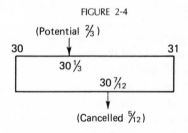

Net Exposure: $\frac{1}{4}$

CASE 2. Entered at age $30\frac{1}{3}$; died at age $30\frac{7}{12}$. See Figure 2-5.

FIGURE 2-5

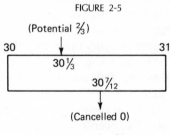

Net Exposure: $\frac{2}{3}$

CASE 3. Entered at age $30\frac{1}{3}$; reached end of observation period at age $32\frac{3}{4}$. See Figure 2-6.

FIGURE 2-6

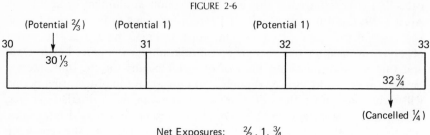

Net Exposures: $\frac{2}{3}$, 1, $\frac{3}{4}$

The exposures created in the first two cases, $\frac{1}{4}$ and $\frac{2}{3}$ year, respectively, become a part of the denominator in the calculation of q_{30}. In the third case, the exposures of $\frac{2}{3}$, 1, and $\frac{3}{4}$ become parts of the denominators of q_{30}, q_{31}, and q_{32}, respectively.

Further consideration of each case should reveal the necessity that a full unit of potential exposure be assigned to each interval subsequent to the one beginning at age 30. Yet exposure beyond the last interval shown in the respective diagrams is zero. In Case 3, for example, the ending date of the study creates a full unit of cancellation for all intervals beginning with that from age 33 to 34. It is important that the student realize that each of our cases would produce one unit each of potential and cancelled exposure for all intervals to the right of the ones depicted, producing an obviously correct net exposure of zero for each such interval.

Finally, it appears tempting to determine the total exposure contribution for any case to be "the distance from the date of entry of any individual to his date of exit." This rule is a perfectly safe one to use, but only if it is remembered that the "date of exit" of a death under the Balducci hypothesis is not the date of death but the end point of the unit age interval in which death occurs. A special warning is necessary in a case in which death occurs but in which the ending date of the observation period is reached prior to the end of the unit age interval in which the death was observed. In such a case, the "date of exit" will be beyond the end of the observation period, causing the phenomenon of an individual life producing exposure not only after death but also, in many cases, for several months after the defined end of the study. The student who clearly understands the effect of assuming that mortality follows the Balducci hypothesis should have no problem in accepting this fact.

As an example, let us consider a fourth case for the earlier illustration, in which our sample life, born on April 1, 1946, died on November 30, 1978, one month before the end of the observation period. Since deaths do not generate cancelled exposure, this case would result in contribution of exposure until the deceased's next "birthday," specifically until April 1, 1979. Exposure is therefore credited for the first three months of the calendar year

1979, regardless of the fact that the ending of the observation period inter-vened at the end of 1978. It might be said, then, that under the Balducci hypothesis, no barrier, including the termination of the study, is sufficiently strong to prevent the crediting of exposure of an observed death to the end of the unit age interval in which the death occurs.

A COMPREHENSIVE ILLUSTRATION

One final example, illustrating many of the concepts introduced in this chapter, should be helpful to the student prior to progressing to Chapter Three and its treatment of the tabulation of actual data upon which mortality investigations will be based.

EXAMPLE 2-3   It is required to find the value of q_x for the mortality experience observed during calendar year z. Assume that 1900 lives attain age x on July 1, z, and that 1000 lives are age $x + \frac{1}{2}$ on January 1, z. No other lives are included in the study, and there are no withdrawals other than by death. Of the groups of 1900 and 1000 lives, there are 100 and 50 observed deaths, respectively, between ages x and $x + 1$ in calendar year z. Indicate the mortality assumptions being used.

SOLUTION   The two-dimensional diagram in Figure 2-7 will be helpful in visualizing the overall problem.

FIGURE 2-7

Calendar Year

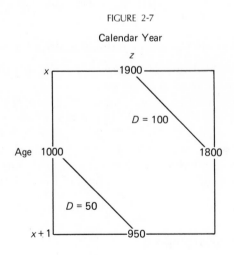

METHOD 1.   The following life contingencies equation is clearly ap-plicable:

$$1900 \cdot {}_{1/2}q_x + 1000 \cdot {}_{1/2}q_{x+(1/2)} = 150.$$

(a) Applying the Balducci hypothesis, we have

$$\frac{950 \cdot q_x}{1 - \frac{1}{2} \cdot q_x} + 500 \cdot q_x = 150,$$

and the solution, $q_x = \frac{1}{10}$, is obtainable from an application of the quadratic formula.

(b) Assuming a uniform distribution of deaths, we have

$$950 \cdot q_x + \frac{500 \cdot q_x}{1 - \frac{1}{2} \cdot q_x} = 150,$$

and the solution, $q_x \doteq .1016$, is also found by use of the quadratic formula. Note that the two results are, as expected, close but not equal, as they are based upon different mortality assumptions.

METHOD 2. The following life contingencies equation is also clearly applicable:

$$1900 \cdot q_x - 1800 \cdot {}_{1/2}q_{x+(1/2)} + 1000 \cdot {}_{1/2}q_{x+(1/2)} = 150.$$

(a) Applying the Balducci hypothesis, we have

$$1900 \cdot q_x - 900 \cdot q_x + 500 \cdot q_x = 150,$$

and the solution, $q_x = \frac{1}{10}$, is trivial.

(b) Assuming a uniform distribution of deaths, we have

$$1900 \cdot q_x - \frac{900 \cdot q_x}{1 - \frac{1}{2} \cdot q_x} + \frac{500 \cdot q_x}{1 - \frac{1}{2} \cdot q_x} = 150,$$

requiring the use of the quadratic formula to obtain $q_x \doteq .1014$.

Several interesting and valuable observations may be made with respect to the four answers obtained in Example 2-3.

It is evident that the two answers obtained by applying the Balducci hypothesis to the two life contingencies identities are equal. However, the assumption of uniform distribution of deaths produced two unequal results. This phenomenon occurs because the given numerical values were designed such that the experience represented by each of the two diagonals would be consistent with each other and with the Balducci hypothesis. Clearly, the upper diagonal gives

$${}_{1/2}q_x = \tfrac{1}{19},$$

while the lower diagonal produces

$${}_{1/2}q_{x+(1/2)} = \tfrac{1}{20}.$$

Each of these results is consistent with the overall solution

$$q_x = \tfrac{1}{10}.$$

Had the numerical input been slightly varied, we would have obtained four different answers to the question, all reasonable and all numerically very close to each other. Thus, we observe the somewhat surprising fact that a given assumption, applied to each of two life contingencies expressions which are identically true, may produce unequal arithmetical results if the numerical values associated with the problem are not consistent with the chosen assumption. We need, therefore, to keep in mind that we may often impose the Balducci hypothesis in problems involving data inconsistent with this assumption. This should not be disturbing when it is recalled that the use of the Balducci hypothesis is chosen for the sake of computational convenience, rather than because it is believed that the pattern of deaths must necessarily be consistent with that anticipated by Balducci.

When approaching a problem of the type illustrated by Example 2-3, a life contingencies identity should be constructed along the lines of that used in Method 2 rather than Method 1, simply because an equation containing only probabilities of the form $_{1-t}q_{x+t}$ is much more easily solvable (using our chosen Balducci hypothesis) than one involving probabilities of the form $_t q_x$. Notice that of the four solutions proposed in Example 2-3, only the first approach of Method 2 led to a simple arithmetical solution. The student must be sure that he understands why this particular approach is recommended when the Balducci hypothesis has been accepted.

Finally, having analyzed Example 2-3 in great detail, it should be observed that the "best" solution has still not been illustrated. Under the Balducci hypothesis, we can determine that the total potential exposure is

$$1900(1) + 1000(\tfrac{1}{2}) = 2400$$

and that the total cancelled exposure is

$$1800(\tfrac{1}{2}) = 900,$$

producing a net exposure of 1500 life-years and a mortality rate of

$$q_x = \tfrac{150}{1500} = \tfrac{1}{10}.$$

The elegant simplicity of the concepts of potential and cancelled exposure under the Balducci hypothesis must not be underemphasized by the student, as it permits ready solutions for otherwise tedious problems.

SUMMARY

The main thrust of this chapter has been a determination of an intra-age mortality assumption which will be both reasonably accurate and convenient for application to studies of mortality. Since several assumptions can be found which are sufficiently accurate for our purposes, our choice has been based almost wholly upon the esthetically satisfying characteristic of the simple diagrammatic representation possessed by the Balducci hypothesis.

The Balducci hypothesis produces a somewhat surprising physical interpretation in the case of an observed death, but it is an interpretation which is simple in its application. Other mortality patterns do not possess such simple interpretations. The student should proceed to the more practical aspects of mortality investigations, presented in subsequent chapters, only if the treatment of individual cases by the Balducci hypothesis is thoroughly understood.

EXERCISES

1. A basic mortality assumption underlies most exposure formulas used in life insurance company mortality studies. State the assumption, and demonstrate algebraically its implication as to treatment of deaths during the unit age interval.

2. Comment upon the validity of the statement "A theoretically correct exposure formula for q_x should count a full year for each person who remained insured and under observation throughout the full year of observation and a fraction of a unit for each other person corresponding to the fraction of the year during which he was insured and under observation."

3. In computing the exposure associated with q_x, under the assumption

$$_{1-t}q_{x+t} = (1 - t)q_x \qquad (0 \le t \le 1),$$

   discuss the validity of each of the following:
   (a) Deaths are treated as if they occurred at the end of the year of age under investigation.
   (b) Deaths are given a full year of exposure in the year of death.
   (c) The total exposure for any life is the distance from the point of entry to the end of the observation period or to the end of the unit age interval, whichever occurs sooner.

4. A mortality study based upon the Balducci hypothesis produces $\mu_{x+t} = .12$ for some t. Based upon the following facts, find t.
   (i) There were 100 lives in the study at exact age x.
   (ii) There were 30 new entrants at age $x + \frac{1}{3}$.
   (iii) There were 44 withdrawals at age $x + \frac{3}{4}$.
   (iv) There were 74 lives remaining in the study at age $x + 1$.

5. One hundred lives enter a mortality study at age x and ten additional lives enter at age $x + \frac{1}{2}$. There are no withdrawals other than by death. Ten deaths are observed prior to age $x + 1$. Three of the deaths are assumed to cease exposure contribution at age $x + \frac{1}{3}$; the remaining

seven contribute until age $x + \frac{2}{3}$. The resulting exposure between ages x and $x + 1$ may be used as the denominator of a specific value of μ_{x+t}. Assuming the Balducci hypothesis throughout, find t.

6. Assume $_{2-t}q_{23+t}$ is a linear function of t, $0 \leq t \leq 2$. If 2000 lives enter a study at age 23, 1000 enter at age $24\frac{1}{2}$, 800 withdraw at age $23\frac{3}{4}$, 10 die between ages 23 and 24, and an additional 15 die between ages 24 and 25, find $_2q_{23}$.

7. In a mortality study ending on December 31, 1976, based upon the Balducci hypothesis, the unit age interval runs from integer to integer. Consider a person born on April 1, 1915. On what date does exposure contribution cease if death occurred on
   (a) February 1, 1975?
   (b) July 1, 1975?
   (c) February 1, 1976?

8. At exact age x, 102 persons were in a group of observed lives. During the following 12-month period 6 lives entered and 10 lives left the group, with each such entry and exit assumed to have occurred at age $x + \frac{1}{2}$. If the number of lives still alive and under observation at age $x + 1$ was 96, calculate the value of q_x to six decimal places if
   (a) $_{1-t}q_{x+t} = (1 - t)q_x$ $\quad (0 \leq t \leq 1)$.
   (b) $_tq_x = t \cdot q_x$ $\quad (0 \leq t \leq 1)$.
   (c) μ_{x+t} is constant $\quad (0 \leq t \leq 1)$.

9. Consider the following five persons contributing exposure to a mortality study in which lives are observed until they leave a defined group. The Balducci hypothesis is imposed. The observation period began on March 1, 1970.

Life	Birth date	Other facts
A	Oct. 1, 1960	Withdrew Feb 1, 1972
B	Dec. 1, 1961	Died Apr. 1, 1973
C	Apr. 1, 1959	Died May 1, 1974
D	Mar. 1, 1960	Died Apr. 1, 1970
E	Nov. 1, 1960	Withdrew Aug. 1, 1974

   (a) If the age continuum is divided into one-year intervals whose end points are integral ages, determine the *total* exposure contribution of each life.
   (b) If unit intervals are constructed, running from half-age to half-age, e.g., from $9\frac{1}{2}$ to $10\frac{1}{2}$, $10\frac{1}{2}$ to $11\frac{1}{2}$, etc., determine the *total* exposure contribution of each life.

10. Let n_{x+t} represent the number of lives entering a mortality study at exact age $x + t$. Let w_{x+t} represent the number of lives who withdraw, for

reasons other than death, at exact age $x + t$ $(0 \leq t \leq 1)$. The number of observed deaths, D, is denoted by the equation

$$D = \sum_{t} (n_{x+t} - w_{x+t})_{1-t}q_{x+t}.$$

Let k be an arbitrary constant $(0 \leq k \leq 1)$. Assuming the Balducci hypothesis, express as a single symbol

$$\frac{D}{\sum_{t} (1 - t)(n_{x+t} - w_{x+t}) - (1 - k)D}$$

11. The unit age interval in a mortality investigation runs from half-ages to half-ages. Assuming the Balducci hypothesis, how much exposure is contributed by each of the following lives between ages $28\frac{1}{2}$ and $29\frac{1}{2}$? The ending date of the investigation is March 31, 1980.

Life	Birth date	Other data
A	Mar. 1, 1950	Died May 1, 1979
B	Mar. 1, 1950	Withdrew May 1, 1979
C	Mar. 1, 1951,	Died Oct. 1, 1979
D	Mar. 1, 1951,	Withdrew Oct. 1, 1979
E	Mar. 1, 1951,	Died Apr. 1, 1980
F	Mar. 1, 1952	Died Mar. 15, 1980

12. A mortality study of an employee group, the members of which were all hired in 1975, terminates on June 30, 1977. If

$$_{1-t}q_{x+t} = (1 - t)q_x \qquad (0 \leq t \leq 1, \ x \text{ an integer}),$$

find the total exposure contributed by each of the following three employees during calendar year 1977:

Employee	Birth date	Other data
A	Nov. 15, 1920	Died Feb. 1, 1977
B	Jan. 15, 1921	Died Jul. 15, 1977
C	Jul. 15, 1919	Died Jun. 15, 1977

13. The age continuum in a Balducci-based mortality study has been divided into unit intervals at integral ages. Consider a life entering the study at age $24\frac{1}{4}$ who later dies at age $29\frac{1}{3}$. Determine the amount of potential and cancelled exposure, respectively, produced for the unit age interval between
    (a) Ages 24 and 25.
    (b) Ages 27 and 28.
    (c) Ages 29 and 30.
    (d) Ages 40 and 41.

14. The following information is available:
    (i) On January 1, 1978, the following lives came under observation:
       (1) 1600 lives of exact age $50\frac{1}{4}$.
       (2) 1600 lives of exact age $50\frac{3}{4}$.
    (ii) 1500 lives came under observation at exact age 50 on April 1, 1978.
    (iii) 1300 lives came under observation at exact age 50 on October 1, 1978.
    (iv) No other lives came under observation, and none of the observed lives left the observed group except by reason of death.
    (v) The observation period started January 1, 1978 and ended December 31, 1978.
    (vi) As of December 31, 1978, there were 1200 survivors at exact age $50\frac{1}{4}$ and 1200 survivors at exact age $50\frac{3}{4}$.
    (vii) During the calendar year 1978, the observed number of deaths between exact ages 50 and 51 was 800.
    Find q_{50}, assuming the Balducci pattern of mortality.
15. Find the exposure between ages 60 and 61, given the following facts:
    (i) The lives were observed only during the first six months of 1978.
    (ii) On January 1, 1978, 600 lives entered the study at age $60\frac{1}{6}$ and 1200 entered at age $60\frac{2}{3}$.
    (iii) On March 1, 1978, 300 lives entered the study at age 60.
    (iv) On May 1, 1978, 600 lives entered the study at age 60.
    (v) On June 30, 1978, the following lives remained:
        588 at age $60\frac{1}{6}$;
        294 at age $60\frac{1}{3}$;
        588 at age $60\frac{2}{3}$;
        1158 at age $61\frac{1}{6}$.
    (vi) There were no withdrawals other than by death.
    (vii) The Balducci hypothesis is assumed.
16. A mortality study, based upon the Balducci hypothesis, is conducted based upon experience during the calendar year 1977. For each of the following lives, determine the amounts of potential and cancelled exposure for the unit age interval from $31\frac{1}{3}$ to $32\frac{1}{3}$:

Life	Entered	Other facts
A	Jan. 1, 1977 at age $30\frac{5}{6}$	Still in group Jan. 1, 1978
B	Jan. 1, 1977 at age $30\frac{1}{2}$	Died Apr. 1, 1977
C	Jul. 1, 1977 at age 32	Withdrew Sep. 1, 1977
D	Jan. 1, 1977 at age $31\frac{2}{3}$	Died May 1, 1977
E	Apr. 1, 1977 at age 32	Died Dec. 1, 1977

17. Rework Exercise 16 if the investigation had been designed to measure withdrawal experience rather than mortality experience.

Methods of Tabulation

INTRODUCTION

In Chapters One and Two we have laid the mathematical foundation for the techniques to be used in the determination of rates of mortality or of other types of decrement such as withdrawal or disability. An assumption as to the distribution of decrements within any one-year age interval has been selected, and the effects of its imposition have been carefully investigated. We have seen that the Balducci hypothesis is elementary in its application and is uniquely suitable for the computation of probabilities of decrement from raw data, as $f(t) = {}_{1-t}q_{x+t}$ is that function whose simplification is most often required.

Many studies of mortality are based upon large quantities of data, often representing millions of life-years of exposure. It is the responsibility of the actuary to tabulate these data in such a way that the aggregate amount of exposure can be calculated with a minimum of error and to see that such exposure is carefully allocated to the unit age intervals defined by the study. To accomplish this task, formal definitions of various classifications of lives must be established. Strict adherence to such definitions makes the initial effort of tabulation a task which is easily effected by data processing machines. Subsequent to such processing, exposures and individual mortality rates are an almost immediate by-product of formulas which have been developed based upon the original methods of tabulation. It seems, then, that the stage in the process demanding the greatest skills and care is that at which we now find ourselves, that is, the segregation of the data into categories which will lead most efficiently to a highly accurate finished product.

Our objectives in Chapter Three are twofold. First, the categories alluded to above must be defined verbally in terms of the language traditionally associated with mortality studies. Second, tabulating rules must be developed for the delineation of these categories, with both great detail and flexibility, so that the actuary may easily and confidently devise tabulating rules for use in any specific instance which may arise.

TABULATING CATEGORIES

The classifications, or categories, into which all exposed lives are placed are generally identical regardless of the period of time over which the study is conducted. The analysis of such categories may be best undertaken, however, only after a brief discussion of the types of groups upon which studies of mortality are commonly based and the types of observation periods which are frequently encountered.

The *observed group* may be defined in any of several ways. For example, it may be defined as the active employees of a given corporation or perhaps as the set of those employees who are covered by a pension plan or by group life insurance. The experience of these groups is usually of primary interest to consulting actuaries who specialize in the area of employee benefit plans. In other instances, it may refer to the entire population of a given region, such as a town, county, city, state, or other political subdivision. The mortality patterns of such a group would be of greatest interest to a demographer or social statistician. The type of observed group most often encountered by actuaries, however, is a group or subgroup of policyholders within one or several life insurance companies. Mortality patterns of such insured lives are of paramount importance to all actuaries, in that the rate-making function depends largely on the experience of policyholders insured under past conditions which may be considered similar to those expected in the future.

Date-to-Date Studies

The date-to-date study is quite simple in concept, as each life is observed between two fixed points in time. For example, the beginning and ending dates of an observation period may be taken as January 1, 1974 and December 31, 1977, respectively, although there is no requirement that a date-to-date study must coincide with calendar years. Any life which was a member of the observed group at any time during such a four-year period would make a contribution to the total exposure and, of course, would make a contribution to the numerator of a mortality rate only if death occurred, during the four-year period, while the life was under observation.

Let us consider the categories generally arising from an observation period covering the calendar years 1974–1977, inclusive. We must keep in mind that every observed life may be represented by an ordered pair, (a, b), indicating the means by which exposure contribution began and was terminated. Each life must fall into two separate categories, one describing its means of entrance and the other describing its means of exit.

The only two ways in which a life may begin to contribute exposure are, first, by already being a member of the observed group when the study commences or, second, by entering the observed group between the starting and ending dates of the study. The categories thus generated are called *starters* and *new entrants*, respectively, and will be denoted by the letters s and n. A starter, then, is a person whose exposure contribution begins simultaneously with the study's beginning, that is, on January 1, 1974 in this instance. A new entrant is a person whose exposure contribution begins later in the observation period. A person whose association with the observed group actually commences on January 1, 1974 is treated as a new entrant rather than as a starter. An easy way for the student to resolve such a borderline decision of classification is to consider the observation period as beginning at the stroke of midnight at which instant the year 1973 ended and the year 1974 began.

The two means by which exposure may terminate are, first, by withdrawal (voluntary or otherwise) from the observed group and, second, by the termination of the observation period. Persons who leave the group prior to the end of the observation period are tentatively labeled *withdrawals*, while those who remain in the group as of the end of 1977 are appropriately referred to as *enders*. Assuming that the decrement being measured is that of death, those persons tentatively labeled *withdrawals* who in fact died while under observation are accorded separate treatment and therefore must be classified as *deaths* rather than *withdrawals*. Similar treatment would be given to *lapses* if determination of lapse rates had been the objective of the study. In a traditional study of mortality, then, the three categories representing exposure termination are withdrawals, enders, and deaths, denoted by the symbols w, e, and θ, respectively.

The five categories defined above are usually the only ones appearing in a given investigation. Exceptions, of course, can be easily envisioned. Mortality may be subdivided into deaths due to heart disease, cancer, and all other causes, in which case additional categories are required. Similarly, withdrawals could be studied by cause, or enders could be segregated on the basis of their state of health. Yet these "new" categories are not really new at all, generating no new theory and only a minimum of added inconvenience.

On occasion, *fewer* than five categories may arise. A study designed to investigate the mortality of a closed group until all its members die would require no ender category. The study of a group of policies issued in 1970 and observed for the years 1972–1977 would have no new entrants, while a 1974–1977 study of the issues of 1974–1976 would have no starters. The student should be able to visualize other situations in which certain categories would be nonexistent.

Birthday-to-Birthday Studies

Rather than possessing a fixed starting and ending point, some mortality studies treat a person as exposed from his birthday in some calendar year to his birthday in a subsequent calendar year. Due to the frequent use of this type of observation period for studies of insured lives, birthday-to-birthday studies are often referred to as *anniversary-to-anniversary* studies. In such cases, the observation period runs from a policy anniversary in a given year to that in a given subsequent year. In either situation, however, there are no changes in the basic five categories identified earlier for date-to-date studies.

Consider a period of observation running from birthdays in 1974 to birthdays in 1977. Persons entering the observed group in 1973 or earlier and who are under observation on their birthdays in 1974 are considered starters, commencing their contribution of exposure on that date. Persons entering the group in 1974 but before their birthdays could be treated as either starters or new entrants. We shall refer to such persons as new entrants, preferring to consider as starters only those persons actually under observation on the date on which the *overall* study begins. Therefore, any person entering the observed group on or after January 1, 1974 and before his 1977 birthday is considered a new entrant unless, of course, he both entered and left the observed group in 1974 prior to his birthday in that year. New entrants begin to contribute exposure on the date of entry or on their 1974 birthday, whichever occurs later. The categories describing exit from the study introduce no new concepts or complications.

The anniversary-to-anniversary type of study of insured lives is somewhat easier to comprehend, as the issuance of a policy automatically creates a policy anniversary, the true date of birth being irrelevant. If the observation period is that enclosed between the 1974 and 1977 policy anniversaries, any policy issued in 1974, 1975, or 1976 is treated as a new entrant. Policies issued in 1977 are automatically excluded from the study, because their dates of entry and exit necessarily coincide.

Variations in the treatment of individual lives in an insured life study, resulting from changes in the nature of the observation period, are illustrated in Table 3-1. The student should verify the composition of the ordered pairs for each of the four cases considered.

Other Periods of Observation

The overwhelming majority of practical studies of mortality either have observation periods defined by fixed end points or are defined in the anniversary-to-anniversary fashion. Hybrids of these two methods are occasionally encountered but require the consideration of no new concepts

TABLE 3-1

			Observation period	
Insured	*Date of issue*	*Other data*	*Calendar years 1974–1977*	*1974 anniversaries to 1977 anniversaries*
A	Nov. 1, 1973	Dec. 1, 1977 (w)	(s, w)	(s, e)
B	May 1, 1970	Jun. 1, 1977 (θ)	(s, θ)	(s, e)
C	Aug. 1, 1977	Oct. 1, 1977 (w)	(n, w)	*
D	Mar. 1, 1971	Feb. 1, 1974 (θ)	(s, θ)	*

* Excluded from study.

or definitions. For example, categories in a study of insured lives running from August 1, 1973 to policy anniversaries in 1976 could be handled quite easily by using only the definitions already considered.

TABULATING RULES

In any study of mortality, we have seen that every exposed life may be treated as an ordered pair. For example, a starter who remains under observation until the termination of a study is labeled as the ordered pair (s, e). A new entrant who dies while under observation is similarly labeled as (n, θ).

The determination of whether an observed life is a starter or new entrant and whether exposure ceases by virtue of the life becoming a withdrawal, death, or ender is generally trivial. However, each element of an ordered pair must be assigned a numerical subscript which gives an indication of the age at which exposure contribution began and was terminated. It is crucially important that the lives comprising each category be subdivided into sub-groupings, or *decks*, with an integer assigned as a subscript for all of the lives within any specific deck.

The ordered pair (s_{30}, w_{33}) is read "starter at tabulated age 30, withdrawal at tabulated age 33." It is essential that the reader understand that this life was not necessarily exactly age 30 at the study's inception, nor was he exactly age 33 when he withdrew. In fact, this same life may be denoted as (s_{31}, w_{33}), (s_{29}, w_{32}), (s_{30}, w_{34}), or as any one of many other ordered pairs by competent actuaries, each of whom can easily justify the choice of subscripts. The subscripts which are assigned to each element of each ordered pair are merely fictitious ages which reflect the techniques being used by the actuary responsible for supervising the study. These subscripts must be thought of as numbers which are somehow related to the true ages of entry and exit but which are not meaningful in the absence of information as to the method of their determination. The devices used by the actuary to establish the proper subscript in any case are known as *tabulating rules*.

The remainder of Chapter Three will be devoted to the development and application of tabulating rules. We shall see that there is generally no "correct" set of tabulating rules for a given situation but that in many instances one set may be superior to another. Rules which may be ideal under one set of circumstances may be of no value whatever when the nature of the mortality investigation is slightly varied. As indicated earlier, the selection of appropriate, efficient tabulating rules is the element of a mortality study necessitating the greatest degree of actuarial expertise. For this reason, we shall launch into an exhaustive study of tabulating rules prior to the development of the mechanical aspects of the calculation of mortality rates from raw data.

Studies of mortality are generally conducted on one of three bases, producing mortality rates based upon true age, insuring age, or fiscal age. With respect to the tabulating rules used, great similarity in concept exists for the three types. For this reason, we shall concentrate in this chapter only upon tabulating rules used in obtaining mortality rates by *true age*. Specific considerations of tabulating rules for insuring and fiscal studies will be undertaken in Chapter Four.

Two primary objectives must be kept in mind as we proceed. First, the student must gain the insights necessary to analyze tabulating rules which are predetermined, rules over which no control may be exercised. Second, the ability necessary to construct tabulating rules which will produce mortality rates with the highest possible degree of accuracy from a given body of data must be developed.

Deaths

Due to the fact that the method of tabulating deaths will define the ages at which mortality rates will ultimately be determined, it is appropriate to consider tabulating rules for the death category before those for other categories.

To permit consideration of several types of tabulating rules, let us assume that the data of Table 3-2 are available for five hypothetical persons whose deaths occurred while under observation.

Calendar age. First, let us consider a quite simple but very useful tabulating rule for deaths, usually referred to as *tabulation by calendar age*:

$$\theta_x : x = \text{Calendar year of death} - \text{Calendar year of birth},$$

or

$$\theta_x : x = \text{CYD} - \text{CYB}.$$

TABLE 3-2

Life	Birth date	Date of death	Actual age at death
A	Feb. 1, 1940	Mar. 1, 1975	$35\frac{1}{12}$
B	Jul. 1, 1940	May 1, 1975	$34\frac{10}{12}$
C	Oct. 1, 1940	Feb. 1, 1975	$34\frac{4}{12}$
D	May 1, 1940	Dec. 1, 1975	$35\frac{7}{12}$
E	Apr. 1, 1940	Sep. 1, 1975	$35\frac{5}{12}$

This rule states that the subscript associated with any death is the numerical difference between the calendar year of death and the calendar year of birth of the life under consideration. Clearly, all five lives in our sample would be tabulated as θ_{35}, although none of the lives were exactly age 35 at death. This underlines the concept that the tabulated subscripts are only fictitious numbers which are, at best, approximations to true ages. It also suggests a question which demands a clear answer before the rule is to be used, that is, "If a death is tabulated as θ_{35}, what is known about the *actual* age of death?" This question may be answered in any of several ways, each dependent on the assumptions imposed.

METHOD 1 (ANALYSIS OF EXTREMES). Let us consider two extreme cases, both of which produce θ_{35}:

Birth date	Date of death
Dec. 31, 1940	Jan. 1, 1975
Jan. 1, 1940	Dec. 31, 1975

Both cases have common calendar years of birth and death, but their actual ages at death are essentially 34 and 36, respectively. Thus we see that the deck θ_{35} may contain persons whose ages at death fall at any point between 34 and 36. This fact is represented symbolically by using *range notation*,

$$\theta_{35}\Big]_{34}^{36},$$

indicating the extreme ages between which all persons in the θ_{35} deck actually fell at the date of their deaths. A quick reference to Table 3-2 substantiates that this range notation is appropriate for the five sample lives, as each died at an age between 34 and 36.

The first example, though elementary up to this point, introduces a complication which must be resolved immediately. As indicated earlier, we are ultimately interested in obtaining rates of mortality which pertain to a *single* year of age, yet we are now faced with a numerator of a mortality rate which includes deaths over an age range of *two* years. This dilemma is handled by the somewhat arbitrary expedient of truncating six months from each of the upper and lower limits of the range notation, producing

$$\theta_{35} \Big]_{34\frac{1}{2}}^{35\frac{1}{2}}.$$

Such action is perhaps justified by the fact that three-fourths of the θ_{35} group arising from 1940 births and 1975 deaths are expected to exhibit true ages at death between $34\frac{1}{2}$ and $35\frac{1}{2}$, a result which is left to the student as an exercise. Perhaps a better justification is that the calendar age tabulation for deaths is so easy to use that we are willing to accept the error introduced by the truncation process. The student can easily observe that if only the calendar years of birth and death are available in a given study, the calendar age tabulation of deaths is almost mandatory. We shall soon see, however, that when data are presented in sufficient detail, we shall usually opt for a tabulating rule which does not present the problem of shaving six months from the upper and lower limits created by the extreme cases as illustrated. In fact, in many cases, blind application of the truncation process just described produces invalid results, as we shall see shortly.

METHOD 2 (ASSUMPTION OF CENTRAL OCCURRENCE). The second method of determining range notation for the tabulation of deaths by calendar age is based upon an assumption as to the distribution of births and deaths within any calendar year. In the absence of any clue that would suggest the contrary, let us assume that all births within any calendar year occur centrally, or on July 1. Similarly, we shall assume that all deaths within any calendar year occur on July 1. These assumptions may produce over-statements or understatements of age at death by several months in specific situations, but they should provide approximately equal amounts, in the aggregate, of such overstatements and understatements. It should be mathematically and logically evident that, regarding births, for example, there are expected to be as many cases of persons born prior to July 1 as those born subsequent to July 1, unless the pattern of births is markedly seasonal. For the moment, we shall assume that it is not.

The assumption of central occurrence may be represented visually by superimposing the appropriate dates upon the tabulating rule itself, that is,

$$\overset{\text{Jul. 1}}{\theta_x} : x = \overset{\text{Jul. 1}}{\text{CYD}} - \text{CYB}.$$

We can see that our assumptions are tantamount to assuming that deaths occur on birthdays. Thus a death θ_x is assumed to be exact age x on the date of death. Then, to obtain range notation covering a range of one year of age, we find it necessary to add six months to x to obtain the upper limit of the range notation and to subtract six months from x to obtain the lower limit. The justification for such adjustments should be clear; in fact, it is quite akin in principle to the truncation approach applied in Method 1. The resulting range notation is

$$\theta_x \Big|_{x-(1/2)}^{x+(1/2)}$$

in general, or

$$\theta_{35} \Big|_{34\frac{1}{2}}^{35\frac{1}{2}}$$

as before.

A simple variation of this approach is valuable in cases in which average birth dates are known to vary from July 1, perhaps due to demographic phenomena or even to the definition of a particular study which might require observation of only those persons born in the winter and spring months. Whatever the reason, let us assume that the average birth date in a given study is May 1. Since it is highly unlikely that such a change in the birth assumption would materially affect the distribution of deaths within any calendar year, we shall leave the July 1 death assumption intact. This produces

$$\begin{array}{cc} \text{Jul. 1} & \text{May 1} \end{array}$$
$$\theta_x : x = \text{CYD} - \text{CYB}$$

and indicates that deaths tabulated at age x occur two months *after* the attainment of age x, or at exact age $x + \frac{2}{12}$. An adjustment of six months in both directions produces

$$\theta_x \Big|_{x-(4/12)}^{x+(8/12)}.$$

This result indicates the danger of blind application of Method 1. Notice that the consideration of extreme cases would still produce a two-year range (from $x - 1$ to $x + 1$) and that the six-month truncation from each limit would produce an incorrect result. The error arises simply because the May 1 birth assumption is not given recognition, suggesting that Method 1 is recommended only in cases in which the "cleanest" of assumptions can safely be made.

METHOD 3 (FIXED BIRTH ASSUMPTION). The third method to be considered combines the better points of Methods 1 and 2 and is definitely the safest and most flexible of the three. Let us assume that births occur on May 1, and let us write the tabulating rule with the *extremes* superimposed above CYD and May 1 superimposed above CYB:

$$\begin{matrix} | \text{Dec. 31} | \\ | \ \text{Jan. 1} \ | \end{matrix} \quad \text{May 1}$$

$$\theta_x : x = \quad \text{CYD} \quad - \text{CYB.}$$

An analysis of this tabulating rule produces the proper range notation without requiring six-month adjustments as in Methods 1 and 2. Since the rule, in conjunction with the May 1 birth assumption, states symbolically that exact integral age x is attained on May 1 of the calendar year of death, we must simply determine the extreme differences from age x should death occur at one of the end points of the calendar year. If death occurred on December 31, the deceased survived eight months beyond the May 1 attainment of age x. Similarly, a January 1 death occurred four months prior to age x, resulting in the symbol

$$\theta_x \Big]_{x-(4/12)}^{x+(8/12)}.$$

In future tabulations of death by calendar age, we shall use Method 3 due to its simplicity and flexibility and, most importantly, its minimization of the probability of error.

It has been observed that, in all three methods, we have assumed that deaths within the calendar year of death tend to occur in such a way that the average date of their occurrence is July 1. This assumption is quite reasonable in studies whose periods of observation cover an integral number of complete calendar years. We shall later see that difficulties, generally of a minor nature, may arise in connection with observation periods which do not begin and end at the end points of calendar years.

Age last, next, or nearest birthday. The tabulating rule

$$\theta_x : x = \text{Age last birthday at death}$$

is extremely simple and quite popular. The deaths θ_x as defined by this rule include all persons whose actual age at death is between x and $x + 1$. Thus, the range notation would be written

$$\theta_x \Big]_x^{x+1}.$$

The five lives illustrated in Table 3-2 would be tabulated as deaths at ages 35, 34, 34, 35, and 35, respectively.

Similarly, the tabulating rule

$$\theta_x : x = \text{Age next birthday at death}$$

generates the symbol

$$\theta_x \Big]_{x-1}^{x}$$

and would produce subscripts for the five sample lives of 36, 35, 35, 36, and 36. It should be obvious that the *age next birthday* rule assigns each death a subscript one unit greater than the *age last birthday* rule. Thus life A is tabulated as θ_{35} in one case and as θ_{36} in the other, substantiating the statement that two reasonable tabulating rules may properly assign different subscripts to the same individual.

Finally, the rule

$$\theta_x : x = \text{Age nearest birthday at death}$$

treats all deaths occurring between ages $x - \frac{1}{2}$ and $x + \frac{1}{2}$ as deaths at tabulated age x. This rule leads to

$$\theta_x \Big]_{x-(1/2)}^{x+(1/2)}$$

and designates our five sample lives as deaths at ages 35, 35, 34, 36, and 35, respectively.

The three tabulating rules just considered have the major advantage that they each uniquely determine a *deck* of deaths which fall between two ages exactly one year apart. They therefore obviate the need for such questionable techniques as adding or subtracting six months in order to create an age range of length one year. Another advantage of these tabulating rules is that they are wholly independent of the nature of the observation period. This is best realized from the fact that no assumption is necessary as to the average date of birth or death, unlike the case of tabulation of deaths by calendar age.

These rules, however, are inapplicable in situations in which data are not available in sufficient detail. For example, if we are given the date, month, and year of an individual's death but only the year of his birth, we are unable to determine the correct tabulated death subscript for the age last, age next, or age nearest tabulating rules. In such cases, we generally resort to a tabulation of deaths by calendar age. An analogy with the computation of mileage traveled using an automobile's odometer may be helpful. If a trip begins with an odometer reading of 147 and ends with a reading of 197, the distance traveled is said to be 50 miles. However, the true distance may be anywhere between 49 and 51 miles. Only if note is taken of the *tenths* digit of the odometer reading may greater accuracy be obtained. Further, if the tenths digit is observed only for the *terminal* reading, the maximum range becomes a single mile. Similarly, when exact dates of death are given but only *years* of birth are known, a one-year death range becomes available for any given death. In summary, the more detail available with regard to dates of birth and death, the greater the number of tabulating rules that can be utilized with confidence.

Other rules. Another type of tabulating rule for deaths is one which, though it may initially seem unduly complicated, provides the student added insight into the nature and interpretation of tabulating rules in general.

Further, rules of this type are closely akin to those which are widely used in the determination of mortality rates by fiscal ages, a subject to be treated in Chapter Four.

Let us consider the tabulating rule

$\theta_x : x =$
Calendar year containing the April 1 following (or coincident with) death – CYB.

For purposes of simplification, let us agree to write this rule as

$$\theta_x : x = \text{CYC Apr. 1 FD} - \text{CYB}.$$

Application of this rule introduces no real difficulties. Consider, for example, a person born in 1940 who dies during 1975. Should death occur on or before April 1, the calendar year containing the next April 1 is clearly 1975. Should death occur after April 1, the year described by the first component of the tabulating rule is 1976. Thus a February 1975 death would be tabulated as a θ_{35}, while a June 1975 death would be treated as a θ_{36}. The five sample lives in Table 3-2 would be tabulated by this rule as deaths at ages 35, 36, 35, 36, and 36, respectively.

The difficulty in using tabulating rules of this type is usually in the determination of the range of the deaths defined by θ_x. However, such determination should be easily mastered with a careful analysis of each such rule, accompanied by a simple diagram. First, it must be reiterated that the tabulated age x is always an integer. Clearly, integral ages are attained by all persons on their birthdays. Assuming that the average birth date within any calendar year is July 1, we may rephrase the tabulating rule by stating that "age x is the integral age which would have been attained on the July 1 of the calendar year containing the April 1 following death."

It is evident from Figure 3-1 that deaths occurring between April 1, z and April 1, $z + 1$ represent a one-year deck of deaths, all of which have $z + 1$ as the "calendar year containing the April 1 following death." Thus all deaths in the illustrated θ_x deck would have attained exact age x on July 1, $z + 1$. It is important to note that all deaths in the θ_x deck of Figure 3-1 were born in the calendar year $z + 1 - x$. This may be seen from the tabulating rule which, for this case, reads

$$\theta_x : x = (z + 1) - \text{CYB}.$$

FIGURE 3-1

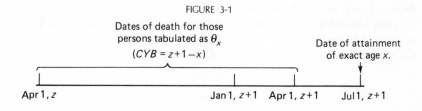

Dates of death for those persons tabulated as θ_x
($CYB = z+1-x$)

Date of attainment of exact age x.

Apr 1, z Jan 1, $z+1$ Apr 1, $z+1$ Jul 1, $z+1$

At this stage, we resort to an analysis of extremes. The earliest deaths among members of this one-year group occurred in early April, z, while the latest deaths occurred in late March, $z + 1$. The extreme cases, then, were deaths at exact ages $x - \frac{15}{12}$ and $x - \frac{3}{12}$, respectively. Thus, the correct range notation for this tabulating rule is

$$\theta_x \Big]_{x-(15/12)}^{x-(3/12)},$$

which, in retrospect, could have been determined immediately from the observation of Figure 3-1.

Indeed, the key step in the determination of the range notation for the deaths was the sketching of Figure 3-1. The objective of such a diagram was to isolate "a full year's worth" of deaths, all of which possessed the common characteristic of having $z + 1$ as the "calendar year containing the April 1 following death." Since the tabulating rule states that exact age x would have been attained in the "right-hand" calendar year, that is, year $z + 1$, it becomes evident that the deaths in question occurred between 15 and 3 months prior to attainment of age x. With a little practice, the student should readily be able to determine the range notation generated by similar tabulating rules.

It should be observed that the true ages at death of the five persons illustrated in Table 3-2 do not necessarily fall in an interval between 15 and 3 months less than the respective ages at death tabulated by the rule

$$\theta_x : x = \text{CYC Apr. 1 FD} - \text{CYB},$$

that is, 35, 36, 35, 36, and 36, because the July 1 birth assumption used in determining the range of the deaths θ_x was not valid in the case of the individual lives. This underlines the important fact that tabulating rules often lead to death ranges only after imposition of a simplifying assumption and that it is therefore dangerous to test the validity of the range notation by considering individual lives for whom the assumption may be invalid. The student should also note that the problem of dealing with a true range of two years for deaths rather than the desirable single year arises with tabulating rules of this type just as with tabulation by calendar age.

Determination of the range notation for the tabulating rule which we have been considering is no more difficult if a different birth assumption is utilized. Suppose, for example, that indications point to the reasonableness of an August 1 birth assumption. The tabulating rule which we have been considering then indicates that integral age x would have been attained on August 1 in the right-hand calendar year of Figure 3-1. Thus, the true ages at death would fall between $x - \frac{16}{12}$ and $x - \frac{4}{12}$, leading to the symbol

$$\theta_x \Big]_{x-(16/12)}^{x-(4/12)}.$$

Finally, let us consider the rule

$\theta_x : x =$ Calendar year containing the September 1 nearest death $-$ CYB,

or, simplified,

$$\theta_x : x = \text{CYC Sep. 1 ND} - \text{CYB.}$$

In determining the range notation for the deaths, consistent with this tabulating rule, we must again isolate a 12-month period during which all deaths must be handled identically. All persons dying between March 1, z and March 1, $z + 1$ have the year z as the calendar year containing the September 1 nearest their date of death. Thus, the tabulating rule states that such persons had (or would have had) their xth birthday in calendar year z. Imposing the standard July 1 birth assumption, we see that the earliest of such deaths occurred 4 months prior to July 1 and that the latest occurred 8 months subsequent to July 1. The desired range notation, then, is

$$\theta_x \Big]_{x-(4/12)}^{x+(8/12)}.$$

The student should construct a diagram similar to Figure 3-1 as an aid in the analysis of this and similar problems. Further, it should be verified that a May 1 birth assumption with this same tabulating rule would lead to

$$\theta_x \Big]_{x-(2/12)}^{x+(10/12)}.$$

Let us observe a slightly modified approach which handles tabulation rules of this type in a fashion which may be helpful. Consider the rule

$\theta_x : x =$

Calendar year containing the June 1 preceding (or coincident with) death $-$ CYB,

or

$$\theta_x : x = \text{CYC Jun. 1 PD} - \text{CYB.}$$

Let us impose an August 1 birth assumption. Suppose a person was born on August 1, 1940. If death occurred between June 1, 1975 and June 1, 1976, the tabulated age at death is 35 (1975 $-$ 1940). Consideration of the extreme cases suggests, however, that the true age at death is between $34\frac{10}{12}$ and $35\frac{10}{12}$, leading to

$$\theta_{35} \Big]_{34\frac{10}{12}}^{35\frac{10}{12}}$$

or, more generally,

$$\theta_x \Big]_{x-(2/12)}^{x+(10/12)}.$$

Whereas this method is clearly equivalent to the more general techniques illustrated earlier, some students may feel more comfortable with the concrete analysis of a special case, followed by generalization.

Starters and Enders

Tabulating rules for starter and ender categories are generally less complex than those for deaths. We shall see, however, that the definition of the period of observation has a major effect upon the analysis of such rules, unlike the situation with deaths where the nature of the observation period rarely affects the determination of the range.

Another important consideration with respect to nondeath categories is that we are generally more concerned with a single age representing an entire deck than with range notation. For example, the symbol $s_x^{x+(1/3)}$ will be read "the set of starters tabulated at age x whose true age at the study's inception is, on the average, $x + \frac{1}{3}$." Notice that such a symbol gives no information as to the age of the youngest and oldest members of the s_x deck but indicates that, for computational purposes, we may treat every person thus included as being of exact age $x + \frac{1}{3}$. Such notation will be referred to as *superscripted notation* as opposed to *range notation*. Nondeath categories lend themselves to range notation in the same manner as deaths. However, range notation is rarely used for starters, new entrants, withdrawals, or enders, because, as we shall see later when exposure formulas are developed, standard formulas are designed for use when the deaths are expressed in range notation with all other categories represented by superscripts.

Calendar year studies. Let us assume a date-to-date mortality study which covers an integral number of calendar years, say 1973–1977, inclusive. The two most commonly used tabulating rules for starters in such studies are

$$s_x : x = 1972 - \text{CYB} \tag{3-1}$$

and

$$s_x : x = 1973 - \text{CYB,} \tag{3-2}$$

each of which is quite simple to apply. A person born in 1940, for example, would be tabulated as s_{32} and s_{33}, respectively, by these rules.

If we make the normal assumption of July 1 births, the superscripted notation is most efficiently determined for Rule (3-1) by using the line of reasoning that starters tabulated at age x attain exact age x on July 1, 1972. We are interested in their age as of the starting date of the study, which is January 1, 1973, or six months *after* attainment of age x. Therefore, given the birth assumption, each member of the s_x deck is exact age $x + \frac{1}{2}$ at the study's inception. This produces the symbol

$$s_x^{x+(1/2)}.$$

It should be easy to see, by similar reasoning, that an August 1 birth assumption with Rule (3-1) produces

$$s_x^{x+(5/12)},$$

as the observation period begins five months after the attainment of age x.

Rule (3-2) for starters leads to a similar analysis, as it states that a starter tabulated at age x attains age x during 1973. The July 1 birth assumption produces the symbol

$$s_x^{x-(1/2)},$$

as the starting date of the study falls six months *prior* to the attainment of age x. A September 1 birth assumption with Rule (3-2) produces

$$s_x^{x-(8/12)},$$

a result which may easily be verified.

In addition to the rules just illustrated, the only other methods commonly used for starter tabulation are the age last birthday, age next birthday, and age nearest birthday bases. If, for example, starters are tabulated by age last birthday, the superscripted symbol would be

$$s_x^{x+(1/2)}$$

in the absence of an unusual distribution of births. If births occur in a reasonably uniform pattern over any given calendar year, it is to be expected that, at any point in time, those persons who are age x last birthday are approximately age $x + \frac{1}{2}$ on the average. Similarly, the age next birthday and age nearest birthday rules lead to

$$s_x^{x-(1/2)} \quad \text{and} \quad s_x^{x},$$

respectively.

It should be noted that two seemingly different tabulating rules may be identical. Consider, for example, an observation period beginning on January 1, 1974 and the following tabulating rules:

$$s_x : x = 1974 - \text{CYB} \tag{3-3}$$

and

$$s_x : x = \text{Age next birthday as of January 1, 1974.} \tag{3-4}$$

These two rules, when applied to any individual starter, must assign the same subscript. The first rule indicates that starters at tabulated age x each attain actual age x on their 1974 birthdays. It follows that, at the beginning of 1974, all such persons are age x next birthday, verifying that Rules (3-3) and (3-4) are always consistent. For example, any starter born in 1930 would be classified by both rules as a member of the s_{44} deck.

Similarly, the identical range notation generated by two tabulating rules does not imply identity of the rules themselves. For example, the symbol

$$\theta_x \Big]_{x-(1/2)}^{x+(1/2)}$$

may result from the tabulation of deaths by calendar age or by age nearest birthday. Yet it should be obvious that the calendar age of a person is not necessarily the same as his age nearest birthday.

Tabulating rules for enders follow the same patterns as those for starters, a fact which makes an exhaustive analysis of such rules unnecessary. Although not mandatory from a theoretical point of view, tabulating rules for enders are usually designed in such a way as to produce the same superscripts as those obtained for starters. For example, suppose we utilize a tabulating rule for starters which produces

$$s_x^{x+(1/2)}.$$

It is common practice to select a rule for enders which will produce

$$e_x^{x+(1/2)}.$$

It would be unusual, though certainly not incorrect, to tabulate starters by age nearest birthday and enders by age last birthday. The justification for the efforts to produce uniformity is simply that we may wish to treat $s_x - e_x$ as a single quantity in some of the exposure formulas yet to be derived. As we shall see, such consolidation will not be feasible unless the starters and enders tabulated at age x have a common superscript.

In a mortality study covering the four calendar years 1974–1977, suppose the tabulating rule for starters is

$$s_x : x = 1973 - \text{CYB},$$

producing the symbol

$$s_x^{x+(1/2)}$$

under the assumption of July 1 births. Then, given a free hand to construct a tabulating rule for enders, we would probably choose

$$e_x : x = 1977 - \text{CYB},$$

which produces

$$e_x^{x+(1/2)}$$

rather than

$$e_x : x = 1978 - \text{CYB},$$

which leads to

$$e_x^{x-(1/2)}.$$

Birthday-to-birthday studies. Tabulating rules for starters and enders generally assume the same forms in birthday-to-birthday studies as in date-to-date studies. Yet different superscripts are often encountered, illustrating the fact that the nature of the observation period is a major factor in the analysis of tabulating rules for nondeath categories.

Consider a mortality study in which lives are observed from birthdays in 1974 to birthdays in 1977. The most convenient tabulating rules for starters and enders are

$$s_x : x = 1974 - \text{CYB}$$

and

$$e_x : x = 1977 - \text{CYB}.$$

These tabulations are said to be on the basis of *exact age*. This results from the fact that on 1974 birthdays exposure measurement for starters begins and exact age x is attained simultaneously. Similarly, for enders, the observation period ends just as exact age x is attained. Notice that no assumption is necessary regarding distribution of births, because a starter begins his exposure contribution on his birthday regardless of the date in 1974 on which his birthday falls. A similar statement is applicable to enders.

It is an interesting theoretical exercise to consider the tabulating rules

$$s_x : x = 1973 - \text{CYB}$$

and

$$e_x : x = 1978 - \text{CYB}$$

for the same observation period discussed above. Whereas these rules would not be the logical choices, they could in no way be considered improper. The starter rule indicates that age x is attained on a person's 1973 birthday. Since the study actually begins exactly one year later, the appropriate symbol is

$$s_x^{x+1}.$$

Similarly, the given rule for enders would produce

$$e_x^{x-1}.$$

Tabulations of starters and enders by age last, next, or nearest birthday are not used in birthday-to-birthday studies, because of the advantage inherent in such studies which makes it possible to tabulate these categories by exact age.

Other periods of observation. Date-to-date studies other than those covering an integral number of calendar years produce little complication in the analysis of tabulating rules for starters and enders. The techniques discussed earlier for calendar year studies are easily applied in such cases.

Consider, for example, an observation period from May 1, 1974 to November 30, 1977. The optimum choices for tabulating rules are

$$s_x : x = 1974 - \text{CYB} \quad \text{and} \quad e_x : x = 1977 - \text{CYB},$$

leading to

$$s_x^{x-(2/12)} \quad \text{and} \quad e_x^{x+(5/12)}$$

under the standard July 1 birth assumption. The starter superscript may be determined by analyzing the extreme birth dates or by writing May 1 and Jul. 1 above the respective components of the tabulating rule, indicating that the study began for the s_x deck two months prior to the attainment of age x. The ender superscript is obtained similarly.

As a somewhat more complicated example, consider the tabulating rules

$$s_x : x = 1975 - \text{CYB}$$

and

$$e_x : x = 1976 - \text{CYB}$$

for the same period of observation just considered but with an August 1 birth assumption. The rule for starters, in conjunction with the birth assumption, indicates that age x is attained on August 1, 1975, or 15 months after the initial date of the observation period, leading to

$$s_x^{x-(15/12)}.$$

Likewise, the ender rule, in conjunction with the birth assumption, states that age x is attained on August 1, 1976. Since the study does not terminate until 16 months later, the enders tabulated at age x would then have become age $x + \frac{16}{12}$, producing

$$e_x^{x+(16/12)}.$$

Although these rules would not be the traditional choices, they are nevertheless satisfactory. We shall later see that all tabulating rules of the form

$$s_x : x = z - \text{CYB}$$

will produce exactly the same exposure values and mortality rates, regardless of the calendar year represented by z, as long as the superscripts are correctly determined.

New Entrants and Withdrawals

The nature of the tabulating rules generally associated with new entrants and withdrawals closely parallels that of the rules used for deaths. In fact, a great deal of the material to be devoted here to new entrants and withdrawals could be significantly condensed merely by treating the tabulating rules for simple cases as if they referred to deaths and then averaging the limits on the range notation to determine the appropriate superscript. Just as is the case with deaths, the form of the observation period is only rarely a factor in the analysis of tabulating rules. The final illustration at the end of this chapter will consider the case in which the observation period is of an irregular nature.

It has been observed that there are certain advantages in using tabulating rules for starters and enders which result in identical superscripts for the two categories. Similarly, it is common practice to follow the same procedure for new entrants and withdrawals. For situations in which this practice is followed, we shall adopt the notational expedient of treating $n_x - w_x$ as the single term m_x, where m_x is defined as "the net migration at tabulated age x." This is not feasible if, for example, we are forced to tabulate new entrants by calendar age and withdrawals by age last birthday. These two rules produce different superscripts for the n_x and w_x decks, and, as we shall later see, such decks can then not be combined when used in standard exposure formulas.

Calendar age. Consider the tabulating rule

$$m_x : x = \text{Calendar year of migration} - \text{CYB}$$

or

$$m_x : x = \text{CYM} - \text{CYB.}^*$$

Such a rule necessitates assumptions as to both the average date of migration and the average date of birth within any calendar year period. The July 1 assumption for each leads to

$$m_x^x,$$

whereas an August 1 migration assumption and a June 1 birth assumption produce

$$m_x^{x+(2/12)}.$$

As indicated during the earlier discussion of calendar age tabulations of deaths, several methods exist which are helpful in the analysis of such rules. Ideally, more than one such method should be mastered for migration rules as well as death rules. However, the student should realize that the superscript for the migration category is found most easily by comparing the date at which age x is attained with the point at which migration is assumed. The assumption that migration, on the average, occurs on birthdays produces the symbol

$$m_x^x$$

with no specific assumption being necessary as to distribution of either births or migration.

---

* In cases of separate tabulating rules for new entrants and withdrawals, the letter N will be used to represent entry and W will be used for withdrawal. For example, CYN stands for "calendar year of new entry" and CYW for "calendar year of withdrawal."

Age last, next, or nearest birthday. Tabulations of migration by the last, next, or nearest birthday rules produce appropriate superscripts effortlessly. Assuming a uniform distribution of birthdays over any 12-month period, the resulting symbols are

$$m_x^{x+(1/2)}, \quad m_x^{x-(1/2)}, \quad \text{and} \quad m_x^x,$$

respectively, simply because, for example, those persons whose migration occurs at age x last birthday are, on the average, 6 months older than age x at the time of such migration.

Other rules. The same relatively complex tabulating rules illustrated earlier for deaths may be applied equally well to migration. Consider the rule

$m_x : x =$ Calendar year containing the November 1 preceding migration $-$ CYB,

or

$$m_x : x = \text{CYC Nov. 1 PM} - \text{CYB}.$$

A July 1 birth assumption leads to the conclusion that exact age x is attained on the July 1 of "the calendar year containing the November 1 preceding migration." As a first step in determining the superscript, we must isolate the 12-month period from November 1, z to November 1, $z + 1$. All migration occurring within this period has calendar year z as the calendar year containing the preceding November 1. Then, since x is attained on July 1, z and the assumed average date of migration is May 1, $z + 1$ (halfway between November 1, z and November 1, $z + 1$), the correct symbol is

$$m_x^{x+(10/12)}.$$

Variations of this example are numerous, but all should be analyzed by this technique. Exercises at the end of the chapter will afford opportunities for the student to develop the ability to determine superscripts generated by rules of this and other types rapidly and accurately.

A FINAL ILLUSTRATION

The following comprehensive illustration is designed to accomplish two purposes. First, it serves as an opportunity for the student to apply many of the concepts and techniques discussed in this chapter. Second, it illustrates the fact, alluded to earlier, that certain categories should be handled with extra care in date-to-date studies which do not comprise an integral number of complete calendar years.

EXAMPLE 3-1   The following tabulating rules are given for use in mortality studies A and B:

$$\theta_x : x = \text{CYC Apr. 1 ND} - \text{CYB},$$

$$s_x : x = 1973 - \text{CYB},$$

$$m_x : x = \text{CYM} - \text{CYB},$$

$$e_x : x = 1979 - \text{CYB}.$$

Assuming that births within any calendar year fall on September 1, determine the range notation for deaths and the superscripted notation for the other categories. The observation period for study A is the calendar years 1974–1978, inclusive. For study B, the observation period runs from March 1, 1974 to May 31, 1979.

SOLUTION   For study A, application of the techniques described in this chapter immediately produces

$$\theta_x \Big]_{x-(11/12)}^{x+(1/12)}, \quad s_x^{x+(4/12)}, \quad m_x^{x-(2/12)}, \quad \text{and} \quad e_x^{x-(8/12)}.$$

To arrive at the above, only one assumption was imposed, that of central occurrence of migration over any calendar year.

The symbols for starters and enders in study B,

$$s_x^{x+(6/12)} \quad \text{and} \quad e_x^{x-(3/12)},$$

involve no new theory. Analysis of the migration category does, however, give rise to a minor complication. It will be helpful to consider such an observation period as consisting of a *head*, a *body*, and a *tail*. In this case, the head comprises the last ten months of 1974, the body is the four calendar years 1975–1978, and the tail consists of the first five months of 1979.

The migration occurring during the calendar years 1975–1978, inclusive, may safely be assumed to fall on July 1. However, the migration occurring during that portion of 1974 which falls during the observation period tends to fall in the middle of such period, or on August 1. Likewise, the observed migration during 1979 is assumed to occur in mid-March. Thus, the 1974 migration at tabulated age x is assigned the superscript $x - \frac{1}{12}$, and the 1979 migration is assigned $x - \frac{11}{24}$. Clearly, $x - \frac{2}{12}$ is the appropriate superscript for the migration of the years 1975–1978. Taking a weighted average of these results, using as weights the lengths of the head, body, and tail, we have

$$\frac{\frac{10}{12}(x - \frac{1}{12}) + 4(x - \frac{2}{12}) + \frac{5}{12}(x - \frac{11}{24})}{\frac{10}{12} + 4 + \frac{5}{12}}$$

or

$$x - \tfrac{89}{504}.$$

Notice that the resulting symbol

$$m_x^{x-(89/504)}$$

varies only slightly from the symbol

$$m_x^{x-(2/12)}$$

obtained in study A. As a general rule, we shall agree to use the migration superscript resulting from a disregard of the unusual nature of the observation period, although the student must be aware of the slight error thus overlooked.

The range notation for the deaths in study B is not affected by the change in observation period from that used in study A, as analysis of the extreme cases in the two studies produces identical results. Granted, the distribution of the deaths θ_x will be somewhat different for the two distinct observation periods, but this distribution is not reflected when the range notation is employed.

SUMMARY

The efficient analysis of large quantities of data is the first major task in the administration of a study of mortality, disability, lapse, or other form of decrement. Such data must be neatly packaged into well-defined categories which describe the means of entry into and exit from the observed group.

Although in certain instances other categories may exist, most studies involve only the five which have been designated as starters, new entrants, withdrawals, enders, and deaths. We have seen how each of these is defined and that there is rarely a problem in properly assigning, to individual lives, two categories which reflect the means of entry and exit. Such assignments are conveniently represented by ordered pairs.

A more complex problem is the determination of unit groupings within each category. Such groupings, which permit the association of realistic ages of entry and exit with tabulated ages which only approximate true ages, are defined by arithmetical guidelines known as tabulating rules. The results of an analysis of these rules are represented by category symbols written either in superscripted notation or range notation, the latter being reserved for the decrement under study, generally the decrement of death. At this stage, then, every life which was under observation is represented as an ordered pair, such as (s_{22}, w_{24}), with the subscripts of each element revealing valuable information regarding the true ages at which exposure measurement began and ceased.

The types of tabulating rules illustrated in this chapter range from extremely elementary to fairly complex. The student must master all types to the extent that any given tabulating rule may be analyzed quickly and accurately, producing range or superscripted notation which, as we shall see, uniquely determines the exposure formulas which are to be applied to the given body of data.

It must be emphasized that the tabulating rules thus far considered relate only to mortality studies based upon *true* ages. However, as we begin to work with fiscal or insuring ages in Chapter Four, we should encounter little difficulty in applying the concepts which have been presented here.

The remaining step in our development of the theory of table construction is the derivation of formulas which will produce, from our tabulated data, exposure values and mortality rates. The objectives of the following three chapters are the development of the necessary exposure formulas and the analysis of such formulas in a manner which will uncover interesting interrelationships and, in some instances, an inherent identity which is undeniable but not immediately obvious.

EXERCISES

1. Dates of birth and death for A, B, C, D, and E are as follows:

Life	Birth date	Date of death
A	Mar. 1, 1950	Oct. 1, 1976
B	Jun. 1, 1951	Aug. 1, 1976
C	Oct. 1, 1950	Feb. 1, 1975
D	Dec. 1, 1949	Jun. 1, 1975
E	Aug. 1, 1951	Jul. 7, 1977

For a study covering the calendar years 1974–1978, inclusive, determine the subscript of θ for each life under each of the following tabulating rules:

(a) $\theta_x : x =$ age next birthday at death.
(b) $\theta_x : x =$ CYC Jul. 1 FD − CYB.
(c) $\theta_x : x =$ CYC Mar. 1 ND − CYB.

2. In analyzing the data used in a mortality study, the following determinations are made:
   (i) Withdrawals in the first half of each calendar year have an average date of occurrence of March 1.
   (ii) Withdrawals in the second half of each calendar year have an average date of occurrence of September 1.

(iii) Twice as many withdrawals occur in the first half of each calendar year as in the second half.

(iv) The average birth date within any calendar year is June 1.

 (v) Withdrawals are tabulated by calendar age.

Determine the appropriate superscript for the w_x deck.

3. Using the tabulating rule

$$\theta_x : x = CYD - CYB,$$

determine the assumption which leads to the symbol

$$\theta_x \Big]_{x-(1/4)}^{x+(3/4)}.$$

4. Using the tabulating rule

$$s_x : x = 1974 - CYB,$$

determine at least two sets of birth assumptions and periods of observation which lead to the symbol

$$s_x^{x+(1/3)}.$$

5. Using the tabulating rule

$$m_x : x = CYC \text{ Mar. } 1 \text{ PM} - CYB,$$

determine at least two sets of birth and migration assumptions which lead to the symbol

$$m_x^x.$$

6. Determine the symbol for deaths in range notation under each of the following tabulating rules, assuming that births within any calendar year fall on July 1:

(a) $\theta_x : x = CYD - CYB.$

(b) $\theta_x : x = CYC \text{ Feb. } 1 \text{ PD} - CYB.$

(c) $\theta_x : x = CYC \text{ Aug. } 1 \text{ FD} - CYB.$

(d) $\theta_x : x = CYC \text{ Nov. } 1 \text{ ND} - CYB.$

(e) $\theta_x : x = $ age next birthday at death.

7. Rework each part of Exercise 6, imposing a May 1 birth assumption.

8. Based upon the tabulating rule

$$s_x : x = 1977 - CYB,$$

determine the superscripted symbol for starters, using an August 1 birth assumption and an observation period which begins on

(a) July 1, 1977.

(b) April 1, 1977.

(c) February 1, 1978.
(d) October 1, 1976.
(e) December 1, 1980.
(f) 1977 birthdays.
(g) 1976 birthdays.

9. Rework each part of Exercise 8, imposing an April 1 birth assumption.

10. The employees of an organization, hired during the five calendar years 1970–1974, are observed from March 1, 1975 until February 29, 1984. Deaths and withdrawals are tabulated by calendar age, and the following rules are used for starters and enders:

$$s_x : x = 1974 - \text{CYB},$$

$$e_x : x = 1983 - \text{CYB}.$$

Determine the category symbols if it is determined that the average birth date within each year is June 15.

11. The observation period of a mortality study runs from May 1, 1975 through August 31, 1979. Stating all assumptions, determine the category symbols based upon the following tabulating rules:

$$\theta_x : x = \text{CYC Dec. 1 PD} - \text{CYB},$$

$$s_x : x = 1975 - \text{CYB},$$

$$n_x : x = \text{CYC Aug. 1 NN} - \text{CYB},$$

$$w_x : x = \text{CYC Feb. 1 FW} - \text{CYB},$$

$$e_x : x = 1978 - \text{CYB}.$$

12. In a mortality study, deaths are tabulated by calendar age and starters are tabulated by the rule

$$s_x : x = 1977 - \text{CYB}.$$

These tabulating rules produce the symbols

$$\theta_x \Big]_{x-(2/3)}^{x+(1/3)} \quad \text{and} \quad s_x^{x-(1/2)}$$

when deaths are assumed to occur centrally within any calendar year. Determine

(a) The birth assumption which was used.
(b) The starting date of the study.
(c) The *range notation* for starters.

13. The following tabulating rules have been used in a mortality study of members of an employee group, observed from March 1, 1975 through October 31, 1977:

$$\theta_x : x = \text{CYC Oct. 1 FD} - \text{CYB},$$

$$s_x : x = 1975 - \text{CYB},$$

$$n_x : x = \text{CYN} - \text{CYB},$$

$$w_x : x = \text{CYC Jul. 1 PW} - \text{CYB},$$

$$e_x : x = 1978 - \text{CYB}.$$

(a) Stating all assumptions, determine the category symbols.
(b) Using the given tabulating rules, represent each of the following lives as an ordered pair with the appropriate subscripts:

Employee	Birth date	Date of hire	Other data
A	Jul. 1, 1945	Jul. 1, 1971	Died Nov. 3, 1976
B	Apr. 1, 1944	Dec. 1, 1971	Still working Oct. 31, 1977
C	Feb. 1, 1946	Mar. 1, 1971	Quit Feb. 1, 1976
D	Oct. 1, 1945	Jul. 1, 1977	Died Sep. 30, 1977
E	Dec. 1, 1945	Oct. 1, 1976	Still working Oct. 31, 1977
F	Aug. 1, 1946	Sep. 1, 1975	Quit Aug. 1, 1976

14. Three separate mortality studies are being designed for a group of employees. Study 1 begins on May 1, 1974 and terminates on August 31, 1978. Study 2 covers the calendar years 1974–1978, inclusive. Study 3 runs from birthdays in 1974 until birthdays in 1978. The following tabulating rules are used for each study:

$$\theta_x : x = \text{Calendar age at death},$$

$$s_x : x = 1973 - \text{CYB},$$

$$n_x : x = \text{CYC Oct. 1 FN} - \text{CYB},$$

$$w_x : x = \text{CYC Apr. 1 NW} - \text{CYB},$$

$$e_x : x = 1978 - \text{CYB}.$$

(a) Stating your assumptions, write the category symbols for each study.
(b) For each study, categorize and assign a subscript to each of the following lives:

Life	Birth date	Date of hire	Other data
A	Apr. 6, 1955	Jul. 3, 1973	Died Oct. 17, 1975
B	May 13, 1955	Dec. 24, 1974	Quit Sep. 15, 1975
C	Jan. 11, 1956	Jun. 7, 1973	Died Apr. 10, 1974
D	Sep. 28, 1956	Feb. 3, 1974	Still working Dec. 31, 1978
E	Oct. 6, 1955	Aug. 15, 1972	Quit Mar. 1, 1974

15. The observation period of a mortality study is from May 1, 1974 through October 31, 1978. The tabulating rule

$$w_x : x = \text{CYW} - \text{CYB}$$

is used in conjunction with assumptions that births occur on June 1 and withdrawals are uniformly distributed within any given calendar year. As a result, the symbol

$$w_x^{x+(1/12)}$$

is selected. Find the theoretical absolute value of the error in the withdrawal superscript resulting from the irregular nature of the observation period.

16. Determine the range notation for deaths produced by the following tabulating rule:

$$\theta_x = A - B,$$

where

A = calendar year containing the September 1 following death;

B = calendar year containing the May 1 nearest birth.

17. Demonstrate that, under a reasonable assumption with respect to distribution of births and deaths, three-fourths of those persons born in calendar year z and dying in calendar year $z + n$ are between ages $n - \frac{1}{2}$ and $n + \frac{1}{2}$ at death.

Individual Record
Exposure Formulas

INTRODUCTION

Having completed an analysis of the means of categorizing lives which contribute exposure to a mortality study, we are now prepared to pursue the ultimate goal of this text, that is, the development of techniques for determining exposures and mortality rates. Three basic methods will be presented. They will be referred to as the seriatim method, the grouped individual record method, and the in-force, or valuation schedule, method. The first two, each designed for use when records of individual lives exposed to risk are available, will be considered in this chapter. The foundation for the concept of grouping individual lives in mortality studies was laid in Chapter Three with the selection and analysis of tabulating rules for the several categories of exposed lives. The in-force method, of a different nature but in many ways very similar to the individual record methods, will be treated in Chapter Five.

THE SERIATIM METHOD

The seriatim method takes its name from the Latin word meaning *series*, and, significantly, the present-day English meaning of the word seriatim is *serially*. Thus, the calculation of exposures by the seriatim method involves the consideration of each exposed life, one by one. The ages at which exposure contribution begins and ceases are determined for each life independently, and the results are then combined to produce numbers of life-years of exposure for each unit age interval as defined by the study.

For mortality studies based upon massive amounts of data, the seriatim method may seem impractical, and some means of grouping the data may seem advisable. However, the extreme simplicity of the seriatim method and the absence of approximating techniques make it quite attractive, especially with the ever-increasing capacity of data processing machines. It seems likely that, in the not-too-distant future, the seriatim method will supersede the grouped individual record method in utility. The in-force method is certain to retain its popularity, however, as it is applicable to aggregate data which do not permit direct use of seriatim techniques.

Two widely held misconceptions surrounding the seriatim method must be dispelled at the outset. For some unexplainable reason, many students of mortality theory have felt that the seriatim method is applicable only to the calculation of mortality rates at integral ages. On the contrary, regardless of the method used to tabulate deaths and the unit age interval thus defined, the seriatim method may easily be employed. The second misconception is that the seriatim method, since it is applied to each life independently, should be used without the imposition of any assumption as to mortality patterns. Whereas such use would theoretically be possible, the seriatim method will be used here only in conjunction with the Balducci hypothesis. Such a ground rule is justified not only because of the demonstrated reasonableness of this mortality assumption but also because its use will permit valuable comparisons of the seriatim method with the two methods to be considered later.

Application of the Method

Without mentioning the seriatim method by name, examples and illustrations earlier in the text have already given the reader an indication of the techniques to be used. The actual age at which exposure began for an individual is subtracted from the actual age at which exposure ceased, leaving as the result the number of units (usually fractional) of exposure contributed by the life. Clearly, a method of tabulation of deaths must be selected before the exposure termination date for deaths can be determined, as we recall that deaths contribute exposure to the end of the unit age interval when the Balducci hypothesis is assumed. Once the total exposure for each person has thus been obtained, the substantial problem of allocating such exposure to the several unit age intervals must be attacked.

Let us assume that, for an observation period covering the calendar years 1972–1978, inclusive, deaths have been tabulated by age nearest birthday. Since θ_x is thus used to describe the deaths occurring between ages $x - \frac{1}{2}$ and $x + \frac{1}{2}$, we shall adopt the notational expedient of denoting the exposure between these same two ages as E_x. The symbol E_x will hereafter always be understood to derive its meaning from that given to θ_x in any given situation.

An analysis of six employees of a given organization, for whom data are given in Table 4-1, should be helpful in illustrating the seriatim method.

TABLE 4-1
Period of Observation: January 1, 1972 through December 31, 1978

Employee	Born	Hired	Other data
A	Mar. 1, 1950	Oct. 1, 1970	Quit Feb. 1, 1975
B	Aug. 1, 1951	Jun. 1, 1971	Died Sep. 1, 1972
C	Jul. 1, 1950	Apr. 1, 1973	Died Feb. 1, 1974
D	Nov. 1, 1950	Feb. 1, 1974	Died Mar. 1, 1975
E	Apr. 1, 1951	Sep. 1, 1973	Still working Jan. 1, 1979
F	Feb. 1, 1951	Dec. 1, 1976	Died Oct. 1, 1978

The total exposure contributed by employees A and E is especially easy to compute, as neither employee died while under observation. Employee A was exposed from the study's inception until the date on which employment was terminated, a total of $3\frac{1}{12}$ years. Similarly, employee E contributed exposure from his date of hire until the study's terminal date, or $5\frac{4}{12}$ years.

Employee A's $3\frac{1}{12}$ units of exposure cover the age interval from $21\frac{10}{12}$ to $24\frac{11}{12}$. His contribution to E_{22} is therefore $\frac{8}{12}$ of a year (from $21\frac{10}{12}$ to $22\frac{1}{2}$). Since A is exposed continuously from age $22\frac{1}{2}$ to age $24\frac{1}{2}$, he contributes one full unit to each of E_{23} and E_{24}. The remaining $\frac{5}{12}$ of a unit (from $24\frac{1}{2}$ to $24\frac{11}{12}$) is credited to E_{25}.

Employee E, age $22\frac{5}{12}$ at his date of hire, contributed only $\frac{1}{12}$ of a year to the value of E_{22} but contributed a full year to each of E_{23}, E_{24}, E_{25}, E_{26}, and E_{27}. Since he remained on the risk until age $27\frac{9}{12}$, he also contributed $\frac{3}{12}$ of a year to E_{28}, producing the obviously correct total exposure of 5 years and 4 months.

Employees B, C, D, and F, each of whom were observed deaths, afford the opportunity to consider the effect when the Balducci hypothesis is applied to a unit age interval with end points which are not integers. It will be recalled that the determination of the date upon which exposure contribution terminates requires great care in the case of deaths, as exposure continues to be generated subsequent to the actual date of death.

Employee B, age $20\frac{5}{12}$ at the inception of the study, clearly contributed $\frac{1}{12}$ of a year to the value of E_{20}. On February 1, 1972, the date on which B attained age $20\frac{1}{2}$, he had the potential to contribute a full year of exposure to E_{21}. Even though death intervened eight months later, the full unit potential was realized as a result of the requirement that no cancellation be created for deaths. Thus, the date on which B ceased exposure contribution was February 1, 1973, on which date he would have attained age $21\frac{1}{2}$, the end of the unit age interval defined by θ_{21}.

Similarly, employees C, D, and F contribute exposure until January 1, 1975, May 1, 1975, and August 1, 1979, respectively. Notice that each one of these employees was assumed to contribute exposure up until his *half-*

birthday which followed death. As we have observed before, we should not be concerned by the result that employee F continued to contribute exposure for ten months after his death, seven months of which were subsequent to the terminal date of the observation period.

A summary of the exposure totals for the six sample lives may be represented as in Table 4-2. Notice that the total exposure of 15 years and 2 months is easily allocated to the various age intervals by relating the beginning and ending for each life to the unit age interval defined by θ_x, $20 \leq x \leq 28$, in this case ranging from age $x - \frac{1}{2}$ to age $x + \frac{1}{2}$. It should be noted from Table 4-2 that $\sum_{y=20}^{28} E_y = 15\frac{2}{12}$, as required.

Once the individual exposures are determined, it is a simple matter to compute the desired rates of mortality. Consider, for example, the interval between ages $22\frac{1}{2}$ and $23\frac{1}{2}$. Table 4-2 indicates a total exposure of $\frac{36}{12}$, or three years. Since no deaths were observed between these ages, we have

$$q_{22\frac{1}{2}} = \frac{0}{3}.$$

TABLE 4-2

Period of Observation:
January 1, 1972 through December 31, 1978

Deaths by Age Nearest Birthday; $\theta_x \Big]_{x-(1/2)}^{x+(1/2)}$

| | Age at Which Exposure | | | Number of Years Contributed To | | | | | | | | |
Employee	Begins	Ends	Total Exposure	E_{20}	E_{21}	E_{22}	E_{23}	E_{24}	E_{25}	E_{26}	E_{27}	E_{28}
A	$21\frac{10}{12}$	$24\frac{11}{12}$	$3\frac{1}{12}$			$\frac{8}{12}$	$\frac{12}{12}$	$\frac{12}{12}$	$\frac{5}{12}$			
B	$20\frac{5}{12}$	$21\frac{6}{12}$	$1\frac{1}{12}$	$\frac{1}{12}$	$\frac{12}{12}$*							
C	$22\frac{9}{12}$	$24\frac{6}{12}$	$1\frac{9}{12}$				$\frac{9}{12}$	$\frac{12}{12}$*				
D	$23\frac{3}{12}$	$24\frac{6}{12}$	$1\frac{3}{12}$				$\frac{3}{12}$	$\frac{12}{12}$*				
E	$22\frac{5}{12}$	$27\frac{9}{12}$	$5\frac{4}{12}$			$\frac{1}{12}$	$\frac{12}{12}$	$\frac{12}{12}$	$\frac{12}{12}$	$\frac{12}{12}$	$\frac{12}{12}$	$\frac{3}{12}$
F	$25\frac{10}{12}$	$28\frac{6}{12}$	$2\frac{8}{12}$							$\frac{8}{12}$	$\frac{12}{12}$	$\frac{12}{12}$*
			$15\frac{2}{12}$	$\frac{1}{12}$	$\frac{12}{12}$	$\frac{9}{12}$	$\frac{36}{12}$	$\frac{48}{12}$	$\frac{17}{12}$	$\frac{20}{12}$	$\frac{24}{12}$	$\frac{15}{12}$

* Observed Death

Although it is clear that $\frac{0}{3} = 0$, it is preferable to indicate the magnitudes of both the numerator and the denominator. Had we obtained a mortality rate with 10 deaths and 120 life-years of exposure, the rate would be best represented as $\frac{10}{120}$ rather than $\frac{1}{12}$, because it is often required to combine two or more rates of mortality, and the form $\frac{10}{120}$ would be much more descriptive than the form $\frac{1}{12}$. Suppose, for example, a study of one group of employees produced $q_x = \frac{10}{120}$ and a study of a similar group produced $q_x = \frac{12}{60}$. The best estimate of the combined rate would be

$$q_x = \frac{10 + 12}{120 + 60} = \frac{22}{180},$$

a result which differs from that obtained by reducing the fractions to $\frac{1}{12}$ and $\frac{1}{5}$ and then combining them to produce $\frac{2}{17}$. The only alternative would be to weight the $\frac{1}{12}$ and $\frac{1}{5}$ with weights of $\frac{2}{3}$ and $\frac{1}{3}$ prior to adding, reflecting the relative magnitudes of the two exposures.

The entire set of mortality rates derived from the experience of the six sample employees is shown in Table 4-3. It should be obvious that the

TABLE 4-3

x	q_x
$19\frac{1}{2}$	$\dfrac{0}{\frac{1}{12}}$
$20\frac{1}{2}$	$\dfrac{1}{1}$
$21\frac{1}{2}$	$\dfrac{0}{\frac{9}{12}}$
$22\frac{1}{2}$	$\dfrac{0}{3}$
$23\frac{1}{2}$	$\dfrac{2}{4}$
$24\frac{1}{2}$	$\dfrac{0}{\frac{17}{12}}$
$25\frac{1}{2}$	$\dfrac{0}{\frac{20}{12}}$
$26\frac{1}{2}$	$\dfrac{0}{2}$
$27\frac{1}{2}$	$\dfrac{1}{\frac{15}{12}}$

magnitude of these rates is essentially meaningless due to the fact that the illustration includes only a handful of lives. Yet it should be equally obvious that the operation of the law of large numbers would tend to eliminate such aberrations where a significant amount of data is present.

The seriatim method involves no concepts other than those already discussed and illustrated in the six-life example just concluded. However, it will be quite instructive to give it further consideration later when we shall be able to uncover interesting relationships between it and the method based upon the grouping of individual records.

GROUPED INDIVIDUAL RECORD METHOD

In many instances, such as, but not restricted to, situations in which high-speed computer facilities are not available, actuaries rely upon grouping devices for exposure calculation rather than upon the seriatim method. Although slight inaccuracies are introduced by the grouping of exposed lives, they may generally be ignored, for reasons which we shall investigate.

The method of calculating exposures based upon grouped individual records is dependent on the selection of a single representative age for each deck of starters, new entrants, withdrawals, and enders. Of major importance, also, is the determination of the proper unit age interval which defines the deaths θ_x. The analysis of actual age tabulating rules in Chapter Three was designed to indicate the techniques through which such ages may be determined.

Once the tabulating rules have been chosen and properly analyzed, every life contributing exposure to a study is assigned a single age at which he began to contribute and a single age at which his contribution ceased. In the case of deaths tabulated at age x, the upper limit of the range notation for θ_x represents the exact age at which exposure contribution terminated, a fact which results from the application of the Balducci hypothesis. The amounts of potential and cancelled exposure for any unit age interval may then be determined by a direct comparison of the superscripts assigned to the nondeath categories with the upper limit of the range for that interval. It should be clear that the above description varies from that of the seriatim method only in that every life in a given deck is assumed to be represented by the superscript assigned by a tabulating rule, rather than being considered on the basis of an exact age which is likely to be different from the superscript. In individual cases, then, the exposure contribution calculated by the seriatim method will differ from that calculated by the grouped method, but only to the extent that the superscript and the true age are not in agreement.

For example, let us consider a study, beginning on April 1, 1975, in which deaths are tabulated by age nearest birthday and starters are tabulated by the rule

$$s_x : x = 1975 - \text{CYB}.$$

Using the July 1 birth assumption, the starter symbol becomes

$$s_x^{x-(1/4)}$$

and must be compared with the death symbol

$$\theta_x \Big|_{x-(1/2)}^{x+(1/2)}.$$

Let us further investigate the exposure contribution of a starter, born on September 1, 1940, who died while under observation on May 1, 1976. This life is a member of the decks s_{35} and θ_{36}. Using the grouped method, he is therefore assumed to have commenced contribution at age $34\frac{3}{4}$ and terminated contribution at age $36\frac{1}{2}$, producing a total exposure of $1\frac{3}{4}$ years. In reality, however, his contribution began at age $34\frac{7}{12}$. His age at the end of the unit age interval in which death occurred does not change from $36\frac{1}{2}$, therefore producing a *true* total exposure of $1\frac{11}{12}$ years, 2 months greater than under the grouped method. This deviation is easily explained, as the July 1 birth assumption of the grouped method was in error by 2 months in this specific case. The seriatim method produced an additional 2 months of exposure because it correctly treated his contribution as having begun at age $34\frac{7}{12}$ rather than at age $34\frac{3}{4}$ as dictated by consideration of the superscript for the s_{35} deck. Of course, the error thus generated by the grouped method would be counterbalanced by another life whose actual birth date was May 1, 1940, varying from the July 1 assumption by 2 months in the opposite direction. Finally, it should be clear that if the 1940 births were uniformly distributed over the calendar year, making the July 1 assumption a realistic one, the errors of understatement and overstatement by the grouped method would tend to be offset, with the resulting exposures therefore approximating those produced by the more accurate seriatim method. It is largely because of the tendency of such understatements and overstatements to counterbalance that the grouped individual record method produces excellent results when the data are of sufficient quantity.

The results of the example discussed above may be represented as in Figure 4-1. The diagram in Figure 4-1 indicates the relative positions of the two decks in question. Note that entry at age $34\frac{3}{4}$ (as represented by G) is based upon the assumption of the grouped method that all lives in s_{35} are centrally located within the deck, consistent with the July 1 birth

FIGURE 4-1

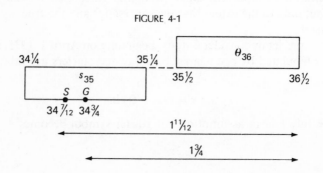

assumption. Entry at age $34\frac{7}{12}$ (as represented by S) is based upon the seriatim method, reflecting the true birth date of the life in question. In either case, the total exposure is taken to be the distance from the point of entry, G or S, to the end of the unit age interval in which death occurred. The additional exposure obtained by the seriatim method resulted simply because the life under investigation did not fall in the center of the s_{35} deck (as assumed by the grouped method) but fell two months to the left of the deck's center.

It should be noted that the resulting exposures of $1\frac{3}{4}$ and $1\frac{11}{12}$ years must be allocated to the unit age intervals involved. The student should verify that the seriatim method produces contributions of $\frac{11}{12}$ and 1 to E_{35} and E_{36}, respectively, while the corresponding contributions by the grouped method are $\frac{9}{12}$ and 1.

Not only is it quite likely for the seriatim method and the grouped individual record method to produce two different exposure values for a given individual, but it is even possible for the grouped method to produce negative amounts of exposure in certain situations. Let us consider the following tabulating rules for new entrants and withdrawals in a study of an employee group:

$$n_x : x = \text{Age nearest birthday at hire,}$$
$$w_x : x = \text{CYC Oct. 1 FW} - \text{CYB.}$$

These rules produce the symbols

$$n_x^x \quad \text{and} \quad w_x^{x-(1/4)}$$

upon the assumptions of July 1 births and uniform distribution of withdrawals between successive October 1's. Applying these rules to an individual who was born on July 1, 1940, hired on February 1, 1971, and fired on March 1, 1971, we see that he belongs to the n_{31} and w_{31} decks. Comparison of the superscripts then suggests that the grouped method treats his age at entry as 31 and his age at withdrawal as $30\frac{3}{4}$, producing an exposure value of negative three months! The seriatim method, on the other hand, simply treats him as exposed for the one-month period during which he was actually a member of the employee group. It is important to be able to account for the four-month discrepancy between the two answers.

First, the grouped method assumed entry on July 1, or the assumed date of birth. However, entry *actually* occurred on February 1, 5 months earlier. Thus, with respect to entry, the grouped method *understated* the true exposure by 5 months. Second, our withdrawal assumption of April 1 (halfway through the 12-month period) was in error for this individual for a single month because withdrawal actually occurred on March 1. Hence the grouped method *overstated* the correct exposure by 1 month as a result of its treatment of withdrawals. The net result is therefore a 4-month understatement, consistent with the earlier observation.

The Single Interval Exposure Formula

The exposure associated with any unit age interval is determined by considering all decks of lives which either enter or leave the study before or during the unit age interval in question. Only such decks will produce potential or cancelled exposure. To formalize a means of computing exposures where large amounts of grouped data are available, it will be necessary to formulate some definitions and to derive some basic exposure formulas.

Let us assume, for the moment, that tabulating rules are selected such that the superscripts i for each nondeath category at tabulated age x fall in the range $a \leq i \leq b$, where a and b are the lower and upper limits on the range of deaths defined by θ_x. For example, if the tabulating rule for deaths produces

$$\theta_x \Big|_{x-(1/3)}^{x+(2/3)},$$

we shall assume that tabulating rules are selected for s_x, n_x, w_x, and e_x such that the superscripts associated with each category will fall in the interval from $x - \frac{1}{3}$ to $x + \frac{2}{3}$, inclusive. If this is true, superscripts for decks subscripted $x - 1$ or less must necessarily be less than or equal to $x - \frac{1}{3}$.

We may now proceed to a consideration of the potential exposure of all starters and new entrants, at subscripted ages $x - 1$ or less, to the unit interval defined by the deaths θ_x. Since all such lives enter the study prior to the beginning of the unit age interval in question, each must have a potential for that interval of one full year or, in the aggregate,

$$\sum_{y=a}^{x-1} (s_y + n_y),$$

where a is the youngest age for which tabulated data are available. Similarly, all withdrawals, enders, and deaths at tabulated ages $x - 1$ and less must necessarily leave the observed group prior to the beginning of the unit age interval represented by θ_x. No such life, then, can possibly make any contribution to E_x. The total amount of cancelled exposure for those lives is

$$\sum_{y=a}^{x-1} (w_y + e_y + \theta_y).$$

Therefore, considering only those lives in decks subscripted $x - 1$ or less, the exposure formula for E_x is

$$E_x = \sum_{y=a}^{x-1} (s_y + n_y - w_y - e_y - \theta_y).$$

To complete the formula for E_x, we need to consider those lives in decks whose subscripts are x. From our tentative assumption, we know that such lives enter or leave the study within the unit age interval for which exposure is sought. Let us suppose that the death symbol is

$$\theta_x \Big|_{x_1}^{x_2}$$

and that the symbols for the other categories are

$$s_x^{x_2 - \alpha}, \quad n_x^{x_2 - \beta}, \quad w_x^{x_2 - \gamma}, \quad \text{and} \quad e_x^{x_2 - \delta},$$

where α, β, γ, and δ all fall within the closed interval from 0 to 1.

The s_x deck, then, has a potential to E_x of α units. Similarly, the n_x deck has β units potential, whereas the w_x and e_x decks generate γ and δ units of cancellation for each life thus included. Finally, based upon the Balducci hypothesis, lives in the θ_x deck generate no cancelled exposure whatever with respect to the unit age interval defined by θ_x.

Introducing actuarial notation, let

$$^{s}\!f_x = \alpha,$$
$$^{n}\!f_x = \beta,$$
$$^{w}\!f_x = \gamma,$$
$$^{e}\!f_x = \delta,$$

and

$$f_x = {}^{s}\!f_x \cdot s_x + {}^{n}\!f_x \cdot n_x - {}^{w}\!f_x \cdot w_x - {}^{e}\!f_x \cdot e_x.$$

The values $^{s}\!f_x$, $^{n}\!f_x$, $^{w}\!f_x$, and $^{e}\!f_x$ are referred to as the *f-factors* for the appropriate categories, the letter f being chosen because f-factors represent the *future* time from entry or exit to the end of the unit age interval defined by θ_x.* Note that f-factors for deaths are not considered because, under the Balducci hypothesis, they must always be zero when rates of mortality are being computed. The final formula then becomes

$$E_x = \sum_{y=a}^{x-1} (s_y + n_y - w_y - e_y - \theta_y) + f_x,$$

often shortened to

$$E_x = \sum_{y=a}^{x-1} j_y + f_x \qquad (4\text{-}1)$$

---

* Note that f-factors, even for categories producing cancellation of exposure (such as withdrawals and enders), are treated as *positive* as long as the category superscript is less than the upper limit of the death range.

by the simplifying definition

$$j_y = s_y + n_y - w_y - e_y - \theta_y,$$

and is called the *single interval exposure formula for E_x*.

As a trivial first example of the use of this formula, let us apply it to the previous illustration concerning the single life represented by the ordered pair (s_{35}, θ_{36}). Since we earlier obtained the symbols

$$s_x^{x-(1/4)} \quad \text{and} \quad \theta_x \Big]_{x-(1/2)}^{x+(1/2)},$$

we see that the f-factor for starters is $(x + \frac{1}{2}) - (x - \frac{1}{4})$, or $\frac{3}{4}$. The single interval formula applicable to this simple case is

$$E_x = \sum_{y=a}^{x-1} j_y + \tfrac{3}{4} \cdot s_x,$$

producing

$$E_{34} = 0,$$

$$E_{35} = \tfrac{3}{4} \cdot s_{35},$$

$$E_{36} = s_{35},$$

and

$$E_{37} = s_{35} - \theta_{36},$$

with the only terms indicated being those which include the s_{35} and/or θ_{36} lives. The exposures thus created are 0, $\frac{3}{4}$, 1, and 0, because $s_{35} = \theta_{36} = 1$. This result is identical to that obtained earlier. Note that E_x, $x \leq 34$, must be zero, as must E_x, $x \geq 37$. The student should realize that, even though the formula produces the proper result for this one-life illustration, the technique of comparing the starter superscript with the upper limit of the range of θ_x is much more efficient. Obviously, the value of the formula is much more significant where large amounts of data, for each category and for several ages, are available.

EXAMPLE 4-1 Suppose tabulating rules have been selected for a study of mortality, producing

$$s_x^{x+(1/4)}, \quad n_x^{x+(1/2)}, \quad w_x^{x+(5/8)}, \quad e_x^{x+(3/4)}, \quad \text{and} \quad \theta_x \Big]_x^{x+1}.$$

Calculate all exposures and rates of mortality which are obtainable from the data in Table 4-4.

TABLE 4-4

x	s_x	n_x	w_x	e_x	θ_x
30	300	400	50	100	10
31	450	200	60	200	20
32	270	300	70	160	20
33	300	200	50	100	30
34	600	400	100	200	20

SOLUTION Formula (4-1), upon incorporating the given superscripts, becomes

$$E_x = \sum_{y=30}^{x-1} j_y + \tfrac{3}{4} \cdot s_x + \tfrac{1}{2} \cdot n_x - \tfrac{3}{8} \cdot w_x - \tfrac{1}{4} \cdot e_x.$$

Taken age by age, this produces

$$E_{30} = \tfrac{3}{4}(300) + \tfrac{1}{2}(400) - \tfrac{3}{8}(50) - \tfrac{1}{4}(100)$$
$$= 381\tfrac{1}{4},$$

$$E_{31} = 540 + \tfrac{3}{4}(450) + \tfrac{1}{2}(200) - \tfrac{3}{8}(60) - \tfrac{1}{4}(200)$$
$$= 905,$$

$$E_{32} = 540 + 370 + \tfrac{3}{4}(270) + \tfrac{1}{2}(300) - \tfrac{3}{8}(70)$$
$$- \tfrac{1}{4}(160)$$
$$= 1196\tfrac{1}{4},$$

$$E_{33} = 540 + 370 + 320 + \tfrac{3}{4}(300) + \tfrac{1}{2}(200) - \tfrac{3}{8}(50)$$
$$- \tfrac{1}{4}(100)$$
$$= 1511\tfrac{1}{4},$$

$$E_{34} = 540 + 370 + 320 + 320 + \tfrac{3}{4}(600) + \tfrac{1}{2}(400)$$
$$- \tfrac{3}{8}(100) - \tfrac{1}{4}(200)$$
$$= 2112\tfrac{1}{2}.$$

A more systematic solution is represented by Table 4-5.

Figure 4-2 should be helpful in permitting the student to visualize the physical interpretation of the single interval formula and its application to Example 4-1. It has been constructed from the given category symbols by assuming that the superscript for each nondeath category represents the age at the exact center of each deck. Thus, for computational purposes, each life in any of the nondeath decks represented by Figure 4-2 is assumed to enter or exit in the middle of the appropriate rectangle, or deck.

TABLE 4-5

x	s_x	n_x	w_x	e_x	θ_x	j_x	$\sum\limits_{y=30}^{x-1} j_y$	f_x	E_x
30	300	400	50	100	10	540	0	$381\frac{1}{4}$	$381\frac{1}{4}$
31	450	200	60	200	20	370	540	365	905
32	270	300	70	160	20	320	910	$286\frac{1}{4}$	$1196\frac{1}{4}$
33	300	200	50	100	30	320	1230	$281\frac{1}{4}$	$1511\frac{1}{4}$
34	600	400	100	200	20	680	1550	$562\frac{1}{2}$	$2112\frac{1}{2}$

Consider, for example, the computation of E_{30}. The s_{30}, n_{30}, w_{30}, and e_{30} decks are assumed to enter or leave the study at ages $30\frac{1}{4}$, $30\frac{1}{2}$, $30\frac{5}{8}$, and $30\frac{3}{4}$, respectively. The potential exposure for the starters and new entrants is

$$\tfrac{3}{4}(300) \quad \text{and} \quad \tfrac{1}{2}(400)$$

as these two decks enter the picture $\frac{3}{4}$ year and $\frac{1}{2}$ year, respectively, from the end of the unit age interval defined by θ_{30}. Similarly, the withdrawals and enders produce cancelled exposure of

$$\tfrac{3}{8}(50) \quad \text{and} \quad \tfrac{1}{4}(100),$$

FIGURE 4-2

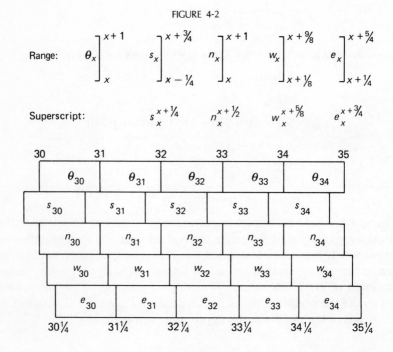

producing total exposure of

$$\tfrac{3}{4}(300) + \tfrac{1}{2}(400) - \tfrac{3}{8}(50) - \tfrac{1}{4}(100) = 381\tfrac{1}{4} \text{ life-years,}$$

as before. Figure 4-2 may also be used as a guide to the calculation of successive exposures. However, once the true visual meaning of the single interval exposure formula is grasped, the student will probably prefer to rely upon the quicker and more systematic computational scheme represented in Table 4-5.

The degree of actuarial sophistication required to compute exposures, such as those in the foregoing example, is not great. The routine is quite mechanical and is generally carried out by a clerical assistant or by an electronic computer. As observed earlier, actuarial skills are more appropriately utilized in connection with the design of the study and with the selection and analysis of tabulating rules, all of which were predetermined by the hypothesis of the preceding example.

The student should verify that the final step in Example 4-1, that of calculating the observed rates of mortality, produces values of

$$\frac{10}{381\tfrac{1}{4}}, \quad \frac{20}{905}, \quad \frac{20}{1196\tfrac{1}{4}}, \quad \frac{30}{1511\tfrac{1}{4}}, \quad \text{and} \quad \frac{20}{2112\tfrac{1}{2}}$$

for q_{30}, q_{31}, q_{32}, q_{33}, and q_{34}, respectively.

It should be evident from the theory thus far developed that different sets of assumptions tend to produce different exposure values when applied to a given body of data. For example, if one formula is based upon July 1 withdrawals and another upon August 1 withdrawals, the two formulas have different f-factors for withdrawals and thus generate different exposure values. It is extremely important, however, to realize that there is a sharp distinction between making two different assumptions and using two different tabulating rules.

Let us consider a mortality study beginning on January 1, 1970. Suppose actuary A utilizes the tabulating rule

$$s_x : x = 1970 - \text{CYB}$$

while actuary B selects the rule

$$s_x : x = 1969 - \text{CYB}.$$

Both actuaries tabulate deaths by age nearest birthday and utilize the July 1 birth assumption.

Ignoring new entrants, withdrawals, and enders, the exposure formulas of actuaries A and B are, respectively,

$$E_x = \sum_{y=a}^{x-1} j_y + s_x$$

and

$$E_x = \sum_{y=a}^{x-1} j_y.$$

Consider a life born on July 1, 1930, who becomes a starter on January 1, 1970. Actuary A classifies him as a member of the s_{40} deck, whereas actuary B concludes that he should be treated as belonging to the s_{39} deck. In the computation of E_{40}, actuary A uses

$$E_{40} = \sum_{y=a}^{39} j_y + s_{40},$$

while actuary B uses

$$E_{40} = \sum_{y=a}^{39} j_y.$$

The individual life under discussion contributes one unit to actuary A's E_{40} by virtue of being in the s_{40} deck. Likewise, he contributes a full unit to actuary B's E_{40} by being an s_{39}, hence appearing in the $\sum_{y=a}^{39} j_y$ component of the formula. Therefore, both actuaries produce the same results even though different tabulating rules were used. In summary, identical results were obtained because identical *assumptions* were imposed. This concept will take on additional meaning in Chapter Six when the idea of counterpart formulas is introduced.

Inconvenient f-Factors

One of the assumptions used to facilitate the development of Formula (4-1) was that f-factors for each category fall within the "convenient" range $[0, 1]$. In most cases, tabulating rules may be judiciously chosen such that this will be the case. On occasion, however, either in a practical or pedagogical situation, we may encounter f-factors which are either negative or greater than 1. The degree of adjustment to Formula (4-1) necessitated by such inconvenient f-factors is determined through application of the same concepts used in its original development.

Although generalized formulas for such adjustments would not be difficult to obtain, it seems preferable to consider each such problem by means of an appeal to basic principles. Therefore, let us assume that the following category symbols are given:

$$s_x^x, \quad n_x^{x-(3/4)}, \quad w_x^{x+1}, \quad e_x^{x+(1/2)}, \quad \text{and} \quad \theta_x \Big|_{x-(1/2)}^{x+(1/2)}.$$

Since the f-factors for the starters and enders provide no difficulty, these categories will appear in our final exposure formula just as they do in

Formula (4-1). However, the new entrant category ostensibly has an f-factor of $\frac{5}{4}$. Blind reasoning might therefore suggest that the n_x term be assigned a coefficient of $\frac{5}{4}$. Such assignment would be fallacious, as it would in effect permit a single life to contribute $\frac{5}{4}$ years of potential exposure to an age interval only 1 year in length. The proper technique involves the realization that each life in the n_{x+1} deck is treated as being age $x - \frac{3}{4} + 1$, or $x + \frac{1}{4}$. Thus, the n_{x+1} deck must become an element of the formula for E_x, as its members begin to contribute exposure one-quarter of a year of age prior to the end of the unit age interval defined by θ_x. The contribution of the new entrants to the single interval formula for E_x is then

$$n_a + \cdots + n_{x-1} + n_x + \tfrac{1}{4} \cdot n_{x+1}.$$

Similarly, the f-factor for the withdrawals is apparently $-\frac{1}{2}$. This circumstance requires that the withdrawal deck at tabulated age $x - 1$ be closely examined. The lives in the w_{x-1} deck are assumed to leave the study at exact age $x + 1 - 1$, or x. Thus, the lives in the w_{x-1} deck should be assigned a coefficient of $-\frac{1}{2}$, whereas the w_x deck should not appear at all in the single interval formula for the determination of E_x. The withdrawal terms in the formula for E_x are therefore

$$-w_a - \cdots - w_{x-2} - \tfrac{1}{2} \cdot w_{x-1}.$$

Finally, the single interval formula is

$$E_x = \sum_{y=a}^{x-1} j_y + \tfrac{1}{2} \cdot s_x + n_x + \tfrac{1}{4} \cdot n_{x+1} + \tfrac{1}{2} \cdot w_{x-1}.$$

Notice that the formula correctly assigns an overall coefficient of $-\frac{1}{2}$ to the w_{x-1} deck, as the w_{x-1} lives appear in the $\sum_{y=a}^{x-1} j_y$ term with a coefficient of -1. The alternative form,

$$E_x = \sum_{y=a}^{x-1} (s_y + n_y - e_y - \theta_y)$$
$$- \sum_{y=a}^{x-2} w_y + \tfrac{1}{2} \cdot s_x + n_x + \tfrac{1}{4} \cdot n_{x+1} - \tfrac{1}{2} \cdot w_{x-1},$$

with which the student may feel more comfortable because all withdrawal terms clearly have negative coefficients, has the disadvantage of added length.

A clear understanding of the above example should permit the student to write the appropriate single interval formulas for the even more unusual cases in which f-factors are larger than 2 or less than -1. For example, if the f-factor for a category is found to be $2\frac{1}{4}$, the deck subscripted $x + 2$ must be considered in addition to those at ages $x + 1$ and less.

Other Formulas

The single interval exposure formula for E_x is the only formula which is an essential tool in the actuary's repertoire for the determination of exposures from individual records. Even though he may occasionally encounter formulas which appear to be of a nature different from that of the single interval formula, these are necessarily direct offshoots of the basic formula and are better derived than memorized. To perform such simple derivations, several notational expedients must be introduced.

Let us denote the complement of the *f*-factor for any category as its *p-factor*. A careful analysis of this definition leads to the realization that the *p*-factor of a given nondeath category represents the positive distance from the *beginning* of the unit age interval defined by θ_x to the point at which entry or exit is assumed to occur. If, for example, we have

$$s_x^x \quad \text{and} \quad \theta_x \Big|_{x-(1/3)}^{x+(2/3)},$$

producing an *f*-factor of $\frac{2}{3}$, the *p*-factor for the s_x deck (^sp_x) is said to be $\frac{1}{3}$, or the length of time between $x - \frac{1}{3}$ and x. It may be helpful to associate the letter p with the word *past*, just as the letter f is associated with the word *future*. Clearly, situations which give rise to inconvenient *f*-factors will likewise produce inconvenient *p*-factors. If we have

$$w_x^{x+(1/2)} \quad \text{and} \quad \theta_x \Big|_{x-1}^{x},$$

producing an *f*-factor of $-\frac{1}{2}$, the appropriate *p*-factor (^wp_x) is $\frac{3}{2}$. Notice that the *p*-factor for deaths is necessarily equal to 1 where the Balducci hypothesis is being utilized. Having defined the *p*-factors, we may now define, analogously to f_x,

$$p_x = {}^sp_x \cdot s_x + {}^np_x \cdot n_x - {}^wp_x \cdot w_x - {}^ep_x \cdot e_x - 1 \cdot \theta_x.$$

As expected, then,

$$f_x + p_x = j_x.$$

Having now defined f_x, p_x, and j_x, we shall define F_x, P_x, and J_x to be their negatives. As an illustration, suppose the tabulating rules in a mortality study produce the following symbols:

$$s_x^x, \quad n_x^{x-(1/4)}, \quad w_x^{x+(1/4)}, \quad e_x^{x+(1/2)}, \quad \text{and} \quad \theta_x \Big|_{x-(1/4)}^{x+(3/4)}.$$

Then,

$$f_x = \tfrac{3}{4} \cdot s_x + \quad n_x - \tfrac{1}{2} \cdot w_x - \tfrac{1}{4} \cdot e_x;$$

$$p_x = \tfrac{1}{4} \cdot s_x \quad\quad - \tfrac{1}{2} \cdot w_x - \tfrac{3}{4} \cdot e_x - \quad \theta_x;$$

$$j_x = \quad s_x + \quad n_x - \quad w_x - \quad e_x - \quad \theta_x;$$

$$F_x = \quad\quad \tfrac{1}{4} \cdot e_x + \tfrac{1}{2} \cdot w_x - \quad n_x - \tfrac{3}{4} \cdot s_x;$$

$$P_x = \quad \theta_x + \tfrac{3}{4} \cdot e_x + \tfrac{1}{2} \cdot w_x \quad\quad - \tfrac{1}{4} \cdot s_x;$$

$$J_x = \quad \theta_x + \quad e_x + \quad w_x - \quad n_x - \quad s_x.$$

The student will recall that when the definitions of f-factors and the linear combination expression f_x were first formulated we were operating on the assumption that the tabulating rules being employed led to convenient f-factors. Although we have now seen that inconvenient f-factors generate only minor problems in the development of single interval exposure formulas, let us agree that *linear combination expressions* for f_x, p_x, F_x, and P_x may not be written unless all f-factors (and hence p-factors) fall within the interval $[0, 1]$. To permit otherwise would result either in utilizing coefficients greater than 1 for some categories or in necessitating the inclusion of categories subscripted other than x in the expression for f_x, which is theoretically a linear combination of only those categories subscripted x. Thus, where inconvenient f-factors are present, we shall treat the *functions* f_x, p_x, F_x, and P_x as undefined, although we are still free to calculate f-*factors* and p-*factors* as before, whether or not all fall between zero and one, inclusive. Where such problems do arise, it is felt that they are better attacked by basic principles than by the formulas to follow.

The symbols which have just been defined, along with the fact that

$$\sum_{y=a}^{y=b} j_y = \sum_{y=a}^{y=b} J_y = 0,$$

where b is the oldest age at which tabulated data are available, lead to the following variations of the standard single interval exposure formula:

$$E_x = \sum_{y=a}^{x} j_y - p_x, \tag{4-2}$$

$$E_x = \sum_{y=x+1}^{b} J_y + P_x, \tag{4-3}$$

$$E_x = \sum_{y=x}^{b} J_y - F_x. \tag{4-4}$$

Of these three, all of which fall into the family of single interval formulas, Formula (4-3) is probably used most often. It is especially applicable in connection with select mortality studies, the reason for which will become clear later in this chapter.

The formula

$$E_{x+1} = E_x + p_x + f_{x+1} \tag{4-5}$$

and its "twin"

$$E_x = E_{x+1} + P_x + F_{x+1} \tag{4-6}$$

are referred to as *continuous* exposure formulas, simply because they are of a recursive nature, producing any given value of E_x through an adjustment to the value already calculated at an adjacent age. Formulas (4-5) and (4-6) are easily derived from the single interval formulas.

EXAMPLE 4-2   In a mortality study, the following category symbols are given:

$$s_x^{x+(1/2)}, \quad n_x^x, \quad w_x^x, \quad e_x^{x+(1/2)}, \quad \text{and} \quad \theta_x\Big|_x^{x+1}.$$

The oldest age at which any data are available is 23, but data at ages younger than 20 have been utilized. The data shown in Table 4-6 are available.

TABLE 4-6

x	s_x	n_x	w_x	e_x	θ_x	E_x
20	25			4		$14\frac{1}{2}$
21	20	7	3	2	2	37
22	35	10	2	4	3	
23	30	5	9		2	39

(a) Find E_{22}.
(b) Find e_{23}.
(c) Find the net migration and the number of deaths at tabulated age 20.

SOLUTION
(a) Using the continuous formula,

$$E_{22} = E_{21} + p_{21} + f_{22},$$

we have

$$p_{21} = \tfrac{1}{2} \cdot 20 + 0 \cdot (7 - 3) - \tfrac{1}{2} \cdot 2 - 1 \cdot 2 = 7$$

and

$$f_{22} = \tfrac{1}{2} \cdot 35 + 1 \cdot (10 - 2) - \tfrac{1}{2} \cdot 4 = 23\tfrac{1}{2}.$$

Therefore,

$$E_{22} = 37 + 7 + 23\tfrac{1}{2} = 67\tfrac{1}{2}.$$

(b) Using the formula

$$E_x = \sum_{y=x+1}^{b} J_y + P_x,$$

we have

$$39 = E_{23} = P_{23}.$$

Since

$$P_{23} = -\tfrac{1}{2} \cdot 30 - 0 \cdot (5 - 9) + \tfrac{1}{2} \cdot e_{23} + 1 \cdot 2 = \tfrac{1}{2} \cdot e_{23} - 13,$$

we have

$$e_{23} = 104.$$

(c) Using the formula

$$E_{20} = E_{21} + P_{20} + F_{21},$$

we have

$$P_{20} = -\tfrac{1}{2} \cdot 25 - 0 \cdot (n - w)_{20} + \tfrac{1}{2} \cdot 4 + 1 \cdot \theta_{20}$$
$$= -10\tfrac{1}{2} + \theta_{20}$$

and

$$F_{21} = -\tfrac{1}{2} \cdot 20 - 1 \cdot (7 - 3) + \tfrac{1}{2} \cdot 2 + 0 \cdot 2 = -13.$$

Then,

$$14\tfrac{1}{2} = 37 - 10\tfrac{1}{2} + \theta_{20} - 13,$$

producing

$$\theta_{20} = 1.$$

There is not sufficient information to determine the net amount of migration at tabulated age 20. Table 4-7, with unknowns a, b, and c, would serve as a solution for the entire example. Equating the E_x column to the given exposure values, we have

$$39 = \tfrac{1}{2} \cdot c - 13,$$
$$E_{22} = c - 36\tfrac{1}{2},$$
$$37 = c - 67,$$

and

$$14\tfrac{1}{2} = c + b - 90\tfrac{1}{2}.$$

This system produces $c = 104$, $E_{22} = 67\tfrac{1}{2}$, and $b = 1$, consistent with the previous solution. No information is available with regard to $a = n_{20} - w_{20}$.

TABLE 4-7

x	s_x	$(n-w)_x$	e_x	θ_x	J_x	$\sum\limits_{y=x+1}^{23} J_y$	P_x	E_x
20	25	a	4	b	$b-a-21$	$c-80$	$b-10\frac{1}{2}$	$c+b-90\frac{1}{2}$
21	20	4	2	2	-20	$c-60$	-7	$c-67$
22	35	8	4	3	-36	$c-24$	$-12\frac{1}{2}$	$c-36\frac{1}{2}$
23	30	-4	c	2	$c-24$	0	$\frac{1}{2}\cdot c-13$	$\frac{1}{2}\cdot c-13$

STUDIES OF INSURED LIVES

All of the theory of table construction and related examples considered have been in connection with mortality studies based upon the *true ages* of the lives exposed to risk. Tabulating rules as developed in Chapter Three were often stated in terms of actual calendar years of birth. Little if any reference has been made thus far to studies based upon records of insured lives. However, practically all mortality investigations and resulting mortality tables used in the life insurance business are based upon an analysis of policies issued by companies to individuals who have met the underwriting criteria specified by such companies. Such criteria include not only the demonstration (or declaration, in the case of nonmedically issued policies) of good health but also the presence of other favorable personal characteristics which tend to assure that the lives represented by such policies constitute a group whose anticipated future lifetime is greater than the average for the overall population. Clearly, mortality rates to be used in the pricing of insurance products for prospective policyholders should be based upon the past experience of insured lives.

When a life insurer computes premium rates for its various products, such rates are quoted only for integral ages. Consequently, upon the issuance of insurance coverage, each insured life is assigned an integral *issue age*, or *insuring age*. All records of the insurer reflect this insuring age in place of the true age of the insured. Thus, mortality rates resulting from a study of such lives necessarily reflect these fictitious insuring ages rather than true ages. For example, a person whose exact age at issue was $33\frac{5}{12}$ and whose insuring age was determined to be 33 would be treated throughout the study as having been *exactly* age 33 at issue. Of course, this is a desirable consequence if these mortality rates are to be used for the pricing of policies to be sold on the basis of insuring ages rather than true ages. In fact, if the sole purpose of developing mortality rates is for use in the pricing of new products, the translation of such mortality rates to a true age basis is unnecessary. If, however, the primary purpose of a mortality study is to contribute to the construction of a mortality table to be used for general purposes, the final results of such a study must first be adjusted to reflect true ages rather than fictitious insuring ages. Such an adjustment is, as we shall see, of an approximate nature but quite easy to effect.

Valuation Year of Birth

In lieu of the actual calendar year of birth associated with every life in an actual age study, each insured life in an insuring age study is assigned a *valuation year of birth* (VYB). This VYB reflects the basis upon which issue ages are determined by the insurer and is defined by

$$\text{VYB} = \text{Calendar year of issue} - \text{Issue age}$$

or, more simply,

$$\text{VYB} = \text{CYI} - \text{IA}.$$

Suppose, as is commonly the case in current practice, an insurer issues policies of a certain category on the basis of the insured's age last birthday. Computation of issue ages is clearly routine. Then, in turn, the determination of the proper valuation year of birth is routine as well, requiring only subtraction of this issue age from the calendar year in which the policy is issued. Consider a person born on July 3, 1940 to whom two policies are issued, policy *A* on February 14, 1976 and policy *B* on December 24, 1976. Since policies *A* and *B* carry issue ages of 35 and 36, respectively, and since the calendar year of issue is common to the two policies, different valuation years of birth must result. Policy *A* and policy *B* are assigned valuation years of birth of 1941 and 1940, respectively, clearly illustrating the fact that valuation years of birth are of a fictitious nature.

Similar examples may be given with regard to policies which are issued on the age next birthday or the age nearest birthday basis. Consider a person born on June 7, 1950, whose issue date is March 10, 1975. Table 4-8 summarizes the possible cases. It is important to realize that the assignment of a valuation year of birth is tantamount to the assignment of a fictitious *date* of birth as well. For example, the person considered in Table 4-8 is treated as if his actual date of birth had been March 10 of the years 1951, 1950, and 1950, respectively. Such an assignment has the effect of ignoring completely the true birthday, once it has been used to determine the issue age.

TABLE 4-8

Insuring basis	Insuring age	VYB
Age last birthday	24	1951
Age next birthday	25	1950
Age nearest birthday	25	1950

Studies of insured lives, then, treat all persons as if their month and date of birth had been replaced by the month and date of policy issue. Such replacement is, of course, responsible for the phenomenon that calculated mortality rates are not on the basis of the true ages of the insured lives.

Tabulating Rules

An analysis of tabulating rules for studies of insured lives produces very little theory to add to that presented in Chapter Three with respect to actual age studies. The two new features which must be observed have both been noted. First, we refer to valuation years of birth (VYB) rather than calendar years of birth (CYB). Second, we refer to insuring ages and policy anniversaries rather than true ages and birthdays.

The following set of tabulating rules is typical for an insured life study covering the calendar years 1972–1977, inclusive:

$$s_x : x = 1972 - \text{VYB},$$

$$n_x : x = \text{Issue age},$$

$$w_x : x = \text{CYW} - \text{VYB},$$

$$e_x : x = 1978 - \text{VYB},$$

$$\theta_x : x = \text{CYD} - \text{VYB}.$$

In the determination of range notation for deaths and superscripted notation for other categories, it is necessary to impose assumptions similar to those suggested earlier in dealing with actual age studies. Let us first assume that the average date of issue of all policies is July 1. Since the date associated with any valuation year of birth is the issue date of the policy, such an assumption is equivalent to assigning July 1 as the valuation date of birth for each included policy. Further, we shall assume that all withdrawals within any calendar year tend to be centrally located; that is, withdrawals are assumed to occur on July 1. The following symbols result directly from these simple and realistic assumptions:

$$s_x^{x-(1/2)}, \quad n_x^{x}, \quad w_x^{x}, \quad e_x^{x-(1/2)}, \quad \text{and} \quad \theta_x \Big]_{x-(1/2)}^{x+(1/2)}.$$

Note, for example, that the tabulating rule for starters given above defines the subscript x to be "the insuring age attained on the 1972 policy anniversary." Since we have assumed that all anniversaries fall on July 1, the starters at tabulated age x are treated as if they were all six months younger than x, as the starting date of the study preceded attainment of insuring age x by one-half of a year. A similar statement could be made with respect to the enders. Withdrawals are said to be tabulated "by calendar insuring age." New entrants, which are simply the policies issued during the observation period, are said to be tabulated "by exact insuring age" or, equivalently, "by issue age." It should be noted that there is no one-year interval associated with such new entrants in an insured life study, simply because new entrants are permitted *only* at integral insuring ages.

Other assumptions which may on occasion be imposed produce variations in the category symbols in exactly the same way as in the case of actual age studies. For example, assumptions of a September 1 average issue date and a May 1 average date of withdrawal produce

$$s_x^{x-(8/12)}, \quad n_x^x, \quad w_x^{x-(4/12)}, \quad e_x^{x-(8/12)}, \quad \text{and} \quad \theta_x \Big|_{x-(8/12)}^{x+(4/12)},$$

based upon the same tabulating rules considered above.

In addition, the assumption that withdrawals occur on policy anniversaries is often encountered in connection with tabulation of withdrawals by calendar insuring age. Such an assumption gives rise to the symbol

$$w_x^x.$$

No assumption with respect to issue dates is necessary in order to arrive at this symbol.

Tabulating rules such as those in the following example are certainly unusual but should present the student with the opportunity to test his understanding of the analysis of tabulating rules in connection with studies of insured lives.

EXAMPLE 4-3   Write the single interval exposure formula for a mortality study running from policy anniversaries in 1973 until the end of 1976, using the following tabulating rules:

$$s_x : x = 1973 - \text{VYB},$$

$$n_x : x = \text{Issue age},$$

$$w_x : x = \text{CYC Sep. 1 NW} - \text{VYB},$$

$$e_x : x = 1976 - \text{VYB},$$

$$\theta_x : x = \text{CYC May 1 PD} - \text{VYB}.$$

Assume that all policies are issued on August 1 and that withdrawals occur uniformly over each calendar year. Ignore the irregularity of the observation period when considering withdrawals and deaths.

SOLUTION   The tabulating rule for deaths requires that we give consideration to one-year decks of deaths occurring between successive May 1's. The issue date assumption indicates that deaths at tabulated age x would have

FIGURE 4-3

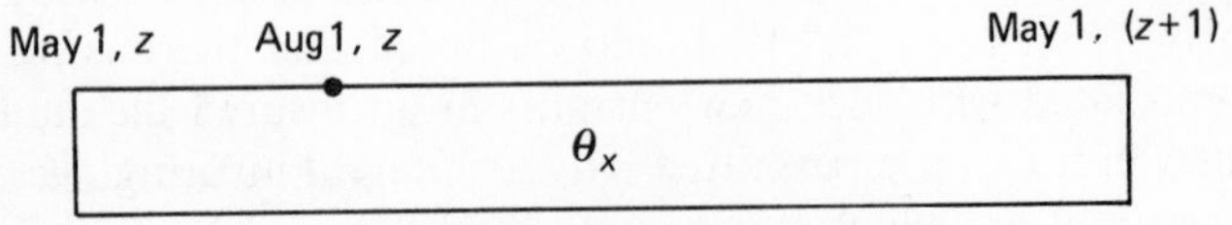

May 1, z Aug 1, z May 1, $(z+1)$

$$\theta_x$$

attained insuring age x on August 1 of the calendar year containing the May 1 preceding death. Figure 4-3 relating to lives with VYB $= z - x$ is helpful. Assuming that death occurs between May 1, z and May 1, $z + 1$, the calendar year containing the preceding May 1 is clearly z. Thus, insuring age x is attained on August 1, z, three months after the beginning of the unit interval under consideration. Thus the proper symbol for deaths is

$$\theta_x \Big|_{x-(3/12)}^{x+(9/12)}.$$

The student should verify that a similar analysis of withdrawals produces the symbol

$$w_x^{x+(1/12)}.$$

It should be clear that the thought processes involved in the analysis of these two categories are identical to those used for actual age tabulating rules.

The remaining three category symbols are found to be

$$s_x^x, \quad n_x^x, \quad \text{and} \quad e_x^{x+(5/12)}.$$

The single interval formula is therefore

$$E_x = \sum_{y=a}^{x-1} j_y + \tfrac{3}{4} \cdot s_x + \tfrac{3}{4} \cdot n_x - \tfrac{2}{3} \cdot w_x - \tfrac{1}{3} \cdot e_x.$$

Translation to Actual Ages

It is of paramount importance that the student realize that Example 4-3 was solved in the total absence of information as to the basis upon which issue ages were determined. It was simply assumed that each observed policy was issued on August 1, but it was unnecessary to know whether issue ages were based upon age last, age nearest, or age next birthday at issue. We must only know that issue ages have been calculated consistently and correctly on *one* of these three bases. Only if it is required to determine mortality rates relating to true ages do we need to know the issue age basis actually used.

Let us suppose that the tabulating rule for deaths in an insured life study is such that the symbol

$$\theta_x \Big|_{x-(1/3)}^{x+(2/3)}$$

results. The mortality rate represented by the fraction θ_x/E_x thus relates to the experience between insuring ages $x - \frac{1}{3}$ and $x + \frac{2}{3}$ and is denoted by

$$q^I_{x-(1/3)},$$

with the superscript I indicating that the age $x - \frac{1}{3}$ is a fictitious one, based upon insuring ages rather than true ages. Again, note that at this stage we neither know nor have we assumed knowledge of the issue age basis, and yet all *insuring age* mortality rates are theoretically available. Now, however, let us suppose that we are required to determine the *true age* to which $x - \frac{1}{3}$ relates.

If the issue age x had been based upon age last birthday, we have in effect treated persons between ages x and $x + 1$ as if they were each exact age x. We have therefore understated their true age by approximately one-half year on the average. Thus, if we have obtained an *insuring age* mortality rate subscripted $x - \frac{1}{3}$, it should, more properly, be subscripted $x - \frac{1}{3} + \frac{1}{2}$, or $x + \frac{1}{6}$, the approximate *true age*. Perhaps it is preferable to utilize this line of reasoning: "Those persons whose age last birthday is $x - \frac{1}{3}$ are, in fact, approximately a half-year older, or age $x + \frac{1}{6}$ on the average." This result is denoted by the approximate expression

$$q^I_{x-(1/3)} \doteq q_{x+(1/6)}.$$

Similarly, if the issue age basis had been age next birthday, the translation would be

$$q^I_{x-(1/3)} \doteq q_{x-(5/6)},$$

as this basis tends to overstate true ages by approximately six months. Finally, if policies had been issued on the age nearest birthday basis, we would have

$$q^I_{x-(1/3)} \doteq q_{x-(1/3)},$$

on the supposition that insuring ages neither systematically overstate nor understate true ages.

EXAMPLE 4-4   If the ratio θ_x/E_x in an insuring age mortality study is translated as $q_{x-(1/4)}$ and if all policies in the study were issued on the age next birthday basis, what was the range notation symbol generated by the tabulating rule for deaths?

SOLUTION   If the true age of this segment of insured lives was between $x - \frac{1}{4}$ and $x + \frac{3}{4}$ and if their issue age basis was age next birthday, their corresponding insuring ages must have been between $x + \frac{1}{4}$ and $x + \frac{5}{4}$. Thus we have the symbol

$$\theta_x \Big|_{x+(1/4)}^{x+(5/4)}.$$

If the mortality rates at true ages are required to be determined with utmost accuracy, additional considerations are necessary because the usual half-age adjustment may not be representative of the true situation. For example, if policies are issued on the age last birthday basis, many persons will tend to obtain policies just prior to their birthdays in order to gain the advantages of the lower rate. In such a situation, policyholders whose issue age is x may well have an average age of $x + \frac{2}{3}$ or greater. The exact adjustment to be made may be determined from a study of the actual distribution of true ages at issue.

The following example should serve as a comprehensive illustration of the steps to be followed in a mortality investigation based upon insuring ages.

EXAMPLE 4-5 Consider a mortality study conducted from policy anniversaries in 1972 to policy anniversaries in 1977. The following tabulating rules are used:

$$s_x : x = 1972 - \text{VYB},$$

$$n_x : x = \text{Issue age} \quad \text{(age last birthday basis)},$$

$$w_x : x = \text{Insuring age next anniversary at withdrawal},$$

$$e_x : x = 1977 - \text{VYB},$$

$$\theta_x : x = \text{Insuring age nearest anniversary at death}.$$

(a) Stating your assumptions, determine the single interval exposure formula.
(b) From the data in Table 4-9, compute as many exposure values as possible.

TABLE 4-9

Insured life	Birth date	Issue date	Other data
A	Apr. 1, 1950	Jun. 1, 1970	Lapsed Aug. 1, 1975
B	Jul. 23, 1950	Apr. 1, 1971	Died Jun. 13, 1973
C	Mar. 20, 1949	Jul. 26, 1972	Died Aug. 14, 1975
D	Oct. 17, 1951	Apr. 20, 1971	Ender
E	Sep. 24, 1952	Mar. 10, 1972	Lapsed Oct. 12, 1973
F	Jun. 20, 1950	Feb. 18, 1970	Died Feb. 20, 1976
G	May 16, 1953	Jan. 14, 1975	Ender
H	Aug. 15, 1951	Dec. 24, 1970	Lapsed Jan. 24, 1972
I	Jan. 9, 1950	Jul. 20, 1974	Died Jul. 19, 1976
J	Jul. 3, 1949	Jun. 7, 1968	Ender

(c) Find the value θ_{22}/E_{22}, and determine the actual age to which the rate applies.

SOLUTION

(a) Assuming only that withdrawals occur halfway between policy anniversaries, we have

$$s_x^x, \quad n_x^x, \quad w_x^{x-(1/2)}, \quad e_x^x, \quad \text{and} \quad \theta_x \bigg|_{x-(1/2)}^{x+(1/2)}.$$

These symbols, in conjunction with the Balducci hypothesis, produce the formula

$$E_x = \sum_{y=a}^{x-1} j_y + \tfrac{1}{2}(s_x + n_x - e_x) - w_x.$$

(b) Prior to performing exposure calculations, it is necessary to analyze the ten insured lives, first determining issue ages, then valuation years of birth, and finally ordered pairs reflecting tabulated ages of entry and exit for each life. It should be noted that since H's policy was not in force on its 1972 anniversary, it must be ignored. The student should verify the entries in Table 4-10. Two approaches may now be used for

TABLE 4-10

Insured life	Issue age	VYB	Ordered pair
A	20	1950	(s_{22}, w_{26})
B	20	1951	(s_{21}, θ_{22})
C	23	1949	(n_{23}, θ_{26})
D	19	1952	(s_{20}, e_{25})
E	19	1953	(n_{19}, w_{21})
F	19	1951	(s_{21}, θ_{25})
G	21	1954	(n_{21}, e_{23})
I	24	1950	(n_{24}, θ_{26})
J	18	1950	(s_{22}, e_{27})

the calculation of exposures. Method A, illustrated in Table 4-11, is the traditional technique and should be used when large numbers of policies

TABLE 4-11
Method A

Age x	s_x	n_x	w_x	e_x	θ_x	j_x	$\sum\limits_{y=19}^{x-1} j_y$	f_x	E_x
19		1				1	0	$\frac{1}{2}$	$\frac{1}{2}$
20	1					1	1	$\frac{1}{2}$	$1\frac{1}{2}$
21	2	1	1			2	2	$\frac{1}{2}$	$2\frac{1}{2}$
22	2				1	1	4	1	5
23		1		1		0	5	0	5
24		1				1	5	$\frac{1}{2}$	$5\frac{1}{2}$
25				1	1	-2	6	$-\frac{1}{2}$	$5\frac{1}{2}$
26			1		2	-3	4	-1	3
27				1		-1	1	$-\frac{1}{2}$	$\frac{1}{2}$

are involved. Method B, very efficient when dealing with only a handful of lives but of true practical value only in indicating the process by which Method A actually operates, is illustrated by Table 4-12. The exposures produced by Methods A and B are clearly equal, as they must be.

(c) The fraction θ_{22}/E_{22} is clearly $\frac{1}{5}$ and is denoted by $q'_{21\frac{1}{2}}$. Since, however, issue ages were determined by age last birthday, the translation to true ages produces

$$q_{22} \doteq \tfrac{1}{5}.$$

TABLE 4-12

Method B

Insured life	Range of exposure	E_x; $x =$								
		19	20	21	22	23	24	25	26	27
A	22-25$\frac{1}{2}$				$\frac{1}{2}$	1	1	1		
B	21-22$\frac{1}{2}$			$\frac{1}{2}$	1					
C	23-26$\frac{1}{2}$					$\frac{1}{2}$	1	1	1	
D	20-25		$\frac{1}{2}$	1	1	1	1	$\frac{1}{2}$		
E	19-20$\frac{1}{2}$	$\frac{1}{2}$	1							
F	21-25$\frac{1}{2}$			$\frac{1}{2}$	1	1	1	1		
G	21-23			$\frac{1}{2}$	1	$\frac{1}{2}$				
I	24-26$\frac{1}{2}$						$\frac{1}{2}$	1	1	
J	22-27				$\frac{1}{2}$	1	1	1	1	$\frac{1}{2}$
		$\frac{1}{2}$	1$\frac{1}{2}$	2$\frac{1}{2}$	5	5	5$\frac{1}{2}$	5$\frac{1}{2}$	3	$\frac{1}{2}$

It is important to realize that Method B is *not* equivalent to the seriatim method, even though the form of the tabulation looks similar to that of Table 4-2, used earlier to illustrate the seriatim technique. The difference is simply that the earlier example based exposure calculations upon *true* ages, whereas the *range of exposure* for this example is determined from the category superscripts. Thus, when asked to determine exposures based upon "your formula," it is perfectly safe to analyze superscripts, rendering the writing of the single interval formula technically unnecessary.

SELECT STUDIES

Select mortality tables, in which the sole variable is the duration since issuance of insurance protection, are of major interest to the life actuary. Mortality rates resulting from select studies tend to be lower than those found in aggregate tables, simply because the latter include experience of all insured lives irrespective of the length of time since issue. For example, the select mortality rate $q_{[34]+1}$ reflects the mortality experience of lives aged 35 who had been accepted for insurance coverage one year earlier. In contrast, the aggregate rate q_{35}, derived from the experience of insured lives aged 35, many of whom were "selected" many years previously, would tend to be greater than its select counterpart. Many insurers base their nonparticipating premium scales upon select mortality experience simply because it is expected to predict policyholder mortality in the early years following issue much more accurately than tables based upon aggregate experience. In addition, comparisons of intracompany select studies are of great value in the evaluation of underwriting practices and agency performance.

The very definition of a select mortality table demands that separate studies be made for each issue age. Often, combination of data for different issue ages will be required for the determination of aggregate mortality rates, but this procedure is effected only after select rates for each issue age have been obtained. In the following examples, it will always be assumed that we are dealing only with data referring to a single issue age, say x.

Tabulating Rules

The procedure for computing select mortality rates differs only slightly from that for computing rates for insured lives on a nonselect basis. The only significant difference is that select studies are performed by duration t since issue, rather than by age x. Tabulating rules for select studies involve no new theory, once it is clearly understood that these rules will generate subscripted *durations* rather than subscripted *ages*. Most tabulating rules which are of practical use with select studies relate the year in which an event occurs to the calendar year of policy issue (CYI).

Let us assume that the observation period for a select study is the calendar years 1973–1977, inclusive. Typical tabulating rules are

$$\theta_t : t = \text{CYD} - \text{CYI},$$

$$s_t : t = 1972 - \text{CYI},$$

$$w_t : t = \text{CYW} - \text{CYI},$$

$$e_t : t = 1977 - \text{CYI}.$$

Note the use of the letter t to represent duration, rather than x, which is generally used to represent age.

Following the pattern of the four rules given above, the tabulating rule for new entrants would be

$$n_t : t = \text{CYN} - \text{CYI}.$$

It should be clear that the calendar year of new entry in a select study must, by definition, coincide with the calendar year of issue, producing $t = 0$ in all cases. Therefore, no tabulating rules will be specified for new entrants in a select study, and all new entrants will be represented by n_0, or simply n. Such a result should be logically clear, as new entrants in a select study must begin to contribute exposure immediately upon issue, specifically at $t = 0$.*

The symbols obtained from the above tabulating rules are

$$\theta_t \bigg|_{t-(1/2)}^{t+(1/2)}, \quad s_t^{t+(1/2)}, \quad n, \quad w_t^t, \quad \text{and} \quad e_t^{t+(1/2)},$$

leading to the single interval formula

$$E_t = n + \sum_{y=0}^{t-1} j_y - \tfrac{1}{2} \cdot w_t.$$

The symbol j_y, in a select study, is defined to *exclude* the new entrants, that is, $j_y = s_y - w_y - e_y - \theta_y$.† The assumptions underlying this formula, other than that of Balducci mortality, are that issues and withdrawals of any calendar year occur on July 1. An assumption that withdrawals occur on policy anniversaries would lead to the same withdrawal term. Note that the range symbol for the deaths is analogous to that obtained from calendar year of death tabulations in Chapter Three, in which an interval of two years in length was shaved down to a range of a single year.

A minor complication arises with the use of this *calendar duration* tabulation rule for deaths. Clearly the ratio

$$\frac{\theta_t}{E_t}$$

measures the mortality experience between durations $t - \tfrac{1}{2}$ and $t + \tfrac{1}{2}$ and is therefore represented by

$$q_{[x]+t-(1/2)}.$$

---

* An exception to this generalization may be found in the case of a study of permanent policies issued as a result of term conversions or guaranteed insurability clauses, where the duration t is to be measured from the date of issue of the *original* policy.

† The student will recall several rearrangements of the basic single interval exposure formula which were developed earlier in this chapter. Specifically, Formula (4-3), when used with a select study, does not involve new entrants since J_y is defined to exclude n. For this reason, the formula

$$E_t = \sum_{y=t+1}^{b} J_y + P_t$$

has found popularity in computing exposures for select studies. Exercise 29 at the end of this chapter is designed to indicate the advantages of this particular form of the single interval formula.

The complication arises when $t = 0$, ostensibly producing the meaningless symbol

$$q_{[x]-(1/2)}.$$

However, an analysis of θ_0/E_0 suggests that the numerator includes those deaths which occur in the calendar year of issue, or, under the July 1 issue assumption, from duration zero to exact duration one-half. The denominator represents a number of annualized exposure units (rather than *life-years*), as evidenced by the coefficient of unity assigned to the new entrant term. The potential exposure of one unit, thus implied for the new entrants, indicates that the interval from $t = 0$ to $t = \frac{1}{2}$ is being treated as if it were one year in length. It thus seems logical to define

$$\frac{\theta_0}{E_0} \doteq {}_{1/2}q_{[x]}.$$

A simple example should be helpful in illustrating this sometimes troublesome concept.

EXAMPLE 4-6   Assume that a select mortality study is to be conducted on the issues of 1975, observed from issue until their first policy anniversary. Of 1000 policies issued at age 35 in 1975, 50 were lapsed and 10 resulted in death claims prior to the end of 1975. Using the following tabulating rules, calculate and interpret θ_0/E_0:

$$\theta_t : t = CYD - CYI,$$

$$w_t : t = CYW - CYI,$$

$$e_t : t = 1976 - CYI.$$

SOLUTION   The tabulating rules and standard assumptions lead to the single interval formula

$$E_t = n + \sum_{y=0}^{t-1} j_y - \tfrac{1}{2} \cdot w_t - \tfrac{1}{2} \cdot e_t,$$

and thus we have

$$E_0 = n - \tfrac{1}{2} \cdot w_0 - \tfrac{1}{2} \cdot e_0.$$

Since we know that $n = 1000$, $w_0 = 50$, and $e_0 = 0$, we easily find that

$$E_0 = 975.$$

The ratio θ_0/E_0, therefore, is $\frac{10}{975}$.

The student might have incorrectly guessed that the value of E_0 would be only half as large as 975, as the number of *life-years* of exposure between durations zero and one-half is really

$$1000(\tfrac{1}{2}) - 50(\tfrac{1}{4}) = 487\tfrac{1}{2},$$

based upon the assumption of July 1 issues and, for the calendar year of issue, October 1 withdrawals. Yet it should now be evident that the exposure formula has the effect of expanding the half-year interval from $t = 0$ to $t = \frac{1}{2}$ into a full "unit" interval. Hence the ratio θ_0/E_0 should be considered to represent mortality for the first half of the first policy year, yielding

$$\frac{\theta_0}{E_0} = \frac{10}{975} \doteq {}_{1/2}q_{[35]}.$$

The coefficient of $-\frac{1}{2}$ for the withdrawals in Example 4-6 represents not the cancellation of exposure for half a *year* but for half of the new, expanded "unit" interval. The ratio θ_1/E_1, not calculable from the given data, is translated as

$$q_{[35]+(1/2)},$$

an annual rate of mortality. Clearly, for $t \geq 1$, no difficulties arise in the interpretation of θ_t/E_t.

Now let us consider an observation period from policy anniversaries in 1974 to policy anniversaries in 1979. The following tabulating rules are typical:

$$\theta_t : t = \text{Policy year of death (PYD)},$$

$$s_t : t = 1974 - \text{CYI},$$

$$w_t : t = \text{CYW} - \text{CYI},$$

$$e_t : t = 1979 - \text{CYI}.$$

A tabulation of deaths by policy year of death produces

$$\theta_t \Big|_{t-1}^{t}$$

simply because the tth policy year begins at the $(t - 1)$th policy anniversary. The "policy year of death" tabulating rule may be equivalently expressed as "duration next anniversary." Only an assumption regarding withdrawals is required, as starters and enders are tabulated by exact duration due to the nature of the observation period. The reasonable assumption that withdrawals occur on policy anniversaries will be made, and the following symbols result:

$$\theta_t \Big|_{t-1}^{t}, \quad s_t^t, \quad n, \quad w_t^t, \quad \text{and} \quad e_t^t.$$

The single interval exposure formula, then, is

$$E_t = n + \sum_{y=0}^{t-1} j_y.$$

When this set of tabulating rules is employed, we see that the term s_0 is nonexistent. A life treated as an s_0 must have a 1974 calendar year of issue. Such issues, however, are treated as new entrants, as their exposure contribution commences at the instant of policy issue. Similarly, the existence of an e_0 would imply a 1979 calendar year of issue. Issues of 1979, however, are excluded from the study, as their dates of entry and exit coincide due to the definition of the period of observation. The student should not rationalize that s_0 and e_0 decks are nonexistent in all select studies, as it is easily seen that the tabulating rules illustrated for calendar year select studies do indeed allow for the presence of such decks.

Example 4-7 illustrates the techniques involved in the process of computing select mortality rates. Further, it indicates the procedure to be followed when it is required to determine aggregate mortality rates from the results of a select study.

EXAMPLE 4-7 A select mortality study is to be conducted on policies issued from 1971 through 1975, observed from anniversaries in 1974 until December 31, 1976. Issue ages are based upon the insured's age nearest birthday at issue. It is desired to obtain select mortality rates at integral durations.

The data in Table 4-13 on 11 sample lives are available.

TABLE 4-13

Insured life	Birth date	Issue date	Other data
A	Apr. 1, 1930	Jun. 11, 1974	Died Oct 30, 1976
B	Apr. 19, 1931	Feb. 19, 1973	In force Jan. 1, 1977
C	Jul. 4, 1929	Dec. 20, 1971	Lapsed Apr. 16, 1975
D	Jun. 8, 1930	Dec. 30, 1973	Died Jun. 1, 1975
E	Nov. 18, 1932	Apr. 1, 1975	In force Jan. 1, 1977
F	Jan 8, 1932	Mar. 5, 1976	In force Jan. 1, 1977
G	May 9, 1931	Nov. 30, 1974	Lapsed Dec. 30, 1974
H	Oct. 24, 1927	Jan. 3, 1972	Died Dec. 30, 1976
I	May 20, 1928	Feb. 9, 1972	In force Jan. 1, 1977
J	Jul. 1, 1930	Mar. 2, 1972	Died Jul. 1, 1974
K	Feb. 9, 1931	Sept. 1, 1972	Died Aug. 1, 1974

(a) Stating your assumptions, determine the single interval exposure formula.

(b) Calculate as many select rates as possible.

(c) Calculate q_{44}^l, indicating the actual age to which it applies.

SOLUTION Before proceeding, it must be observed that all policies were not issued at the same age. Application of the age nearest birthday rule indicates that the lives B, C, E, and J were insuring age 42 at issue, while A, D, G, H, and I were insuring age 44. Life F is ignored because of the 1976 issue date. Similarly, life K is excluded because the policy was not in force on his 1974 anniversary.

(a) Due to the requirement that rates be obtained at integral durations, we may tabulate deaths either by next duration (policy year of death) or last duration (often denoted by *curtate duration*). Let us arbitrarily select the former, or

$$\theta_t : t = \text{PYD},$$

which gives

$$\theta_t \Big]_{t-1}^{t}.$$

For the other categories, let us use

$$s_t : t = 1974 - \text{CYI},$$
$$w_t : t = \text{CYW} - \text{CYI},$$
$$e_t : t = 1977 - \text{CYI}.$$

Assumptions of July 1 issues and July 1 withdrawals lead to the symbols

$$s_t^t, \quad w_t^t, \quad \text{and} \quad e_t^{t-(1/2)}.$$

The single interval formula then becomes

$$E_t = n + \sum_{y=0}^{t-1} j_y - \tfrac{1}{2} \cdot e_t.$$

(b) Considering only A, D, G, H, and I, the issues at age 44, we see that ordered pairs should be assigned as follows:

A: (n, θ_3),
D: (s_1, θ_2),
G: (n, w_0),
H: (s_2, θ_5),
I: (s_2, e_5).

An interesting situation is presented by life G, as this policy may be retained in the study or may be ignored without loss of accuracy. Although G would contribute one month of exposure if this study were based upon the seriatim method, the formula treats a new entrant and a withdrawal at tabulated duration zero as entering and exiting from the study at exact duration zero, thus creating no exposure whatsoever. For the sake of simplicity, then, let us choose to ignore life G. Calculating the exposures for issue age 44 by the simple method of examining super-scripts rather than applying the single interval formula, we have the data in Table 4-14. By following the same procedure for the policies

TABLE 4-14

	Duration at which exposure		E_t				
Insured life	*Begins*	*Ends*	*t = 1*	*t = 2*	*t = 3*	*t = 4*	*t = 5*
A	0	3	1	1	1		
D	1	2		1			
H	2	5			1	1	1
I	2	$4\frac{1}{2}$			1	1	$\frac{1}{2}$
			1	2	3	2	$1\frac{1}{2}$

issued at age 42, the student should verify that the following exposures result:

$$E_1 = 1; \quad E_2 = 1\tfrac{1}{2}; \quad E_3 = 2; \quad E_4 = 1\tfrac{1}{2}.$$

Table 4-15 indicates the results of the study.

TABLE 4-15

t	$E_{[42]+t}$	$E_{[44]+t}$	$q_{[42]+t-1}$	$q_{[44]+t-1}$
1	1	1	0/1	0/1
2	$1\frac{1}{2}$	2	$0/1\frac{1}{2}$	1/2
3	2	3	1/2	1/3
4	$1\frac{1}{2}$	2	$0/1\frac{1}{2}$	0/2
5	0	$1\frac{1}{2}$	—	$1/1\frac{1}{2}$

(c) In the determination of the aggregate insuring age rate q'_{44}, it is necessary to combine, without respect to duration, all data based upon the interval from insuring age 44 to insuring age 45. Thus, by adding the numerators and denominators, respectively, of the fractions $\frac{1}{2}$ and $\frac{0}{1}$, we have

$$q'_{44} = \frac{1+0}{2+1} = \frac{1}{3}.$$

Finally, since policies were issued on the age nearest birthday basis, we have

$$q_{44}^l = \tfrac{1}{3} \doteq q_{44}.$$

One final observation regarding Example 4-7 may be helpful. Had the tabulations been performed in the usual manner, we would have obtained $E_0 = 1$ for each of the issue ages for which data were available. Yet these values are seen to have been unimportant, as they were not used in the computation of mortality rates. This phenomenon is due to the tabulating rule for deaths,

$$\theta_t : t = \text{PYD},$$

for which it is easily seen that θ_0 and hence E_0 are meaningless. The exposure formula developed in part (a) of the solution to Example 4-7,

$$E_t = n + \sum_{y=0}^{t-1} j_y - \tfrac{1}{2} \cdot e_t,$$

deteriorates, when $t = 0$, into

$$E_0 = n - \tfrac{1}{2} \cdot e_0,$$

a formula which is technically correct but which has no concrete interpretation. It may only be used as a check on the computations. Since for each age at issue there was one new entrant and no members of the e_0 deck, we see that we should have obtained $E_0 = 1$ in each tabulation. Had this expected result not been verified in the tabulations, it would have been a clear indication of an error in some stage of the process of exposure determination.

FISCAL YEAR STUDIES

In addition to performing both select and aggregate mortality studies on insured lives, it is often required that the actuary conduct mortality studies on the members of certain organizations without regard to the existence of individual insurance policies. For example, a measure of the mortality experience of members of a large pension plan, labor union, or employee group may be desired. Consulting actuaries, involved in the administration of employee benefit plans for a number of groups, may wish to examine the overall mortality experience of these groups in lieu of conducting independent studies for each group separately. In situations such as these, the utilization of data related to the fiscal year of the organizations in question is often the most efficient course to follow.

A fiscal year is simply the 1-year period between two successive annual balancings of the financial records of an enterprise. Theoretically, any 1-year period may satisfy this definition, but in reality only a few cases are often observed. Probably the most common fiscal year is the 12-month period which coincides with the calendar year. Insurance companies, for example, operate with a fiscal year which is the same as the calendar year. Individual citizens invariably handle their personal finances on a calendar year basis due to the fact that taxes are generally levied against income earned over a calendar year period. Some businesses and governmental entities operate with a fiscal year ending on June 30, while the federal government of the United States terminates its fiscal year on September 30. A school system may choose to operate on a September 1–August 31 fiscal year basis, for obvious reasons.

The advantage of choosing an observation period for a mortality study which consists of an integral number of successive fiscal years is simply that the records of many organizations are readily available at the end points of fiscal years, the dates on which annual accountings are made. The number of terminating employees during a *calendar* year would be difficult to ascertain from the records of a business whose fiscal year ends in April, whereas the number of terminations for any *fiscal* year would be immediately available from company records. In addition, the number of employees at the close of business on the final day of a fiscal year can be used as starters in a study whose observation period begins the following day. Also, the current employees on some subsequent fiscal year end point may be used as the enders for the study.

Fiscal year studies are generally associated with the in-force method of determining mortality rates, a method which will be developed in Chapter Five. In fact, the large majority of fiscal year mortality studies are effected by the in-force method rather than from records of individual lives. However, the principles involved are best illustrated using individual record techniques, and, for this reason, they will be treated here initially and investigated further in Chapter Five.

As the fiscal year ending on May 31, 1976, for example, is generally designated as "fiscal 1976," we shall agree to denote the fiscal year under discussion by the calendar year containing its terminal date (T) rather than its initial date (I), unless otherwise indicated. This is consistent with standard practice, which, for example, defines the 1977 fiscal year for the U.S. government as the one-year period which began on October 1, 1976 and ended on September 30, 1977. In addition, in our mortality investigations, we shall assign a fiscal year to each birth, new entrant, withdrawal, and death, according to rules which must be clearly specified.

It is of utmost importance to realize that, in this text, the term *event* is used to refer to new entry, withdrawal, or death but *not* birth, because a single rule is usually chosen to assign "fiscal year of event" for any particular study, by which all new entrants, withdrawals, and deaths are treated consistently.

It will often be the case, however, that the fiscal year of birth will be assigned on a totally different basis. It must be clear, then, that the term "fiscal year of event" does not include, as a special case, "fiscal year of birth" but does, for example, include "fiscal year of death."

Fiscal Year of Birth

The assignment of a fiscal year of birth to every life in a fiscal year study is in several ways analogous to the assignment of a valuation year of birth in studies of insured lives. Most notably, whatever the rule by which fiscal years of birth are assigned, the effect is to replace true ages by fictitious ages. As a result, upon the completion of the exposure calculations, a final adjustment must be made if it is required that mortality rates be prepared according to true ages rather than according to fictitious fiscal ages. In addition, just as in studies of insured lives, we do not need to know the basis by which fiscal years of birth were assigned in order to compute exposures. We simply need to know that fiscal years of birth have been consistently determined according to whatever basis may have been chosen. Finally, once fiscal years of birth are assigned, the true dates of birth become irrelevant for the remainder of the study. Just as the assignment of valuation years of birth led to the attainment of exact insuring ages on policy anniversaries, the assignment of fiscal years of birth leads to the attainment of *exact fiscal ages* on the terminal date T of every succeeding fiscal year.

A major advantage produced by the assignment of fiscal years of birth is that the actuary is then permitted to conduct a single mortality study on several groups even though their fiscal years do not coincide. As we shall see, a study whose observation period is from T, 1972 to T, 1977 may begin for one group on March 1, for another on June 1, and for another on September 1, without introducing the complications which might be expected to arise because of the three different fiscal year periods involved and the three apparently different periods of observation.

Just as there are three basic methods for the assignment of issue ages and hence valuation years of birth in an insured life study, there are three methods of determining fiscal years of birth. We need to investigate carefully not only the methods themselves but the effect of each method upon the interpretation of the resulting exposure values.

Method 1. First, the fiscal year of birth may be taken as the calendar year containing the T *following*, or coincident with, the true date of birth. For example, if $T =$ April 30 for a given enterprise, the fiscal year of birth 1957 would be assigned to all persons born on or after May 1, 1956 but not later than April 30, 1957. Let us consider a person born on October 1, 1956, who is in the employ of this enterprise on April 30, 1976, on which date his true age is $19\frac{7}{12}$. As the fiscal year of birth of this employee is 1957, his exact fiscal age on April 30, 1976 would be 19 (1976 − 1957), recalling that his true birthday has been replaced by the date April 30, 1957. A consideration of all births between May 1, 1956 and April 30, 1957, inclusive, all of which are treated as if April 30, 1957 had been their true birth date, shows that each such person would be tabulated as exact fiscal age 19 on an April 30, 1976 valuation. Their true ages, however, may fall anywhere between 19 and 20. It then follows that this first method of assigning fiscal years of birth has the effect of understating the age of each person on any subsequent valuation date by an average of six months.

Alternatively, we may analyze Method 1 as follows: If the true birth date is arbitrarily replaced by a fictitious birth date which on the average is six months *after* birth, then the fiscal age of such persons at any subsequent valuation date must *understate* the true age. Such understatement, given a uniform distribution of births, would be of six months' magnitude. When this method of assignment is used, then, we shall treat persons whose fiscal age on a valuation date is x as if they were actually age $x + \frac{1}{2}$ on the average. Valuation figures may therefore be seen to produce data by true age *last* birthday when fiscal years of birth are determined by this first method. Any actuary, then, who consistently assigns fiscal years of birth according to Method 1, finds that all age data computed on a terminal date T are necessarily tabulated by age last birthday, regardless of the fact that the various groups in the study do not operate on a common fiscal year basis.

Suppose group A has a fiscal year whose T = March 31; the T for group B is October 31. Table 4-16 indicates that, as long as fiscal years of birth are determined according to Method 1, all fiscal ages as of the respective valuation dates in 1977 are on a true age last birthday basis. Each of the six persons illustrated is assigned 1961 as his fiscal year of birth, meaning that each such person must be exact fiscal age 16 on T, 1977. Table 4-16 displays the fact that the true ages have a lower and upper bound of 16 and 17, respectively.

TABLE 4-16

Birth date	Employee of group	Fiscal age/true age as of T, 1977
Apr. 1, 1960	A	16/17
Oct. 1, 1960	A } T = March 31	16/16½
Mar. 30, 1961	A	16/16
Nov. 1, 1960	B	16/17
Apr. 30, 1961	B } T = Oct. 31	16/16½
Oct. 30, 1961	B	16/16

Method 2. A second method of assigning fiscal years of birth is to select the calendar year containing the T *preceding*, or coincident with, the true date of birth. In the special case of a fiscal year which coincides with the calendar year, Method 1 assigns fiscal year of birth z to all births of calendar year z, while Method 2 assigns fiscal year of birth $z - 1$ to such lives. Since this method assigns a fiscal year of birth to each life which is one unit less than that assigned by Method 1, it may be analyzed in a way similar to that used for Method 1.

The overall effect of Method 2 is to produce an *overstatement* of age at any valuation date T, because true birth dates are replaced with fictitious birth dates which, on the average, fall six months *earlier*. Such an approach clearly has the effect of treating all persons as if they were six months older than is actually the case. Therefore, actuaries who select Method 2 for the assignment of fiscal years of birth are in effect obtaining fiscal ages, as of any T, which are indicative of true ages on an age *next* birthday basis. Again, this is true without regard to the number of different fiscal years which are included in the study.

The relationship between Methods 1 and 2 is perhaps best illustrated by a reconsideration in Table 4-16. Method 2 assigns 1960 as the fiscal year of birth for each of the six individuals, so each would have an exact fiscal age of 17 on T, 1977 rather than the fiscal age of 16 produced by Method 1. As it is obvious that the true ages do not change, we see that Method 2 does indeed generate fiscal ages which are true ages on the age next birthday basis.

Method 3. Intermediate to the first two methods, Method 3 is defined so as to assign, as a fiscal year of birth, the calendar year containing the T *nearest* the true date of birth. For example, if $T =$ September 30, the fiscal year of birth z is assigned to all births between April 1, z and March 31, $z + 1$, inclusive.

In an enterprise whose $T =$ September 30, consider those persons born between April 1, 1950 and March 31, 1951, inclusive. Each such person is assigned 1950 as a fiscal year of birth. On September 30, 1975, their exact fiscal age is 25, while their true ages fall between $24\frac{1}{2}$ and $25\frac{1}{2}$. Thus, we have the result which the reader surely anticipated, that Method 3 results in fiscal ages, on fiscal year end points T, which duplicate the true age *nearest* birthday for all observed lives. Method 3 produces fiscal ages which neither systematically overstate nor understate true ages. As a result, actuaries consistently applying Method 3 find that fiscal ages are produced on an age nearest birthday basis, again regardless of the fact that the experience of organizations having different fiscal years is being combined in a single study.

As indicated earlier, it is often required to translate exposures and mortality rates, resulting from any of the three methods, from a fiscal age basis to an actual age basis. The justification for such translations should be evident from the discussion of the definition and effect of each method. However, the determination of the proper technique for making such translations must wait until the concept of the assignment of "fiscal years of event" has been introduced and the appropriate tabulating rules analyzed.

Fiscal Year of Event

Fiscal years of event (generally entry, withdrawal, and death) may be assigned upon any one of the three bases used for fiscal years of birth. However, since it has been established that common usage suggests that a fiscal year be denoted by the calendar year containing its terminal date, let us agree that we shall adopt this tradition unless we are given ample warning that a different assignment is being made. For example, unless stated otherwise, the fiscal year of withdrawal (FYW) assigned to any individual will be taken to mean the calendar year in which the current fiscal year terminates. A withdrawal, new entrant, or death occurring after $T, z - 1$ but not later than T, z will therefore be assigned the year z as the fiscal year of the appropriate event. Although, as stated above, assignment in this manner is standard practice, the student must ever be aware that he may encounter situations in which the fiscal years of event are stated to have been assigned as the calendar year containing the T preceding, or nearest, the actual date of event.

Tabulating Rules

Let us consider the following typical tabulating rules for a mortality study whose beginning and ending points are T, 1972 and T, 1978, respectively:

$$\theta_x : x = \text{FYD} - \text{FYB},$$

$$s_x : x = 1972 - \text{FYB},$$

$$n_x : x = \text{FYN} - \text{FYB},$$

$$w_x : x = \text{FYW} - \text{FYB},$$

$$e_x : x = 1978 - \text{FYB}.$$

The student should note that the tabulating rule for deaths is equivalent to

$$\theta_x : x = \text{Calendar year containing the } T \text{ following the actual date of death} - \text{FYB}.$$

Unwieldy tabulating rules of this general form, analyzed in Chapter Three, were introduced at that time in order to lay the foundation for a thorough understanding of tabulating rules couched in fiscal year language.

The tabulating rule for deaths indicates that exact fiscal age x would have been attained on the T of the fiscal year in which death occurred. Consider an individual with FYB = 1950 and FYD = 1975, clearly tabulated as a θ_{25}. The actual date of death must have fallen in the 12-month period preceding T, 1975, on which date exact fiscal age 25 would have been attained had death not intervened. Therefore, death actually occurred between fiscal ages 24 and 25, producing the symbol

$$\theta_{25}\Big]_{24}^{25}$$

or, more generally,

$$\theta_x\Big]_{x-1}^{x}.$$

It should be clear that the upper limit of the range of deaths is the same as the tabulated subscript because the fiscal year of death is defined to be the calendar year containing the *following* T.

The rules for new entrants and withdrawals are easily analyzed by the same process as was the rule for deaths. As both new entrants and withdrawals tabulated at fiscal age x are between fiscal ages $x-1$ and x at entry or withdrawal, the symbols

$$n_x^{x-(1/2)} \quad \text{and} \quad w_x^{x-(1/2)}$$

arise simply by assuming that migration within any fiscal year occurs, on the average, at the fiscal year midpoint.

The starter and ender categories introduce no difficulties whatever. The tabulating rule for starters indicates that starters tabulated at fiscal age x attain exact fiscal age x on T, 1972, the starting date of the study. Similarly, the e_x deck attains exact fiscal age x on T, 1978, the study's terminal date. Hence, starters and enders are said to be tabulated by exact fiscal age, and the symbols

$$s_x^x \quad \text{and} \quad e_x^x$$

result. Note the similarity of the treatment of starters and enders in fiscal year studies with that in insuring age studies with anniversary-to-anniversary observation periods.

This set of tabulating rules easily produces the exposure formula

$$E_x = \sum_{y=a}^{x-1} j_y + \tfrac{1}{2}\cdot(n-w)_x.$$

The resulting values of E_x refer to the units of exposure between exact fiscal ages $x-1$ and x, a fact which is easily determined by observing the range notation for the deaths θ_x. Thus, the ratio

$$\frac{\theta_x}{E_x}$$

is seen to represent

$$q^F_{x-1}$$

in which the superscript indicates that the subscripted age $x - 1$ is not a true age but rather an assigned age that has resulted from the replacement of true ages with fiscal ages.

It must be clearly noted that we have taken a set of tabulating rules, determined the appropriate category symbols, written the single interval exposure formula, and interpreted the ratio θ_x/E_x in the total absence of information regarding the method used to assign fiscal years of birth. We did, however, need to know the definition used to assign fiscal years to the events of entry, withdrawal, and death.

Finally, suppose that we wish to find the true meaning of q^F_{x-1} in terms of an actual age mortality rate. Now we must inquire as to how fiscal years of birth were assigned. Suppose Method 1 has been used. Since this method produces data on valuation dates T which *understate* true ages by an average of six months, the fiscal age $x - 1$ is best approximated by the actual age $x - \frac{1}{2}$, producing

$$\frac{\theta_x}{E_x} = q^F_{x-1} \doteq q_{x-(1/2)}.$$

Method 2, similarly, would produce

$$\frac{\theta_x}{E_x} = q^F_{x-1} \doteq q_{x-(3/2)},$$

as this method of assigning fiscal years of birth *overstates* true ages by approximately six months. Finally, the approximate translation

$$\frac{\theta_x}{E_x} = q^F_{x-1} \doteq q_{x-1}$$

arises from Method 3, which neither systematically understates nor overstates true ages.

The overall effects of Methods 1, 2, and 3 for the assignment of fiscal years of birth are summarized by Table 4-17.

TABLE 4-17

Basis for assignment of F YB	*Produces data by*	*Translation of q^F_x*
Method 1 (following T)	True age last birthday (understates true age)	$q^F_x \doteq q_{x+(1/2)}$
Method 2 (preceding T)	True age next birthday (overstates true age)	$q^F_x \doteq q_{x-(1/2)}$
Method 3 (nearest T)	True age nearest birthday (approximates true age)	$q^F_x \doteq q_x$

Let us now suppose that, with the same set of tabulating rules being prescribed, we are told that "fiscal year of event" has been defined as the calendar year containing the T *preceding*, or coincident with, the actual date of the event. The student should verify that this definition leads to the category symbols

$$s_x^x, \quad n_x^{x+(1/2)}, \quad w_x^{x+(1/2)}, \quad e_x^x, \quad \text{and} \quad \theta_x \Big]_x^{x+1},$$

to the interpretation

$$\frac{\theta_x}{E_x} = q_x^F,$$

and to the translation of q_x^F to

$$q_{x+(1/2)}, \quad q_{x-(1/2)}, \quad \text{and} \quad q_x,$$

under Methods 1, 2, and 3, respectively.

Similarly, the definition of fiscal year of event which assigns the calendar year containing the T nearest the event leads to the following category symbols:

$$s_x^x, \quad n_x^x, \quad w_x^x, \quad e_x^x, \quad \text{and} \quad \theta_x \Big]_{x-(1/2)}^{x+(1/2)}.$$

The ratio θ_x/E_x is then interpreted as $q_{x-(1/2)}^F$ and is translated as

$$q_x, \quad q_{x-1}, \quad \text{and} \quad q_{x-(1/2)}$$

under Methods 1, 2, and 3, respectively. The student should take pains to verify that each of these results is correct, rather than merely identifying certain "patterns" which would aid in a memorization process but which would be of little value in gaining a true understanding of the underlying concepts.

On occasion, the actuary may be confronted with tabulating rules in fiscal studies which do not follow the simple form "fiscal year of event − fiscal year of birth." Although such rules may require additional insights not required for the simple rules, they are generally handled with little extra effort merely through an appeal to basic principles and through a clear understanding of the terminology being used.

EXAMPLE 4-8   The observation period of a mortality study runs from March 1, 1972 through February 28, 1978. Tabulations have been prepared on the following basis:

$\theta_x : x =$ Age last birthday as of the May 31 preceding death,

$s_x : x =$ Age last birthday as of May 31, 1972,

$n_x : x$ = Age last birthday as of the May 31 preceding entry,

$w_x : x$ = Age last birthday as of the May 31 preceding withdrawal,

$e_x : x$ = Age last birthday as of May 31, 1977.

(a) State the tabulating rules in simplest form, being careful to obtain convenient f-factors where possible.
(b) Write the single interval exposure formula.
(c) Interpret θ_x/E_x.

SOLUTION   The first step in the analysis of this example must be a close examination of the tabulating rules, which are obviously not stated in the traditional form. Four key facts must be recognized at the outset.

First, the study may be treated as a fiscal year study based upon a fiscal year with T = May 31, simply because all tabulated data clearly could relate to an enterprise whose records are summarized as of May 31. It seems quite likely that we are in fact dealing with a fiscal age study based upon May 31 valuations, but even if such is not the case, we may still treat the problem in this manner because the availability of data as of some fixed date in each year is the *sine qua non* for the feasibility of a fiscal age study.

Second, since all data are tabulated by age last birthday, it should be evident that we may consider this as a fictitious age study based upon the selection of fiscal years of birth by Method 1. It will be recalled that Method 1 assigns the fiscal year of birth as the calendar year containing the T following birth, resulting in fiscal ages which understate true ages, thus reflecting true ages last birthday.

Third, as the tabulating rules for deaths, new entrants, and withdrawals are based upon the May 31 *preceding* death, entry, and withdrawal, respectively, the term "fiscal year of event" is now seen to be the calendar year containing the May 31 *preceding* the actual date of the event.

Fourth, it has been stated earlier that the standard observation period for fiscal year studies is the interval between two terminal dates T. In this example, however, the stated observation period is inconsistent with the ordinary situation. Although we have no control over this unusual observation period, we shall see that it creates little if any added complication in the solution of the example.

(a) Based upon the first and second of the above observations, we conclude that the tabulating rule for deaths may be more simply written as

$\theta_x : x$ = Fiscal age as of the May 31 preceding death,

merely replacing the words "age last birthday" with "fiscal age." Then, based upon the third observation above, we may further simplify the tabulating rule for deaths to read

$$\theta_x : x = \text{FYD} - \text{FYB},$$

as this rule clearly produces fiscal age as of the May 31 preceding the actual date of death. Similar analyses lead to the simplified rules

$$n_x : x = \text{FYN} - \text{FYB}$$

and

$$w_x : x = \text{FYW} - \text{FYB}.$$

The given tabulating rules for starters and enders are clarified with much less effort than were those for the three "event" categories. The rule for starters at tabulated age x indicates that fiscal age x is attained as of May 31, 1972. A simplified rule for starters, then, is

$$s_x : x = 1972 - \text{FYB}.$$

Similarly, the simplified rule for the tabulation of enders is

$$e_x : x = 1977 - \text{FYB}.$$

The following category symbols are easily obtained, now that the tabulating rules have been simplified:

$$\theta_x \Big]_x^{x+1}, \quad s_x^{x-(1/4)}, \quad n_x^{x+(1/2)}, \quad w_x^{x+(1/2)}, \quad \text{and} \quad e_x^{x+(3/4)}.$$

The only assumption imposed is that migration occurred at the midpoint of each fiscal year, or November 30. We have been asked, in the first part of this example, to rewrite the tabulating rules in such a way as to obtain convenient f-factors where possible. It is essential that the student recognize that we have merely *restated* the tabulating rules and had no leeway to adjust them to suit our own purposes. For example, we would have preferred the starter category to have a superscript of $x + \frac{3}{4}$. This could only be accomplished by changing the starter rule to

$$s_x : x = 1971 - \text{FYB}.$$

The student must understand that to make such a change would be to violate the tabulating rule stated in the original problem. Starters tabulated at age x in the original set of rules would be tabulated at age $x - 1$ after the rule change, a change which would wreak havoc with the numerical computation of exposures.

(b) The single interval formula is now easily seen to be

$$E_x = \sum_{y=a}^{x-1} j_y + s_x + \tfrac{1}{4} \cdot s_{x+1} + \tfrac{1}{2} \cdot n_x - \tfrac{1}{2} \cdot w_x - \tfrac{1}{4} \cdot e_x.$$

(c) It is also immediately obvious from the range notation for deaths that

$$\frac{\theta_x}{E_x} = q_x^F.$$

Since we have observed that the method of assignment of fiscal years of birth had the effect of understating ages, we have

$$q_x^F \doteq q_{x+(1/2)}.$$

Another frequently encountered form of tabulating rule for fiscal year studies incorporates "calendar year of event" rather than "fiscal year of event." Although no new theoretical considerations are created by such rules, it is important to realize that these rules may be used only when the fiscal year is clearly delineated. It will be recalled that the tabulating rule

$$\theta_x : x = \text{FYD} - \text{FYB}$$

may be analyzed without any reference to the actual T which is associated with the enterprise under consideration. The fact that this is not true for the tabulating rule

$$\theta_x : x = \text{CYD} - \text{FYB}$$

should be evident from Example 4-9 and further clarified by Example 4-10.

EXAMPLE 4-9   A mortality study is being performed on the members of a pension fund which operates on the basis of fiscal years which terminate on March 31. The period of observation is January 1, 1973 through December 31, 1977. The tabulating rules are as follows:

$$s_x : x = 1973 - \text{FYB},$$
$$n_x : x = \text{CYN} - \text{FYB},$$
$$w_x : x = \text{CYW} - \text{FYB},$$
$$e_x : x = 1977 - \text{FYB},$$
$$\theta_x : x = \text{CYD} - \text{FYB}.$$

The fiscal year of birth for each observed life was taken to be the calendar year containing the March 31 preceding birth.

(a) Construct the single interval exposure formula.
(b) Interpret θ_x/E_x in terms of both fiscal and actual ages.

SOLUTION

(a) The starter rule indicates that exact fiscal age x is attained by the s_x deck on the "fiscal birthday" of 1973, specifically March 31. Thus, the fiscal age of such lives on the study's initial date is $x - \frac{1}{4}$. A similar analysis leads to the realization that the enders tabulated at age x are in fact fiscal age $x + \frac{3}{4}$. The resulting symbols are

$$s_x^{x-(1/4)} \quad \text{and} \quad e_x^{x+(3/4)}.$$

The rules for the other categories are handled in a similar manner. One approach for analyzing the rule for deaths is to note that exact fiscal age x for the θ_x deck is attained on March 31 of the calendar year in which death occurs. Thus, the range symbol for the deaths is

$$\theta_x \Big]_{x-(1/4)}^{x+(3/4)}.$$

One then only needs to make the assumption that all migration during any given calendar year occurs on July 1 in order to obtain the symbols

$$n_x^{x+(1/4)} \quad \text{and} \quad w_x^{x+(1/4)}.$$

Finally, the single interval exposure formula is

$$E_x = \sum_{y=a}^{x-1} j_y + s_x + \tfrac{1}{2} \cdot n_x - \tfrac{1}{2} \cdot w_x.$$

(b) From a glance at the range for the deaths θ_x, we see that

$$\frac{\theta_x}{E_x} = q_{x-(1/4)}^F.$$

Then, by referring to the method by which fiscal years of birth were assigned, it is recalled that fiscal ages overstate actual ages. Thus,

$$q_{x-(1/4)}^F \doteq q_{x-(3/4)}.$$

The following example is designed to facilitate a comparison of tabulating rules which combine fiscal years and calendar years in various ways. In its solution, the student must be careful to note that fictitious ages and the resulting need to translate to actual ages arise only when a fiscal year of *birth* is a component of the tabulating rule.

EXAMPLE 4-10   In a mortality investigation of the members of a certain organization, fiscal years of birth and death have each been defined as the calendar year containing the October 31 preceding the actual date of birth or death.

For each of the following tabulating rules, write θ_x in range notation and interpret θ_x/E_x in terms of actual ages:

(a) $\theta_x : x = \text{FYD} - \text{CYB}.$
(b) $\theta_x : x = \text{CYD} - \text{FYB}.$
(c) $\theta_x : x = \text{FYD} - \text{FYB}.$
(d) $\theta_x : x = \text{CYD} - \text{CYB}.$

SOLUTION

(a) The assumption that births occur on July 1 of each calendar year indicates the attainment of exact age x by the θ_x deck on the July 1 of "the calendar year containing the October 31 preceding death." Thus, the earliest that such a death could occur would be 4 months after the attainment of age x; the latest would be an additional 12 months later. The death symbol, then, is

$$\theta_x \Big]_{x+(1/3)}^{x+(4/3)} .$$

Translation of θ_x/E_x to actual ages is unnecessary in this case, as no fictitious ages have been introduced. The final interpretation is

$$\frac{\theta_x}{E_x} = q_{x+(1/3)} .$$

(b) This rule is identical to that used to tabulate deaths in Example 4-9. Taking T to be October 31, we have

$$\theta_x \Big]_{x-(5/6)}^{x+(1/6)} .$$

The overstatement of true ages introduced by the rule for determination of fiscal years of birth then leads to

$$\frac{\theta_x}{E_x} = q^F_{x-(5/6)} \doteq q_{x-(4/3)} .$$

(c) It will be recalled that this rule produces

$$\theta_x \Big]_{x}^{x+1}$$

once it is seen that fiscal years of event are based on the "preceding" rather than the more common "following" definition. Thus, the translation, as in Rule (b), is

$$\frac{\theta_x}{E_x} = q^F_x \doteq q_{x-(1/2)} .$$

(d) This rule clearly has nothing whatever to do with the fiscal year concept. As indicated in Chapter Three, it simply leads to

$$\theta_x \Big]_{x-(1/2)}^{x+(1/2)} ,$$

based upon a July 1 birth assumption. As with Rule (a), no translation is needed, so we have

$$\frac{\theta_x}{E_x} = q_{x-(1/2)} .$$

The mechanics of performing fiscal age studies have been described and illustrated with examples. Yet the true significance and flexibility of the fiscal year technique is probably best illustrated through an example which shows how the mortality experience of groups with different fiscal years may be combined.

EXAMPLE 4-11 You are asked to study the combined mortality experience under four group life insurance policies (A, B, C, and D) for the fiscal year beginning in 1976. In all cases, the fiscal year of birth is the calendar year containing the policy anniversary nearest the actual date of birth.

The information in Table 4-18 is available. Assume that, for each policy, new entrants and withdrawals are uniformly distributed.

TABLE 4–18

Policy	Policy anniversary	Fiscal year of birth	For fiscal year beginning in 1976			
			s	n	w	θ
A	May 1	1920	45	6	15	3
		1921	60	3	9	3
B	January 1	1920	10	2	3	0
		1921	15	5	0	1
C	July 1	1920	30	6	10	2
		1921	40	10	4	2
D	October 1	1920	24	8	4	0
		1921	36	12	16	4

(a) Determine the tabulating rules, the category symbols, and the single interval formula.

(b) Calculate all mortality rates which are available from the given data, and translate to actual ages.

SOLUTION

(a) Since this study is to be effected on a fiscal year basis, it seems appropriate to use the following tabulating rules:

$$\theta_x : x = \text{FYD} - \text{FYB},$$

$$s_x : x = 1976 - \text{FYB},$$

$$n_x : x = \text{FYN} - \text{FYB},$$

$$w_x : x = \text{FYW} - \text{FYB},$$

$$e_x : x = 1977 - \text{FYB}.$$

The standard assumption with respect to migration, in conjunction with the definition of fiscal year of event as the calendar year containing the policy anniversary *preceding* the event, produces

$$s_x^x, \quad n_x^{x+(1/2)}, \quad w_x^{x+(1/2)}, \quad e_x^x, \quad \text{and} \quad \theta_x \Big]_x^{x+1}.$$

The resulting formula is

$$E_x = \sum_{y=a}^{x-1} j_y + s_x + \tfrac{1}{2} \cdot n_x - \tfrac{1}{2} \cdot w_x - e_x.$$

(b) Two approaches are available for the calculation of exposures. The first to be presented is the usual tabulating routine which does little to enhance the student's understanding of the fiscal year study. It is essential, however, that the student test his ability to interpret fiscal year tabulating rules by verifying each entry in the following tabulation:

x	s_x	n_x	w_x	e_x	θ_x	j_x	$\sum\limits_{55}^{x-1} j_y$	f_x	E_x
55	151	30	29		10	142	0	$151\tfrac{1}{2}$	$151\tfrac{1}{2}$
56	109	22	32	142	5	-48	142	-38	104
57				94		-94	94	-94	0

Completing the exercise, we have

$$\frac{\theta_{55}}{E_{55}} = \frac{10}{151\tfrac{1}{2}} = q_{55}^F \doteq q_{55}$$

and

$$\frac{\theta_{56}}{E_{56}} = \frac{5}{104} = q_{56}^F \doteq q_{56}.$$

It would be instructive for the student to rework this exercise by this method, using the alternative definition of "fiscal year of event." A second approach to the completion of the exercise requires no tabulation but a clear understanding of the fiscal year terminology and the assumptions which have been imposed. Consider the lives with a 1920 fiscal year of birth and who were therefore fiscal age 56 at the beginning of the study. Policy A, for example, contributed

$$45 + \tfrac{1}{2}(6 - 15) = 40\tfrac{1}{2}$$

life-years of exposure during the period from May 1, 1976 to April 30, 1977, based upon the stated assumption with regard to migration. It is important that the student understand that the fiscal year nature of the observation period permits the combination of all four groups, obtaining 109 starters, 22 new entrants, and 32 withdrawals. Thus we obtain

$$109 + \tfrac{1}{2}(22 - 32) = 104$$

units of exposure for the period from fiscal age 56 until fiscal age 57. Similarly, the exposure for the preceding age interval is

$$151 + \tfrac{1}{2}(30 - 29) = 151\tfrac{1}{2}$$

life-years. The rates q_{55}^F and q_{56}^F are then immediately available. This second method obviated the necessity of determining the number of enders and, more importantly, did not even involve the selection of tabulating rules or the conscious defining of the fiscal year of the various events.

SUMMARY

There are two broad categories of methods used to compute mortality rates. In Chapter Four we have given consideration to those methods based upon individual records rather than upon pregrouped data.

Regardless of whether a mortality study is based upon insured lives or lives with some other defining characteristic and whether the study is select, aggregate, or fiscal, the basic ingredient of grouped individual record studies is constant. That is, each observed life is categorized into each of two cells, determined by application of tabulating rules and represented by an ordered pair. The observed lives are then grouped into decks, such as the s_{25} deck or the w_{27} deck. By considering the ages at which such decks are assumed to enter or leave the study in comparison to the unit age interval over which mortality is being measured, it is possible to apply the concepts of potential and cancelled exposure to compute total exposure and then rates of mortality. Of course, it is often feasible to treat each life individually, determining exposure contributions without regard to any grouping techniques or to tabulating rules other than that for deaths. This approach, known as the seriatim method, produces exposures which are exact for each individual, while the grouped method is inexact for most individuals but produces extremely accurate results through an attempt to have overstatements and understatements counterbalance each other.

Although exposure formulas have been derived, most notably the single interval exposure formula for use with the grouped method, these formulas act only as mechanical guidelines for the computation of exposures. They simply aid in routinizing the computational procedure, and students must guard against blind application of exposure formulas without a true understanding of the underlying theory.

An entirely different approach is often taken with respect to computing exposures when the available data include only aggregate in-force figures and observed deaths rather than data with respect to new entrants and withdrawals. In Chapter Five we shall derive formulas for calculating exposures in terms *only* of in-force figures and deaths. Such formulas are often referred to as valuation schedule formulas. These formulas, quite interestingly, will be seen to produce exposures identical to those calculated by individual record techniques if identical assumptions have been made with respect to such factors as birth or issue dates, mortality patterns, and migration. The demonstration of the true equivalence of such individual record formulas and valuation schedule formulas will then form the basis of Chapter Six.

EXERCISES

Note: *Several of the exercises in Chapters Four, Five, and Six require that the student impose assumptions prior to obtaining a final solution. Answers in the back of the text are predicated upon the most logical, or "common," assumptions. In many cases, however, alternative solutions are equally correct if based upon slightly different assumptions.*

1. The seriatim method is to be used to calculate exposure values in a mortality study of an employee group running from November 1, 1975 through April 30, 1978. The deaths have been grouped so that the symbol $\theta_x]_{x-(1/3)}^{x+(2/3)}$ results. The following individuals are included:

Life	Birth date	Hired	Other data
A	Jul. 1, 1950	Oct. 1, 1975	Died Feb. 1, 1978
B	Oct. 1, 1950	Oct. 1, 1975	Still active May 1, 1978
C	Feb. 1, 1951	Aug. 1, 1976	Died Sep. 1, 1976
D	Jun. 1, 1951	May 1, 1977	Withdrew Mar. 1, 1978
E	Aug. 1, 1949	Jun. 1, 1973	Died May 15, 1976
F	Dec. 1, 1950	Jan. 1, 1977	Died Jan 2, 1978
G	May 1, 1950	Mar. 1, 1976	Withdrew Jul. 1, 1976
H	Nov. 1, 1950	Oct. 1, 1976	Died Feb. 15, 1978

(a) For each of the eight lives separately, determine the amount of contributed exposure.

(b) Allocate the total exposure for the observed lives into the cells E_{25}, E_{26}, and E_{27}.

2. For a study beginning April 1, 1975, with deaths tabulated by age next birthday, find the superscript for the starters and the *f*-factor for the starters if

$$s_x : x = 1975 - \text{CYB}$$

is the prescribed tabulating rule.

3. Given the following tabulating rules, write the single interval exposure formula:

$$s_x : x = \text{Age next birthday},$$

$$n_x : x = \text{Age nearest birthday},$$

$$w_x : x = \text{Calendar age},$$

$$e_x : x = \text{Age last birthday},$$

$$\theta_x : x = \text{Age last birthday}.$$

4. Your tabulating rules in a given mortality investigation have led to the following symbols:

$$s_x^{x-(1/2)}, \quad n_x^x, \quad w_x^x, \quad e_x^{x+(1/2)}, \quad \text{and} \quad \theta_x \Big]_{x-(1/2)}^{x+(1/2)}.$$

What is the f_x associated with θ_x?

5. The observation period for a mortality study runs from January 1, 1975 to December 31, 1976. There are no withdrawals other than by death. July 1 births are assumed. Actuary *A* uses the following tabulating rules:

$$s_x : x = 1974 - \text{CYB},$$

$$e_x : x = 1976 - \text{CYB}.$$

Actuary *B* uses the following tabulating rules:

$$s_x : x = 1975 - \text{CYB},$$

$$e_x : x = 1977 - \text{CYB}.$$

Each actuary determines the exposure to be

$$E_x = \sum_{y=a}^{x-1} (s_y - e_y - \theta_y) + \tfrac{1}{2} \cdot s_x - \tfrac{1}{2} \cdot e_x.$$

Which, if any, of the following is (are) true?

(i) Although using different rules to tabulate *s* and *e*, the actuaries are using identical rules to tabulate deaths.

(ii) $q_x^A = q_x^B$.

(iii) $q_x^A = q_{x+1}^B$.

6. The observation period of a mortality study is January 1, 1975 through December 31, 1977. Deaths are tabulated by calendar age, and the following rules are used:

$$s_x : x = 1975 - \text{CYB},$$

$$e_x : x = 1978 - \text{CYB}.$$

Determine the f-factors for s_x and e_x.

7. The observation period of a mortality study runs from October 1, 1975 through September 30, 1979. The following tabulating rules are prescribed:

$$\theta_x : x = \text{CYC Apr. 1 FD} - \text{CYB},$$

$$s_x : x = 1976 - \text{CYB}.$$

(a) Stating the necessary assumptions, find the f-factor for the starters.
(b) Consider a person born on July 1, 1951, who died on March 1, 1978. On what date does he cease to contribute exposure if the seriatim method is used? If the exposure formula based upon the tabulating rules is used?

8. Consider the following tabulating rule for deaths:

$$\theta_x : x = P - Q,$$

where

$P = \text{CYC Sep. 1 FD};$
$Q = \text{CYC May 1 NB}.$

If $\theta_x / E_x = q_k$, find k.

9. A mortality study covering the calendar years 1973–1976 is based upon the following tabulating rules and the assumption that all births occur on June 1:

$$s_x : x = 1973 - \text{CYB},$$

$$n_x : x = \text{CYC Sep. 1 NN} - \text{CYB},$$

$$w_x : x = \text{CYC Jan. 1 FW} - \text{CYB},$$

$$e_x : x = 1976 - \text{CYB},$$

$$\theta_x : x = \text{CYC Apr. 1 PD} - \text{CYB}.$$

(a) Determine the single interval exposure formula.

(b) Determine the total exposure contributed by each of the following persons using (1) the seriatim approach and (2) the formula derived in (a). Explain any differences.

> A: Born Jun. 1, 1950; entered May 1, 1973; withdrew Feb. 1, 1975.
> B: Born Jun. 1, 1950; starter; died Jul. 1, 1975.
> C: Born Jun. 1, 1950; entered Dec. 1, 1973; died Feb. 1, 1974.

10. An aggregate mortality study is being conducted on policies issued during the calendar years 1967–1969, observed from March 1, 1970 through February 29, 1980. Assume issues on July 1, deaths tabulated by insuring age last anniversary, and Balducci mortality. All f-factors are "convenient"; age 20 is the youngest age for which data are available.

x	s_x	w_x	e_x	θ_x	E_x
20	90	20	60	6	42
21	110	10	90	8	
22	100	20	60	6	56
23	90	30	75	5	52

(a) Find p_{22}.
(b) Find E_{21}.
(c) What is the most likely tabulating rule for enders?

11. Your company has been issuing small 20-year endowments to members of the graduating classes of a large university; the policies are issued on June 1 of the year of graduation with the university as beneficiary. The issue age is the age last birthday at the date of issue. Following are extracts from the records kept by the university officer responsible for the administration of this program:

Insured	Graduating class	Age (last birthday) at issue	Terminations Year	Terminations Type
A	1969	20	*	
B	1969	20	1973	Withdrawal
C	1969	21	1969	Death
D	1969	21	1971	Death
E	1970	20	1972	Death
F	1971	20	1972	Death
G	1971	21	*	
H	1972	20	1974	Withdrawal
I	1972	21	*	
J	1973	20	*	
K	1973	21	1975	Withdrawal

* Still in force Jan. 1, 1975.

Using these records and assuming an observation period covering the calendar years 1970–1974, inclusive,

(a) Develop an exposure formula to be used in computing aggregate mortality rates by attained insuring age.

(b) Compute the mortality rates, and specify the ages to which they apply.

12. A 1975–1977 mortality study was made on persons from their birth or subsequent immigration into the United States until their emigration or prior death. The following tabulating rules were used:

$$s_x : x = 1975 - \text{CYB},$$

$$n_x : x = \text{CYC Jun. 1 FN} - \text{CYB},$$

$$w_x : x = \text{CYC Oct. 1 NW} - \text{CYB},$$

$$e_x : x = 1977 - \text{CYB},$$

$$\theta_x : x = \text{CYC Mar. 1 PD} - \text{CYB}.$$

(a) Determine the single interval exposure formula, stating all assumptions.

(b) How much exposure does your formula produce for each of the following? How does this compare with that produced by the seriatim method? Explain any differences.

	Born	*Other information*
A	Jul. 1, 1945	Native; emigrated Sep. 1, 1977
B	Jul. 1, 1946	Immigrated Feb. 1, 1976; died Aug. 1, 1976
C	Jul. 1, 1947	Immigrated Nov. 1, 1976; died Feb. 1, 1978
D	Jul. 1, 1946	Native; died Jun. 1, 1975

13. To what age does the mortality rate θ_x/E_x refer if

$$\theta_x : x = \text{CYC Oct. 31 PD} - \text{CYB}$$

is the tabulating rule for deaths?

14. If c and k are constants between 0 and 1, determine an expression for

$$E_x - \sum_{y=a}^{x-1} j_y,$$

given the following category symbols:

$$s_x^{x+(1/2)+k}, \quad n_x^{x+(1/2)}, \quad w_x^{x+(1/2)}, \quad e_x^{x-(1/2)-c}, \quad \text{and} \quad \theta_x \Big]_{x-(1/2)}^{x+(1/2)}.$$

15. Write the single interval formula for the exposure associated with μ_x, given the following category symbols:

$$s_x^{x-(1/2)}, \quad n_x^{x+(1/6)}, \quad w_x^{x+(5/6)}, \quad e_x^x, \quad \text{and} \quad \theta_x\Big]_{x-(1/3)}^{x+(2/3)}.$$

Exercises 16–19 relate to an aggregate study based upon insuring ages, with an observation period running from January 1, 1975 through December 31, 1979. Issue age is age nearest birthday at issue. The following tabulating rules have been used in the study:

$$s_x : x = 1974 - \text{VYB},$$

$$n_x : x = \text{CYN} - \text{VYB},$$

$$w_x : x = \text{CYW} - \text{VYB},$$

$$e_x : x = 1979 - \text{VYB},$$

$$\theta_x : x = \text{Insuring age on policy anniversary preceding death.}$$

16. What are the f-factors for starters and withdrawals, respectively?
17. Policy X was issued on August 1, 1973 to a person born May 3, 1943. The policy was terminated by surrender on December 1, 1978. At what tabulated ages does the policy enter and leave the study?
18. Policy Y was issued on February 4, 1977 to a person born October 10, 1933. It was still in force on January 1, 1980. At what tabulated ages does the policy enter and leave the study?
19. Policy Z was issued on April 1, 1979 and was terminated by death on June 1, 1979. How much exposure does it contribute?

Exercises 20–22 relate to a select study of insured lives, in which deaths have been tabulated by policy year of death, while starters, withdrawals, and enders have been tabulated in such a way that their f-factors are each equal to zero. The following data pertain to issue age 35:

t	s_t	w_t	e_t	θ_t	E_t
1	20	5	23	1	80
2	19	5	20	1	
3					
4	18	3	17	1	

20. What is the value of E_2?
21. What is the value of n?
22. Given that $\sum_{y=5}^{b} J_y = 53$, what is the value of E_4?

Exercises 23–24 relate to a select mortality study for which the tabulating rules imply the following category symbols:

$$s_t^{t+(1/2)}, \quad w_t^t, \quad e_t^{t+(1/2)}, \quad \text{and} \quad \theta_t \Big]_t^{t+1}.$$

The highest value of t for which any data exist is 15. Following are some of the data for durations 13–15:

t	s_t	w_t	e_t	θ_t	E_t
13	0	6	38	2	
14	0	4	32	2	54
15	0			0	15

23. What is the value of E_{13}?
24. What is the value of e_{15}?
25. In a select mortality study, policies issued in 1970–1977, inclusive, were observed from issue until March 31, 1978. Given the following data for issue age 40, calculate all possible values of $q_{[40]+t}$, stating all assumptions used:

Withdrawals		Deaths		In force Mar. 31, 1978	
Calendar duration	Number	Curtate duration	Number	Year of issue	Number
0	50	0	10	1970	1200
1	100	1	10	1971	1200
2	90	2	10	1972	1200
3	80	3	10	1973	1600
4	70	4	10	1974	1600
5	60	5	10	1975	1600
6	50	6	10	1976	2000
7	40	7	10	1977	2000
8	0	8	2		

26. In a select mortality study with data available for durations 0–10, inclusive, express each of the following with a single symbol:
   (a) $E_8 - E_9 - P_8$.

   (b) $\sum_{y=6}^{10} J_y - \sum_{y=0}^{5} j_y$.

   (c) $E_0 - n$.

   (d) $\sum_{y=8}^{10} J_y - F_8$.

27. A mortality investigation of insured lives is made on an aggregate basis, with observation from March 1, 1975 until October 31, 1980. The following tabulating rules are used:

$$s_x : x = 1974 - \text{VYB},$$

$$n_x : x = \text{CYC Apr. 1 FN} - \text{VYB},$$

$$w_x : x = \text{CYC Nov. 1 NW} - \text{VYB},$$

$$e_x : x = 1981 - \text{VYB},$$

$$\theta_x : x = \text{CYD} - \text{VYB}.$$

Stating your assumptions, write the single interval exposure formula.

28. An insurance company is making a select study of the mortality experience of issues at age x of calendar years 1972–1974, observed from anniversaries in 1975 to anniversaries in 1978.

  (a) Devise tabulating rules, and construct the appropriate single interval formula.

  (b) From the following data, compute as many select mortality rates as possible:

	Withdrawals				In force on anniversary in	
CYI	1975	1976	1977	1978	1975	1978
1972	20	50	40	10	1000	860
1973	22	40	50	15	1100	950
1974	26	60	40	18	1050	859

Calendar duration at death	Number of deaths
1	20
2	13
3	15
4	12
5	20
6	10

  (c) Calculate $\mu_{[x]+5}$ from the above data.

29. The following tabulation includes the policies issued at age x. The number of new entrants is 2700. Deaths have been tabulated by policy year of death, starters and enders by exact duration, and withdrawals by

calendar duration. Compute the exposures by the most convenient method, and write the mortality rates in fractional form.

Duration t	θ_t	s_t	w_t	e_t
0	—	—	100	—
1	5	650	450	845
2	6	550	250	694
3	7	450	200	543
4	5	0	200	495
5	4	0	150	396

30. You are given the following data for issue age 45. The period of observation runs from anniversaries in 1970 to anniversaries in 1975. Tabulate the deaths by policy year of death and the withdrawals by calendar duration. Compute the exposures, and write the values of $q_{[45]+t}$ in fractional form.

Starters		Enders	
Year of issue	No. of policies	Year of issue	No. of policies
1964	1	1966	1
1965	0	1967	0
1966	2	1968	1
1967	5	1969	0
1968	3	1970	2
1969	2	1971	4
		1972	3
		1973	1

Withdrawals		Deaths	
Issue	Withdrawal	Issue	Death
Jan. 7, 1964	Jul. 7, 1972	Jul. 6, 1971	Sep. 10, 1971
Sep. 6, 1967	Mar. 6, 1975	Aug. 10, 1970	Sep. 5, 1973
Nov. 10, 1969	Nov. 10, 1970	Feb. 12, 1968	Dec. 12, 1973
Nov. 15, 1969	Nov. 15, 1970	Mar. 22, 1968	Apr. 30, 1974
Sep. 10, 1971	Jun. 10, 1973		
Jul. 12, 1967	Jun. 12, 1971		
Mar. 10, 1967	Mar. 10, 1972		
Jul. 12, 1967	Apr. 12, 1972		
Aug. 5, 1967	Sep. 10, 1972		
Apr. 13, 1966	Jul. 13, 1973		

31. You have been asked to investigate mortality rates, by number of policies, among permanent policies issued as conversions from individual term insurance. The observation period for this study is to be January 1, 1970 to December 31, 1976. The issue age is age nearest birthday. The study is to be based upon individual policy records giving information as to the dates of birth, original issue of term insurance, and conversion. These records also show the date of termination of the permanent policy and the reason for termination.

(a) Derive a single interval formula for computation of the exposures for this study in select form, by original issue age and duration since issue of the term policy. State any assumptions and approximations involved in your derivation, and state the tabulating rules involved.

(b) The following table contains information relating to six of the policies in the study. Using the formula and tabulating rules derived in (a), calculate the total contributions of these six policies to the exposures for each applicable age and duration cell.

Policy	Birth date	Term policy issued	Term policy converted	Permanent policy terminated
A	Oct. 21, 1927	Mar. 10, 1973	Jun. 10, 1975	*
B	Jan. 4, 1924	Nov. 16, 1968	Nov. 16, 1969	Lapsed Jan. 16, 1971
C	Oct. 22, 1934	Jan. 13, 1970	Oct. 13, 1970	Lapsed Nov. 13, 1970
D	Nov. 10, 1936	Apr. 8, 1972	Jul. 8, 1976	*
E	Mar. 7, 1925	Nov. 21, 1969	May 21, 1972	Died Jul. 2, 1972
F	Dec. 8, 1930	May 24, 1966	May 24, 1968	Died Apr. 5, 1970

* In force as of December 31, 1976.

Exercises 32–33 relate to a calendar year mortality study by fiscal ages. Fiscal year of birth is defined as the calendar year containing the September 30 following the actual date of birth. The observation period begins January 1, 1975. The following tabulating rules are used:

$$s_x : x = 1975 - \text{FYB},$$

$$\theta_x : x = \text{CYD} - \text{FYB}.$$

32. What is the *f*-factor for starters?

33. What is the interpretation of the resultant q's in terms of the actual ages to which they apply?

34. In a mortality study,

$$\theta_x : x = \text{FYD} - \text{FYB}$$

is the tabulating rule for deaths.

(a) In determining the range notation for the deaths, what fact, if any, must be given or assumed?

(b) How would your answer be different if the rule had been

$$\theta_x : x = CYD - FYB?$$

35. You are conducting a mortality study for the observation period January 1, 1972 through December 31, 1976. The fiscal year runs from April 1 to March 31, and fiscal years of birth are assigned. The tabulating rules are

$$s_x : x = 1972 - FYB,$$

$$n_x : x = FYN - FYB,$$

$$w_x : x = CYW - FYB,$$

$$e_x : x = 1977 - FYB,$$

$$\theta_x : x = CYD - FYB.$$

If $\theta_x/E_x = q_z^F$, find z.

36. Births assumed to occur on June 1 in a mortality study for which deaths are tabulated by $\theta_x : x = FYD - CYB$. If $T = $ March 31 and if FYD is defined in the usual manner, find the actual age to which θ_x/E_x relates.

37. In a mortality study, the following tabulating rules for deaths are suggested:

(i) $\theta_x : x = FYD - FYB.$

(ii) $\theta_x : x = CYD - FYB.$

Rule (i) leads to the symbol

$$\theta_x \Big]_x^{x+1} ;$$

Rule (ii) leads to the symbol

$$\theta_x \Big]_{x-(3/4)}^{x+(1/4)} .$$

If Rule (ii) is used, $\theta_x/E_x \doteq q_{x-(1/4)}$. How are the fiscal years of death and the fiscal years of birth assigned?

38. The following assignment of fiscal years has been made:

$$FYD = CYC \text{ Mar. 31 FD,}$$

$$FYB = CYC \text{ Mar. 31 PB.}$$

For each of the following tabulating rules for deaths, translate θ_x/E_x in terms of actual ages:

(a) $\theta_x : x = FYD - FYB.$

(b) $\theta_x : x = FYD - CYB.$

39. Given the tabulating rule

$$\theta_x : x = \text{FYD} - \text{CYB},$$

it is determined that

$$\frac{\theta_x}{E_x} = q_k.$$

(a) List the facts which must be known or assumed in order to find k.
(b) Determine a set of facts or assumptions which leads to $k = x + \frac{1}{6}$.

40. Repeat Exercise 39 if

$$\theta_x : x = \text{CYD} - \text{FYB}$$

is the tabulating rule for deaths.

41. The observation period of a mortality study runs from March 1, 1972 through February 28, 1978. A fiscal year of birth was used for each life. Tabulations have been prepared on the following basis:

$s_x : x = $ Age last birthday as of June 1, 1972,

$n_x : x = $ Age last birthday as of the June 1 preceding entry,

$w_x : x = $ Age last birthday as of the June 1 following withdrawal,

$e_x : x = $ Age last birthday as of June 1, 1977,

$\theta_x : x = $ Age last birthday as of the June 1 preceding death.

(a) How was the FYB assigned?
(b) State the tabulating rules in simplest form, being careful to obtain "convenient" f-factors if possible.
(c) Interpret θ_x/E_x both as a rate for actual ages and for fiscal ages.
(d) Write the single interval exposure formula.

42. The following definitions are given for "fiscal age at new entry," "fiscal year of new entry," and "fiscal year of death":

$$\text{FAN} = \text{Age next birthday on May 1 FN},$$

$$\text{FYN} = \text{CYC May 1 PN},$$

$$\text{FYD} = \text{CYC May 1 FD}.$$

If $\theta_x : x = \text{FAN} + \text{FYD} - \text{FYN}$ is the tabulating rule for deaths, to what actual age would θ_x/E_x apply?

43. In a mortality study running from May 1, 1973 to April 30, 1977, the following tabulating rules were used ($T = $ April 30):

$$s_x : x = 1973 - \text{FYB},$$

$$n_x : x = \text{FYN} - \text{FYB},$$

$$w_x : x = \text{FYW} - \text{FYB},$$

$$e_x : x = 1977 - \text{FYB},$$

$$\theta_x : x = \text{FYD} - \text{FYB}.$$

Fiscal year of event is defined as the calendar year containing the April 30 following the event. When translated to actual ages, $\theta_x/E_x \doteq q_{x-(3/2)}$.

(a) What FYB was assigned to a person born February 1, 1955? December 1, 1955?

(b) Write the single interval exposure formula.

(c) How much exposure does your formula credit to a person born Apr. 1, 1955 who is a new entrant on Dec. 1, 1975 and a death on Feb. 1, 1977?

(d) With how much exposure would the seriatim method credit the person in (c)?

Valuation Schedule Exposure Formulas

INTRODUCTION

Methods of computing exposure which have been considered thus far have been based upon analyses of the records of individual lives exposed to risk. In some cases the seriatim approach has been used, while in others a grouping technique has given rise to formulas which permit collective consideration of exposed lives in well-defined groups, or decks. The formulas themselves merely consist of linear combinations of these various decks of starters, new entrants, withdrawals, enders, and deaths. It is especially significant to note that these formulas would be inapplicable in their standard form if the only available data consisted of numbers of starters, enders, and deaths.

The second major category of exposure formulas does in fact permit exposure calculations in the absence of specific data with respect to new entrants and withdrawals. These formulas, based only upon the number of observed deaths and periodic counts of the number of lives in the observed group, are known as *valuation schedule* formulas, simply because the only required input is often automatically available from data routinely compiled for purposes of valuation. For example, an annual valuation of the assets of a pension plan, including membership data, may easily be adapted for use in a mortality study of the plan's participants. Similarly, the number of policies in force with a given insurer at year-end may be taken as "starters" for a mortality study of insured lives beginning on January 1, although the primary purpose of the compilation of these data is in all likelihood to make an annual report to regulatory authorities, stockholders, and/or policy-holders. For obvious reasons, then, valuation schedule exposure formulas are often referred to simply as in-force formulas.

It is our objective in this chapter to introduce exposure formulas of the valuation schedule genre, containing no terms involving "movement" such as that associated with new entrants and withdrawals. We shall see that astute use of two-dimensional diagrams will often permit calculation of exposures from these formulas much more readily than from the formulas developed in Chapter Four. In fact, we shall often be able to compute exposures merely by inspecting a carefully constructed diagram.

DEMOGRAPHIC CONSIDERATIONS

Occasionally, we may encounter valuation schedule formulas in terms of only starters, enders, and deaths, s, e, and θ, with

$$E_x \Big]_{x-(1/2)}^{x+(1/2)} = \tfrac{3}{4} \cdot s + \tfrac{1}{4} \cdot e + \tfrac{1}{4} \cdot \theta$$

being a specific example. Much more often, however, these formulas will be expressed in terms of symbols whose origins are found in demography, a discipline which deals with the scientific analysis of census data and vital statistics records. Prior to further consideration of valuation schedule formulas, then, we must introduce some key demographic concepts and notation.

Even though most mortality studies which are of interest to the actuary are based upon insured lives, it is convenient to employ, for such studies, demographic notation, which is generally used in connection with data for an entire population. Let us therefore consider the following definitions:

$P_x^z =$ the number of persons who, at the beginning of calendar year z, are between the integral ages x and $x + 1$;

$E_x^z =$ the number of persons who, during calendar year z, attain exact age x;

$_aD_x^z =$ the number of deaths observed between the attainment of age x in calendar year z and the end of z;

$_\delta D_x^z =$ the number of deaths observed between the beginning of calendar year z and the date in z on which exact age $x + 1$ would have been attained;

$D_x^z =$ the number of deaths observed at age x last birthday during calendar year z, i.e., $_aD_x^z + _\delta D_x^z$.

It should be clear from the foregoing definitions that the calendar years of birth of the P_x^z, E_x^z, $_aD_x^z$, and $_\delta D_x^z$ groups are $z - x - 1$, $z - x$, $z - x$, and $z - x - 1$, respectively.

Just as the definitions of $_aD_x^z$ and $_\delta D_x^z$ classify deaths by whether they occur prior to or subsequent to the birth date in the calendar year of death, new entrants and withdrawals are similarly subdivided. Let

$_an_x^z =$ the number of new entrants who enter the observed group between the attainment of age x in year z and the end of z;

$_\delta n_x^z =$ the number of new entrants who enter the observed group between the beginning of calendar year z and the attainment of age $x + 1$ in year z;

$n_x^z =$ the number of new entrants at age x last birthday during calendar year z, i.e., $_an_x^z + _\delta n_x^z$.

Clearly, the members of the $_\alpha n_x^z$ and $_\delta n_x^z$ groups are born in calendar years $z - x$ and $z - x - 1$, respectively. The symbols $_\alpha w_x^z$, $_\delta w_x^z$, and w_x^z are defined in exactly the same manner as the corresponding new entrant terms.

Figure 5-1 should facilitate the student's effort to become comfortable with standard demographic symbols. As in all such diagrams with which we shall be working, age progresses in a downward direction while time progresses at

FIGURE 5-1

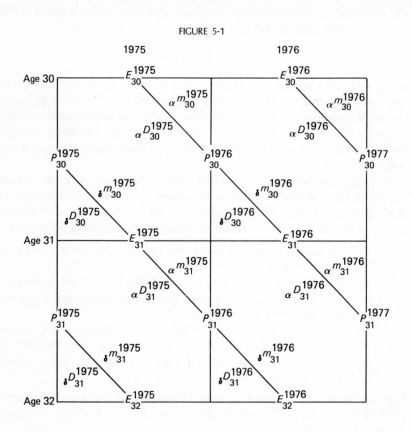

the same rate in a horizontal manner, moving from left to right. It must be understood that such diagrams represent an idealized display in which all persons born in a given calendar year are placed on a single diagonal. Such a representation is tantamount to the assumption that all births in any calendar year fall on a single day. This single day is generally taken as July 1, as in Figure 5-1, but, as will be evident later in this chapter, other birth assumptions are not unusual. To keep diagrams as uncluttered as possible, we shall adopt the symbols

$$_\alpha m_x^z \quad \text{and} \quad _\delta m_x^z$$

to represent the algebraic excess of new entrants over withdrawals within the appropriate regions of the diagrams. Also, it will be standard procedure to indicate the amount of net migration just above the diagonal on which it occurs. Similarly, deaths will be indicated just below the corresponding diagonals. Where it is not obvious, arrows will be used to indicate the exact point at which the various groups are located on the diagram.

The student should note that the following equations are but a few of the many relationships which may be read directly from Figure 5-1:

$$P_{30}^{1975} + {}_{\delta}m_{30}^{1975} - {}_{\delta}D_{30}^{1975} = E_{31}^{1975},$$

$$P_{31}^{1977} - {}_{\alpha}m_{31}^{1976} + {}_{\alpha}D_{31}^{1976} = E_{31}^{1976},$$

$$E_{31}^{1976} + {}_{\delta}D_{30}^{1976} - P_{30}^{1976} = {}_{\delta}m_{30}^{1976}.$$

The third of these equations should provide initial insight into the capacity of valuation schedule formulas to produce exposures without specifically containing migration terms. Clearly, amounts of migration are easily expressible in terms of in-force data and observed deaths, making it evident that the mere absence of specific migration terms in an exposure formula does not indicate that such formulas are independent of the magnitude of the migration.

The fact that demographic symbols were not originally developed with an eye toward use in mortality measurement generates some potential confusion of which the student should be keenly aware. Formal definitions which have been given for D_x^z, n_x^z, and w_x^z require that the subscripts x be taken to represent the *age last birthday* of the observed lives as of their dates of death, entry, or withdrawal. Yet we have seen that, in exposure determinations based upon groupings of individual records, tabulations by age nearest birthday or age next birthday are quite common. As a major conclusion of this text will be that individual record formulas and valuation schedule formulas are essentially identical when based upon the same assumptions, it will be necessary in Chapter Six to effect minute comparisons of such pairs of formulas. At that time, we shall face the dilemma that strict adherence to either set of notation must necessarily result in at least a partial disregard of the other. Additional attention will be devoted to this problem later; for the present, however, we shall adhere to strict demographic usage when the subscript x is attached to a death or a migration symbol.

The student will further note that demographic notation has been strictly defined in the context of calendar year periods and numbers of lives in an entire population. We shall, however, find it easy to apply the resulting formulas to fiscal year periods and to insured lives. In fact, we shall often find ourselves resorting to two-dimensional diagrams on which numerical values have been placed and determining exposures without a conscious realization that the formulas being used actually had demographic origins.

BALDUCCI-BASED FORMULAS

All demographic formulas which will be of use to us are merely composites of *single-diagonal* or *double-diagonal* formulas. By first considering these two basic building blocks in detail, we shall find that progression to the more complicated formulas will be routine. Although primary emphasis will be placed upon those formulas founded upon the Balducci hypothesis, formulas based upon uniform deaths will be considered later in this chapter.

Single-Diagonal Formulas

A single-diagonal formula is one which is based only upon lives with a common calendar year of birth. This definition may be expanded to include a common valuation year of birth, calendar year of issue, or fiscal year of birth in insured life studies, select studies, or fiscal age studies.

The creation of a single-diagonal formula or a double-diagonal formula results from a combination of the choice of observation period and the method of grouping the deaths. Two such combinations lead to single-diagonal formulas. Separate examination of each such combination is advisable and will now be undertaken.

Calendar year study, deaths by calendar age. Let us first consider an observation period of the single calendar year z, with a grouping of deaths by calendar age. If we make the usual assumption of July 1 births, the immediate implication is that all persons are exactly halfway between birthdays at the inception of the observation period. Considering only the unit age interval between $x - \frac{1}{2}$ and $x + \frac{1}{2}$, we have the situation depicted in Figure 5-2. The method of grouping deaths and the choice of observation period, taken together, force the diagram to consist of a single diagonal. The various exposure formulas which may be derived from Figure 5-2 depend on the assumptions imposed with respect to mortality pattern and migration.

Let us assume initially that both α- and δ-migration in Figure 5-2 occur at exact age x, an assumption clearly equivalent to the familiar tabulation of migration by age nearest birthday. By application of the concepts of potential and cancelled exposure with respect to the unit interval $[x - \frac{1}{2}, x + \frac{1}{2}]$, which, it will be recalled, is valid only when the Balducci hypothesis is assumed, we see that the net exposure is

$$E_x \bigg|_{x-(1/2)}^{x+(1/2)} = P_{x-1}^z + \tfrac{1}{2} \cdot (\delta m_{x-1}^z + {}_a m_x^z). \tag{5-1}$$

It should be clear that the death terms and the P_x^{z+1} term do not appear, as each continues to contribute exposure until the end of the unit age interval, thus generating no cancellation. The E_x^z term does not specifically appear, although each of the E_x^z lives actually is given recognition, either

FIGURE 5-2

Calendar Year z

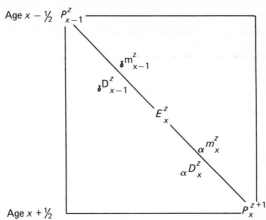

as a member of the P_{x-1}^z or $_\delta m_{x-1}^z$ group, and their potential exposure is duly recorded at the time of their entry. Any cancelled exposure which may be required for the E_x^z lives is likewise handled by the $_\alpha m_x^z$ term.

Formula (5-1), while absolutely valid in that it reflects the underlying assumptions, does not qualify as a valuation schedule formula because it contains migration terms. This shortcoming is easily remedied by substituting, into Formula (5-1), the identity

$$_\delta m_{x-1}^z + _\alpha m_x^z = P_x^{z+1} + _\alpha D_x^z + _\delta D_{x-1}^z - P_{x-1}^z,$$

leading to

$$E_x \bigg|_{x-(1/2)}^{x+(1/2)} = \tfrac{1}{2} \cdot (P_{x-1}^z + P_x^{z+1}) + \tfrac{1}{2} \cdot (_\alpha D_x^z + _\delta D_{x-1}^z).$$

Introduction of the simplifying definition

$$D_{x\backslash}^z = _\delta D_{x-1}^z + _\alpha D_x^z$$

(where the *slash* indicates that the deaths being considered fall on a single diagonal within a single calendar year) produces the formula in simplest form:

$$E_x \bigg|_{x-(1/2)}^{x+(1/2)} = \tfrac{1}{2} \cdot (P_{x-1}^z + P_x^{z+1}) + \tfrac{1}{2} \cdot D_{x\backslash}^z. \qquad (5\text{-}2)$$

It should be noted, for future reference, that the placement of migration at the midpoint of the single diagonal results in a formula which gives equal weight to the census figures at the end points of the diagonal. Formula (5-2), the first true valuation schedule formula which we have encountered, clearly produces the desired exposure values from year-end in force figures and the appropriate deaths.

Again referring to Figure 5-2, let us now assume that the δ-migration occurred an instant *after* age $x - \frac{1}{2}$ and that the α-migration occurred an instant *before* age $x + \frac{1}{2}$.* Imposing the Balducci hypothesis and considering potential and cancelled exposure, we have

$$E_x \Big]_{x-(1/2)}^{x+(1/2)} = P_{x-1}^z + {}_\delta m_{x-1}^z. \tag{5-3}$$

Substituting the identity

$${}_\delta m_{x-1}^z = E_x^z + {}_\delta D_{x-1}^z - P_{x-1}^z$$

into Equation (5-3), the valuation schedule formula

$$E_x \Big]_{x-(1/2)}^{x+(1/2)} = E_x^z + {}_\delta D_{x-1}^z \tag{5-4}$$

results. Again, for future reference, the student should note that placement of migration at the end points of the diagonal results in a formula whose only *census* component is the count of lives at the center of the diagonal.

Now let us generalize the problem by assuming that the δ-migration term is placed m months ($0 \le m \le 6$) below the upper end of the diagonal and that the α-migration term is placed n months ($0 \le n \le 6$) above the lower end of the diagonal. Consideration of Figure 5-2 in light of these migration assumptions leads to

$$E_x \Big]_{x-(1/2)}^{x+(1/2)} = P_{x-1}^z + \frac{12-m}{12} \cdot {}_\delta m_{x-1}^z + \frac{n}{12} \cdot {}_\alpha m_x^z. \tag{5-5}$$

By substituting the identities

$${}_\delta m_{x-1}^z = E_x^z + {}_\delta D_{x-1}^z - P_{x-1}^z$$

and

$${}_\alpha m_x^z = P_x^{z+1} + {}_\alpha D_x^z - E_x^z$$

into Formula (5-5), we have

$$E_x \Big]_{x-(1/2)}^{x+(1/2)} = \frac{m}{12} \cdot P_{x-1}^z + \frac{12-m-n}{12} \cdot E_x^z + \frac{n}{12} \cdot P_x^{z+1}$$

$$+ \frac{12-m}{12} \cdot {}_\delta D_{x-1}^z + \frac{n}{12} \cdot {}_\alpha D_x^z, \tag{5-6}$$

---

* We must avoid careless statements such as "α-migration is assumed at age $x + \frac{1}{2}$," as it would then be unclear whether the P_x^{z+1} term was determined before or after the α-migration took place.

of which Formulas (5-2) and (5-4) are special cases. Another special case of Formula (5-6) which is often encountered specifies placement of migration at the midpoints of each half of the diagonal, that is, at ages $x - \frac{1}{4}$ and $x + \frac{1}{4}$. This produces, letting $m = n = 3$,

$$E_x \Big|_{x-(1/2)}^{x+(1/2)} = \tfrac{1}{4} \cdot P_{x-1}^z + \tfrac{1}{2} \cdot E_x^z + \tfrac{1}{4} \cdot P_x^{z+1} + \tfrac{3}{4} \cdot {}_\delta D_{x-1}^z + \tfrac{1}{4} \cdot {}_\alpha D_x^z.$$

Having exhausted all assumptions as to placement of migration, let us now consider the assumption that the average date of birth within each calendar year is other than July 1. Still adhering to the Balducci hypothesis and the grouping of deaths by calendar age, variations in assumed birth dates seem to represent the only possible means of producing single-diagonal exposure formulas other than those included in the family represented by Formula (5-6).

It should be clear that the primary effect on Figure 5-2 of a change in the birth assumption is to produce a different unit age interval. The single-diagonal nature of the problem is preserved. Of course, such a change is accompanied by placement of E_x^z at a point other than at the center of the diagonal, as birthdays clearly occur on some date other than July 1. For example, the assumption that the average date of birth is May 1 leads to the construction of Figure 5-3, in which the E_x^z group is placed at a point one-third of the distance from the upper end to the lower end of the diagonal, which now runs from ages $x - \frac{1}{3}$ to $x + \frac{2}{3}$.

As before, let us assume that δ-migration occurs m months $(0 \le m \le 4)$ below the upper end of the diagonal and that α-migration occurs n months

FIGURE 5-3

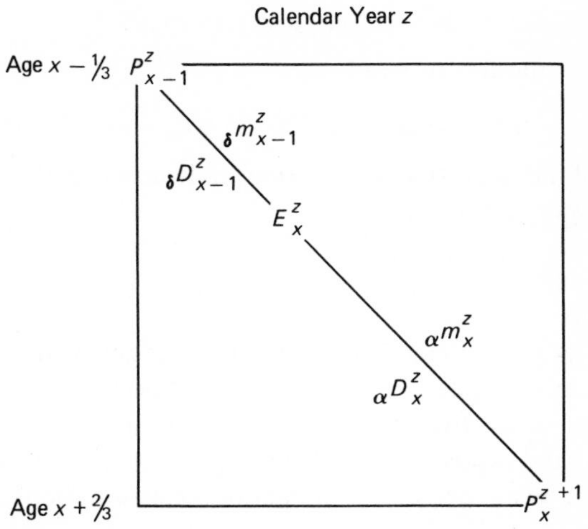

Calendar Year z

$(0 \leq n \leq 8)$ above the lower end of the diagonal. Analysis of potential and cancelled exposure leads to

$$E_x \Big]_{x-(1/3)}^{x+(2/3)} = P_{x-1}^z + \frac{12 - m}{12} \cdot {}_\delta m_{x-1}^z + \frac{n}{12} \cdot {}_\alpha m_x^z,$$

which, significantly, has the same form as Formula (5-5). Appropriate substitution of the identities for the migration terms then produces the valuation schedule formula

$$E_x \Big]_{x-(1/3)}^{x+(2/3)} = \frac{m}{12} \cdot P_{x-1}^z + \frac{12 - m - n}{12} \cdot E_x^z + \frac{n}{12} \cdot P_x^{z+1}$$

$$+ \frac{12 - m}{12} \cdot {}_\delta D_{x-1}^z + \frac{n}{12} \cdot {}_\alpha D_x^z.$$

This formula is visually identical to Formula (5-6) with the only dissimilarity being that m and n are bounded in a slightly different manner. Thus, we may conclude that it may be used for any combination of birth and migration assumptions within the category of single-diagonal formulas with a calendar year observation period, grouping of deaths by calendar age, and the assumption of the Balducci pattern of mortality.

An alternative approach to the derivation of Formula (5-6) is not only enlightening with respect to the handling of the various assumptions, but it should provide the student with a fail-safe technique for deriving formulas from only an inspection of a diagram. We know that the ultimate formula must be in the form of a linear combination of the three demographic symbols and the two death terms:

$$E_x \Big]_{x-(1/3)}^{x+(2/3)} = a_1 \cdot P_{x-1}^z + a_2 \cdot E_x^z + a_3 \cdot P_x^{z+1}$$

$$+ a_4 \cdot {}_\delta D_{x-1}^z + a_5 \cdot {}_\alpha D_x^z. \tag{5-7}$$

Let us consider the five ordered pairs

$$(P_{x-1}^z, {}_\delta w_{x-1}^z), \quad ({}_\delta n_{x-1}^z, {}_\alpha w_x^z), \quad ({}_\alpha n_x^z, P_x^{z+1}), \quad ({}_\delta n_{x-1}^z, {}_\delta D_{x-1}^z), \quad \text{and} \quad ({}_\alpha n_x^z, {}_\alpha D_x^z).$$

An analysis of the migration assumptions indicates that the contribution to E_x of these ordered pairs is

$$\frac{m}{12}, \quad \frac{12 - m - n}{12}, \quad \frac{n}{12}, \quad \frac{12 - m}{12}, \quad \text{and} \quad \frac{n}{12},$$

respectively. As the ordered pairs have been selected in such a way that each involves exactly one of the five terms of Formula (5-7), each uniquely determines one of the five unknown coefficients. This follows directly from the fact that a valid exposure formula must produce the exact correct amount of exposure for any ordered pair in light of the assumptions imposed. Thus, since we have now determined that $a_1 = m/12$, $a_2 = (12 - m - n)/12$, $a_3 = n/12$, $a_4 = (12 - m)/12$, and $a_5 = n/12$, Formula (5-6) has again surfaced. This technique of producing exposure formulas is known as the *method of undetermined coefficients*.

A close examination of the generalized formula represented by (5-6) reveals several characteristics which the student may use as a partial verification of the derivation process. First, the coefficient of P_{x-1}^z is simply the distance from the beginning of the unit age interval to the point at which the first migration occurs. Second, the coefficient of E_x^z is the distance between the two migration points. Finally, the coefficient of P_x^{z+1} is the distance between the second migration point and the end of the unit age interval. The student may wish to use these observations as a device for recalling the form of this general formula without having to resort to rote memorization. Of course, once the coefficients of the in-force terms are so determined, the necessity for obtaining the coefficients of the death terms remains.

EXAMPLE 5-1 Determine the valuation schedule exposure formula resulting from the following assumptions:

(a) Deaths are grouped by calendar age;
(b) The average birth date is September 1;
(c) δ-Migration occurs on March 1;
(d) α-Migration occurs on October 1;
(e) The observation period is the calendar year 1976;
(f) Mortality follows the Balducci pattern.

SOLUTION Figure 5-4 is helpful. Subsequent to the determination of the bounds of the unit age interval and the construction of the diagram (Figure 5-4), the next step is the partitioning of the diagonal into three segments of length two, seven, and three months, the end points of which represent the points of migration and the end points of the diagonal. Thus, we have, by using the observations made above,

$$E_x \Big|_{x-(2/3)}^{x+(1/3)} = \tfrac{2}{12} \cdot P_{x-1}^{1976} + \tfrac{7}{12} \cdot E_x^{1976} + \tfrac{3}{12} \cdot P_x^{1977}$$
$$+ a_1 \cdot {}_\delta D_{x-1}^{1976} + a_2 \cdot {}_\alpha D_x^{1976}.$$

Then by consideration of the ordered pair $({}_\delta n_{x-1}, {}_\delta D_{x-1})$ we see that $a_1 = \tfrac{10}{12}$. Finally, the ordered pair $({}_\alpha n_x, {}_\alpha D_x)$ must receive three months of exposure, producing $a_2 = \tfrac{1}{4}$ and completing the solution.

The derivation of exposure formulas reflecting unusual birth and migration assumptions, such as in Example 5-1, has traditionally proved troublesome for students. The technique which has been introduced here

FIGURE 5-4

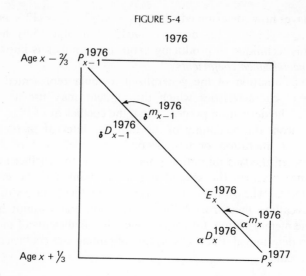

should make such derivations both rapid and routine. The student is cautioned, however, against blind application of the technique without a thorough understanding of the means by which it produces results identical to those produced by the more traditional methods.

EXAMPLE 5-2   Determine the birth and migration assumptions implicit in the formula

$$E_x \bigg]_{x-(1/4)}^{x+(3/4)} = \tfrac{2}{3} \cdot P_{x-1}^z + \tfrac{1}{3} \cdot P_x^{z+1} + \tfrac{1}{3} \cdot D_{x\backslash}^z.$$

SOLUTION   The indicated range of E_x leads to the conclusion that the average date of birth has been taken as April 1, as this is clearly a single-diagonal formula with a calendar year observation period. Further, since the ordered pairs $(P_{x-1}^z, \,_\delta w_{x-1}^z)$ and $(P_{x-1}^z, \,_\alpha w_x^z)$ each are seen to receive eight months' exposure, both types of migration must have been placed at a point $\tfrac{2}{3}$ of a unit below the upper end of the diagonal. This indicates that all migration during any calendar year z has been assumed to occur on August 31. This result is clearly consistent with earlier observations with respect to the relative weights of the in-force terms.

Birthday-to-birthday observation period, deaths by age last birthday. Now let us consider an observation period which runs from birthdays in z to birthdays in $z + 1$. To produce another single-diagonal situation, let us select a grouping of deaths by age last birthday. Upon imposition of a July 1 birth assumption, Figure 5-5 results, and, again, the determination of exposures is dependent only on mortality and migration assumptions.

FIGURE 5-5

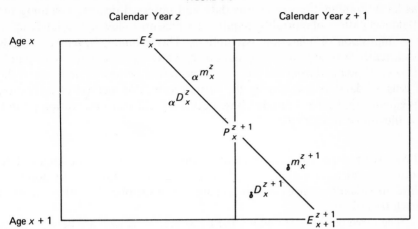

Calendar Year z — Calendar Year $z + 1$

Age x — E_x^z

$_\alpha m_x^z$

$_\alpha D_x^z$

P_x^{z+1}

$_\delta m_x^{z+1}$

$_\delta D_x^{z+1}$

Age $x + 1$ — E_{x+1}^{z+1}

Proceeding directly to the general case, let us assume that α-migration occurs m months $(0 \le m \le 6)$ after the attainment of age x and that δ-migration occurs n months $(0 \le n \le 6)$ prior to the attainment of age $x + 1$. Analysis of potential and cancelled exposure consistent with the Balducci hypothesis produces

$$E_x \Big]_x^{x+1} = E_x^z + \frac{12 - m}{12} \cdot {}_\alpha m_x^z + \frac{n}{12} \cdot {}_\delta m_x^{z+1}. \tag{5-8}$$

Upon elimination of the migration terms as before, we have

$$\cdot E_x \Big]_x^{x+1} = \frac{m}{12} \cdot E_x^z + \frac{12 - m - n}{12} \cdot P_x^{z+1} + \frac{n}{12} \cdot E_{x+1}^{z+1}$$

$$+ \frac{12 - m}{12} \cdot {}_\alpha D_x^z + \frac{n}{12} \cdot {}_\delta D_x^{z+1}. \tag{5-9}$$

When the coefficients of ${}_\alpha D_x^z$ and ${}_\delta D_x^{z+1}$ are equal, the symbol $D_x^{z\backslash z+1}$ is often used to simplify the notation, where $D_x^{z\backslash z+1} = {}_\alpha D_x^z + {}_\delta D_x^{z+1}$. The symbol indicates, through its subscript, that all deaths are by age last birthday, while its superscript indicates that the observation period runs from birthdays in z to birthdays in $z + 1$.

The student should verify that variation from the July 1 birth assumption generates no change in the form of Formula (5-9). Further, it should be verified that the form of Formula (5-9) is consistent with that of Formula (5-6), in that the coefficients of census terms are immediately available from analysis of the migration assumptions. The student should also select a set of five ordered pairs which could be used for a formal derivation of Formula (5-9) by the method of undetermined coefficients.

In summary, all single-diagonal exposure formulas are easily expressed as linear combinations of census data and observed deaths. Assuming the Balducci pattern of mortality, required coefficients follow immediately upon the imposition of migration assumptions. The technique developed here is sufficiently flexible to handle situations in which in-force data are available at several points during the one-year observation period. In addition, if the "census" data are available in the desired form, this method of derivation is equally applicable to studies based upon a fiscal year observation period, as illustrated in Example 5-3.

EXAMPLE 5-3   The fiscal year of a pension fund runs from August 1 to July 31, and a valuation is made each year as of July 31. In addition, interim valuation schedules are prepared as of October 31 and April 30 of each fiscal year.

The three periods into which the fiscal year is divided are designated as follows:

> The a-period, from August 1 to October 31;
> The b-period, from November 1 to April 30; and
> The c-period, from May 1 to July 31.

Let $_k m$ and $_k \theta$ denote net migration and deaths, respectively, during any period k. Tests have indicated that the following may be assumed:

(a) $_a m$ occurs on August 1.
(b) $_b m$ occurs on April 30.
(c) $_c m$ occurs on May 31.

During a particular fiscal year Y, the numbers of active members are known to be as shown in Table 5-1. Derive an expression for the exposure for fiscal year Y in terms of the above T's and the corresponding deaths. Assume that mortality follows the Balducci hypothesis.

TABLE 5-1

Valuation schedule date	Number active
July 31, $Y - 1$	T_1
Oct. 31, $Y - 1$	T_2
April 30, Y	T_3
July 31, Y	T_4

SOLUTION   The in-force values, T_1, T_2, T_3, and T_4, clearly all fall on a single diagonal in a diagram on which the age range is from one un-

FIGURE 5-6

Fiscal Year Y

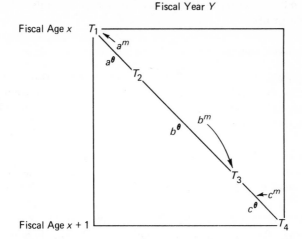

Fiscal Age x

Fiscal Age $x + 1$

determined integral fiscal age, say x, to another. See Figure 5-6. The final exposure formula must be of the form

$$E_x \Big]_x^{x+1} = a_1 \cdot T_1 + a_2 \cdot T_2 + a_3 \cdot T_3 + a_4 \cdot T_4 + a_5 \cdot {}_a\theta + a_6 \cdot {}_b\theta + a_7 \cdot {}_c\theta.$$

The seven ordered pairs in Table 5-2 may be used to effect a unique determination of the seven unknowns. The end result, then, is

$$E_x \Big]_x^{x+1} = \tfrac{3}{4} \cdot T_2 + \tfrac{1}{12} \cdot T_3 + \tfrac{1}{6} \cdot T_4 + {}_a\theta + \tfrac{1}{4} \cdot {}_b\theta + \tfrac{1}{6} \cdot {}_c\theta.$$

Two observations with respect to the preceding example should be helpful. First, the T_1 term is absent, as the a-migration was assumed to occur just after the year-beginning count was made. Second, the coefficients of the in-force terms (including T_1) are seen to be the lengths of time during which each such term represented the number of lives being observed,

TABLE 5-2

Ordered pair	Correct exposure	Conclusion
$(T_1, {}_aw)$	0	$a_1 = 0$
$(T_1, {}_a\theta)$	1	$a_5 = 1$
$({}_an, {}_bw)$	$\tfrac{3}{4}$	$a_2 = \tfrac{3}{4}$
$({}_bn, {}_b\theta)$	$\tfrac{1}{4}$	$a_6 = \tfrac{1}{4}$
$({}_bn, {}_cw)$	$\tfrac{1}{12}$	$a_3 = \tfrac{1}{12}$
$({}_cn, T_4)$	$\tfrac{1}{6}$	$a_4 = \tfrac{1}{6}$
$({}_cn, {}_c\theta)$	$\tfrac{1}{6}$	$a_7 = \tfrac{1}{6}$

specifically 0, 9, 1, and 2 months, respectively. Clearly the sum of these coefficients must be unity, as the ordered pair (T_1, T_4) must be credited a full year of exposure.

Double-Diagonal Formulas

A double-diagonal formula involves lives arising from two adjacent calendar years of birth, or, as the case may be, two adjacent calendar years of issue, fiscal years of birth, or valuation years of birth. Our initial discussion will relate to the simple case of two adjacent calendar years of birth.

The situation most often giving rise to double-diagonal diagrams is that in which deaths are grouped by age last birthday in a calendar year period of observation. Since the unit age interval must then run from integer to integer, the only means of avoiding a double-diagonal situation is to make the absurd assumption that births within any calendar year have January 1 as their average date of occurrence. The typical double-diagonal diagram is shown in Figure 5-7, in which the standard July 1 birth assumption is

FIGURE 5-7

Calendar Year z

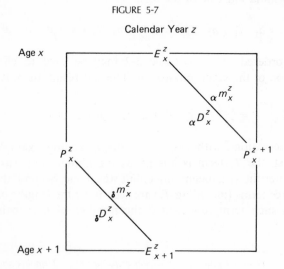

imposed. Other birth assumptions would result in similar diagrams, but the lengths of the two diagonals in such cases would no longer be equal.

Exposure formulas arising from Figure 5-7 vary with mortality and migration assumptions, as was the case with single-diagonal formulas. Still adhering to the Balducci hypothesis, let us impose flexible migration assumptions, leading to the general double-diagonal formula. Assuming that α-migration occurs m months ($0 \le m \le 6$) after age x and that δ-migration occurs n months $(0 \le n \le 6)$ prior to age $x + 1$, the net of potential and cancelled exposure is

$$E_x \Big]_x^{x+1} = E_x^z + \frac{12 - m}{12} \cdot {}_am_x^z - \frac{1}{2} \cdot P_x^{z+1} + \frac{1}{2} \cdot P_x^z + \frac{n}{12} \cdot {}_\delta m_x^z. \qquad (5\text{-}10)$$

In determining such an expression, one must realize that the Balducci hypothesis requires that all terms on the upper diagonal be considered with respect to the *entire* unit age interval even though the diagonal itself seemingly terminates at age $x + \frac{1}{2}$.

Upon substituting the identities

$$_am_x^z = P_x^{z+1} + {}_aD_x^z - E_x^z$$

and

$$_\delta m_x^z = E_{x+1}^z + {}_\delta D_x^z - P_x^z$$

into Formula (5-10), we obtain

$$E_x \Big]_x^{x+1} = \frac{6 - n}{12} \cdot P_x^z + \frac{n}{12} \cdot E_{x+1}^z + \frac{m}{12} \cdot E_x^z + \frac{6 - m}{12} \cdot P_x^{z+1}$$

$$+ \frac{12 - m}{12} \cdot {}_aD_x^z + \frac{n}{12} \cdot {}_\delta D_x^z. \qquad (5\text{-}11)$$

Special cases of Formula (5-11) include

$$E_x \Big]_x^{x+1} = \tfrac{1}{2} \cdot P_x^z + \tfrac{1}{2} \cdot P_x^{z+1} + {}_aD_x^z,$$

$$E_x \Big]_x^{x+1} = \tfrac{1}{2} \cdot E_x^z + \tfrac{1}{2} \cdot E_{x+1}^z + \tfrac{1}{2} \cdot D_x^z,$$

and

$$E_x \Big]_x^{x+1} = \tfrac{1}{4} \cdot P_x^z + \tfrac{1}{4} \cdot E_{x+1}^z + \tfrac{1}{4} \cdot E_x^z + \tfrac{1}{4} \cdot P_x^{z+1} + \tfrac{3}{4} \cdot {}_aD_x^z + \tfrac{1}{4} \cdot {}_\delta D_x^z,$$

when migration is placed on birthdays $(m = n = 0)$, at the end points of the calendar year $(m = n = 6)$, and at the midpoints of the diagonals $(m = n = 3)$, respectively.

It should be clear that the coefficients of the four *corner points* in Formula (5-11) may be easily determined by observing the distances between each such point and the point at which migration occurs. For example, if δ-migration is assumed on February 1 and α-migration on November 1, we immediately obtain

$$E_x \Big]_x^{x+1} = \tfrac{1}{12} \cdot P_x^z + \tfrac{5}{12} \cdot E_{x+1}^z + \tfrac{4}{12} \cdot E_x^z + \tfrac{2}{12} \cdot P_x^{z+1} + a_1 \cdot {}_aD_x^z + a_2 \cdot {}_\delta D_x^z.$$

The ordered pairs $(_an_x^z, \, _aD_x^z)$ and $(_\delta n_x^z, \, _\delta D_x^z)$, which contribute eight and five months of exposure, respectively, may then be used to conclude that $a_1 = \frac{2}{3}$ and $a_2 = \frac{5}{12}$.

The assumption that births occur on a date other than July 1 not only changes the appearance of the diagram but also has an effect upon the double-diagonal formula represented by Formula (5-11). If we assume that births occur k months after the beginning of the typical calendar year, and if we assume that migration is located as before, with the further stipulation that $n \le k$ and $m \le 12 - k$, we obtain the following result:

$$E_x \Big]_x^{x+1} = \frac{m}{12} \cdot E_x^z + \frac{12 - k - m}{12} \cdot P_x^{z+1} + \frac{k - n}{12} \cdot P_x^z$$

$$+ \frac{n}{12} \cdot E_{x+1}^z + \frac{12 - m}{12} \cdot {}_aD_x^z + \frac{n}{12} \cdot {}_\delta D_x^z. \tag{5-12}$$

This derivation is left to the student as an exercise. Although it is desirable to develop the understanding necessary to derive such a formula, it is of at least equal importance that the student recognize that the coefficients of the census terms follow the pattern observed earlier.

EXAMPLE 5-4   Determine the valuation schedule exposure formula which reflects the following assumptions:

(a) Deaths are grouped by age last birthday;
(b) The average birth date is August 1;
(c) δ-Migration occurs on March 1;
(d) α-Migration occurs on December 1;
(e) The observation period is the calendar year 1976;
(f) Mortality follows the Balducci pattern.

SOLUTION   Figure 5-8 is helpful. By comparing the position of the corner points with the points of migration, we have

$$E_x \Big]_x^{x+1} = \frac{1}{3} \cdot E_x^{1976} + \frac{1}{12} \cdot P_x^{1977} + \frac{1}{6} \cdot P_x^{1976}$$

$$+ \frac{5}{12} \cdot E_{x+1}^{1976} + a_1 \cdot {}_aD_x^{1976} + a_2 \cdot {}_\delta D_x^{1976}.$$

The ordered pairs $(_an_x^{1976}, \, _aD_x^{1976})$ and $(_\delta n_x^{1976}, \, _\delta D_x^{1976})$, to which eight and five months' exposure, respectively, is credited, then may be used to determine that $a_1 = \frac{2}{3}$ and $a_2 = \frac{5}{12}$.

Alternatively, the desired formula is available by setting $k = 7$, $m = 4$, and $n = 5$ in Formula (5-12). However, the difficulty inherent in the memorization of Formula (5-12) is evident, and the efficient student will surely prefer the first solution outlined above.

FIGURE 5-8

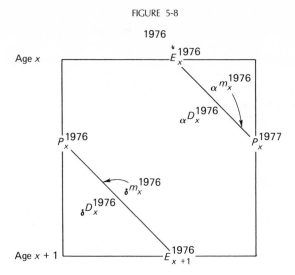

Composite Formulas

The single-diagonal and double-diagonal formulas which have been developed represent the building blocks from which practical valuation schedule exposure formulas are constructed. At this stage we have given consideration only to valuation schedule formulas related to an observation period of a single year, either a calendar year or a 12-month period between two successive birthdays. In reality, however, most mortality studies are performed over an observation period which is several years in length. Fortunately, the student who has grasped the concepts underlying the derivation of the "building block" formulas will find the transition to multiyear, or composite, formulas to be a trivial exercise. Further, it is not at all difficult to construct and apply composite formulas when the data relate to insured lives or to fiscal ages.

Suppose we are dealing with the single-diagonal situation in which deaths are grouped by calendar age, migration occurs on birthdays (July 1), and the period of observation is the three calendar years z through $z + 2$. Since we already know, or can easily determine, that the appropriate formula for the exposure E_x, in calendar year z, is

$$E_x \Big|_{x-(1/2)}^{x+(1/2)} = \tfrac{1}{2} \cdot (P_{x-1}^z + P_x^{z+1} + D_{x\backslash}^z),$$

the desired composite formula is simply

$$E_x \Big|_{x-(1/2)}^{x+(1/2)} = \tfrac{1}{2} \cdot \sum_{k=z}^{k=z+2} (P_{x-1}^k + P_x^{k+1} + D_{x\backslash}^k). \tag{5-13}$$

The diagram illustrating this formula merely consists of three contiguous squares; see Figure 5-9. The most efficient method of applying Formula (5-13) is to add the nine quantities shown in the diagram and then to halve this sum. Finally, we have

$$q_{x-(1/2)} = \frac{\sum\limits_{k=z}^{k=z+2} D_{x\backslash}^k}{\frac{1}{2} \cdot \sum\limits_{k=z}^{k=z+2} (P_{x-1}^k + P_x^{k+1} + D_{x\backslash}^k)}. \tag{5-14}$$

Had we been confronted with a different migration assumption, leading to coefficients of the in-force terms which were other than one-half, no complications would have been encountered. The appropriate single-

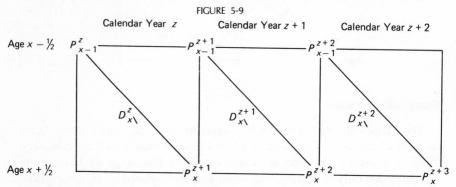

FIGURE 5-9

diagonal formula would have simply been summed over the indicated three-year interval in order to determine the numerical value of the exposure. The numerator of the mortality rate would be identical to that of Formula (5-14).

The examples which follow should clarify the application of composite formulas to various types of mortality data.

EXAMPLE 5-5 The data in Table 5-3 have been obtained from the records maintained by a certain community. Calculate as many mortality rates as possible.

SOLUTION The fact that deaths are grouped by calendar age suggests that we should apply a formula which is a composite of several single-diagonal formulas with calendar year observation periods. Had we been required to determine a single mortality rate for only a year or two of observation, it might have proved efficient to try to identify only the specific input needed. However, since several rates are required over a multiyear period, the effort expended in constructing a diagram such as Figure 5-10 will almost surely·prove to be productive. The census and death terms are clearly indicated.

TABLE 5-3

Number of People Living on January 1 of Each Year

Year of birth	1970	1971	1972	1973	1974
1920	4800	4600	4500	4400	4000
1921	5100	4900	4800	4800	4700
1922	5400	5200	5000	4700	4600
1923	6000	5900	5800	5500	5300
1924	6600	5600	5600	5400	5900
Number of Deaths During Each Calendar Year					
1920	30	32	44	42	—
1921	26	34	36	40	—
1922	36	42	33	40	—
1923	28	44	50	58	—
1924	30	38	48	48	—

The values of the rates of mortality are now easily read from the diagram by using the basic formula

$$E_x \Big|_{x-(1/2)}^{x+(1/2)} = \tfrac{1}{2} \cdot (P_{x-1}^z + P_x^{z+1} + D_{x\backslash}^z)$$

repeatedly. Inherent in this formula are the assumptions of July 1 births and migration on birthdays. Notice that any other migration assumption would require that values of E_x^z be given and that the form of the data thus forced us into a specific migration assumption. Finally, the results are as follows:

$$q_{45\frac{1}{2}} = \frac{30}{\tfrac{1}{2} \cdot (6600 + 5600 + 30)} = \frac{30}{6115};$$

$$q_{46\frac{1}{2}} = \frac{28 + 38}{\tfrac{1}{2} \cdot (6000 + 5900 + 5600 + 5600 + 28 + 38)} = \frac{66}{11,583};$$

$$q_{47\frac{1}{2}} = \frac{36 + 44 + 48}{\tfrac{1}{2} \cdot (5400 + 5200 + 5900 + 5800 + 5600 + 5400 + 36 + 44 + 48)} = \frac{128}{16,714};$$

$$\vdots$$

$$q_{51\frac{1}{2}} = \frac{44 + 40}{\tfrac{1}{2} \cdot (4500 + 4400 + 4800 + 4700) + 44 + 40)} = \frac{84}{9242};$$

$$q_{52\frac{1}{2}} = \frac{42}{\tfrac{1}{2} \cdot (4400 + 4000 + 42)} = \frac{42}{4221}.$$

FIGURE 5-10

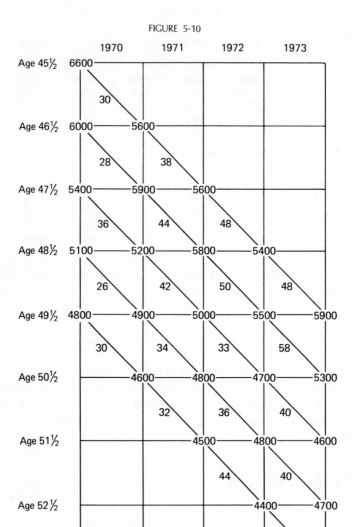

EXAMPLE 5-6   A mortality investigation is to be performed on a group of insured lives observed for the three calendar years 1973–1975. All policies are assumed to have been issued on September 1. It is further assumed that the α- and δ-migration occurred on October 1 and April 1, respectively. If deaths are tabulated by insuring age last anniversary and if the Balducci hypothesis is assumed, determine the value of q_{32} from the following data:

$$E_{32}^{1973} = 1040, \qquad P_{32}^{1973} = 1000,$$

$$E_{32}^{1974} = 1100, \qquad P_{32}^{1974} = 1040,$$

$$E_{32}^{1975} = 1200, \qquad P_{32}^{1975} = 1100,$$

$$E_{33}^{1973} = 1020, \qquad P_{32}^{1976} = 1220,$$

$$E_{33}^{1974} = 1030, \qquad _{\alpha}D_{32}^{z} = 5, \; \Big\}$$

$$E_{33}^{1975} = 1080, \qquad _{\delta}D_{32}^{z} = 15, \Big\} \quad \text{for all } z.$$

SOLUTION   The calendar year observation period with a grouping of deaths by last insuring age suggests that the basic building block for this study is a double-diagonal formula. See Figure 5-11.

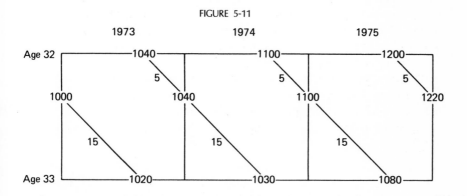

FIGURE 5-11

Based upon the diagram and the migration assumptions, the exposure formula for 1973, for example, is easily shown to be

$$E_{32}\Big]_{32}^{33} = \tfrac{1}{4} \cdot P_{32}^{1973} + \tfrac{5}{12} \cdot E_{33}^{1973} + \tfrac{1}{12} \cdot E_{32}^{1973} + \tfrac{1}{4} \cdot P_{32}^{1974}$$

$$+ \tfrac{11}{12} \cdot {}_{\alpha}D_{32}^{1973} + \tfrac{5}{12} \cdot {}_{\delta}D_{32}^{1973}.$$

It remains simply to compute exposures for the three years separately or to effect a formal summation of the basic double-diagonal formula shown above.

The latter, probably somewhat more efficient, produces

$$E_{32}\Big]_{32}^{33} = \tfrac{1}{4} \cdot 3140 + \tfrac{5}{12} \cdot 3130 + \tfrac{1}{12} \cdot 3340$$

$$+ \tfrac{1}{4} \cdot 3360 + \tfrac{11}{12} \cdot 15 + \tfrac{5}{12} \cdot 45 = 3240.$$

Finally, we have

$$q_{32}^I = \tfrac{60}{3240}.$$

One observation must be made with respect to insured life studies in general. In-force data available from life insurance company records are usually in *year-end* form. Demographic symbols, on the contrary, are based upon the number of persons alive at the *beginning* of calendar years. Let us define the symbol F_x^z to be the number of lives who are insuring age x *last anniversary* as of December 31, z. Thus we see that F_x^z has the same meaning in the context of insured lives as the demographic symbol P_x^{z+1}. Although we shall not rewrite our general formulas to reflect this new symbol, we must be prepared to adapt these formulas to insured life studies when data are given in F_x^z form.

EXAMPLE 5-7   On July 1, 1975 your company adopted stricter under-writing standards with regard to military risks. You are to make a study of the mortality among policies issued since that date. The observation period is to be July 1, 1975 to December 31, 1978, except that, in order to obtain as much experience as possible in the fourth policy year, issues of 1975 are to be followed to June 30, 1979.

The data in Tables 5-4 and 5-5 are available for policies issued after June 30, 1975 to males at age 20. The amount of death claims in the first six months of 1979 among 1975 issues was $20,000.

From the above experience, calculate the mortality rates for the first and fourth years.

SOLUTION   First, let us consider the assumptions which must be imposed. With respect to issue dates, the logical assumptions are that issues of

TABLE 5-4

Amount in force on December 31 of year
(000 omitted)

Year of issue	1975	1976	1977	1978
1975	$14,000	$12,000	$11,000	$10,000
1976		30,000	27,000	25,000
1977			32,000	28,000
1978				34,000

TABLE 5-5

Amount of death claims in year (000 omitted)

Policy year of death	1975 After anniv.	1976 Before anniv.	1976 After anniv.	1977 Before anniv.	1977 After anniv.	1978 Before anniv.	1978 After anniv.
1	$0	$10	$10	$20	$ 0	$10	$10
2			10	20	30	20	20
3					10	20	30
4							10

1976, 1977, and 1978 fell on July 1 and that 1975 issues were dated October 1 due to the fact that only issues during the last six months of 1975 are to be included. Further, since available in-force figures represent year-end data, we have no choice other than to treat withdrawals as having occurred on policy anniversaries. The only additional assumption is that the Balducci hypothesis is applicable.

This example contains features which are slightly different from any which we have previously encountered. Not only can there be no single issue date assumption for the four calendar years of issue, but the nature of the observation period for 1975 issues does not fall neatly into a simple category. These unusual characteristics are obvious from Figure 5-12.

Taking the computation of E_0 first, we may consider the desired value as the sum of three single-diagonal exposures plus that from the *half-diagonal* representing the experience of the 1978 issues. The first three diagonals produce exposures of

$$14{,}000 + 0, \quad 30{,}000 + 10, \quad \text{and} \quad 32{,}000 + 0,$$

respectively, giving a total of 76,010 life-years. These exposures are obtained from the standard single-diagonal formula for an anniversary-to-anniversary observation period with deaths grouped by insuring age last anniversary,

$$E_t \Big]_t^{t+1} = F_t^z + {}_a D_t^z.$$

Although the formula has not specifically been presented, it is merely an adaptation of

$$E_x \Big]_x^{x+1} = P_x^{z+1} + {}_a D_x^z$$

FIGURE 5-12

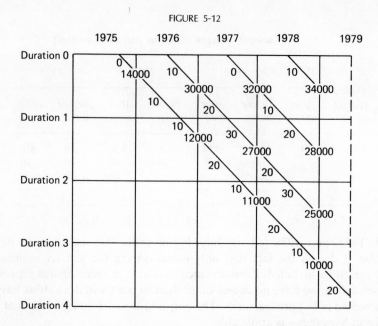

for use with insured life data. Then, considering the final half-diagonal, the F_0^{1978} lives are credited with a half-year of exposure, whereas the $_\alpha D_0^{1978}$ term has a coefficient of unity. A derivation substantiating this intuitive result is simple: For the year 1978,

$$E_0 \Big]_0^{1/2} = n^{1978} - _\alpha w_0^{1978} - \tfrac{1}{2} \cdot F_0^{1978}$$

$$= F_0^{1978} + _\alpha D_0^{1978} - \tfrac{1}{2} \cdot F_0^{1978}$$

$$= \tfrac{1}{2} \cdot F_0^{1978} + _\alpha D_0^{1978}$$

$$= 17{,}000 + 10.$$

Finally, we have

$$E_0 = 76{,}010 + 17{,}010 = 93{,}020$$

and

$$q_0 = \frac{60}{93{,}020}.$$

An alternative, somewhat more tedious, method for calculating E_0 is to consider separately the four calendar years of experience. The formulas for the years 1975 and 1976, easily derived but also intuitively evident, are

$$E_0^{1975} = \tfrac{1}{4} \cdot F_0^{1975} + _\alpha D_0^{1975}$$

and

$$E_0^{1976} = \tfrac{3}{4} \cdot F_0^{1975} + \tfrac{1}{2} \cdot F_0^{1976} + {}_aD_0^{1976}.$$

The formulas for the years 1977 and 1978 are special cases of double-diagonal formulas developed earlier, adapted to select study notation:

$$\left. E_t \right]_t^{t+1} = \tfrac{1}{2} \cdot (F_t^{z+1} + F_t^z) + {}_aD_t^z.$$

Thus we have

$$E_0^{1975} = \tfrac{1}{4} \cdot (14{,}000) + 0 = 3500,$$

$$E_0^{1976} = \tfrac{3}{4} \cdot (14{,}000) + \tfrac{1}{2} \cdot (30{,}000) + 10 = 25{,}510,$$

$$E_0^{1977} = \tfrac{1}{2} \cdot (30{,}000) + \tfrac{1}{2} \cdot (32{,}000) + 0 = 31{,}000,$$

$$E_0^{1978} = \tfrac{1}{2} \cdot (32{,}000) + \tfrac{1}{2} \cdot (34{,}000) + 10 = 33{,}010,$$

producing

$$E_0 = 93{,}020,$$

as before.

Now let us examine the exposure during the fourth policy year, in which only nine months' experience is available. A derivation of the appropriate formula, using undetermined coefficients, is as follows: Let

$$\left. E_3 \right]_3^4 = a_1 \cdot E_3^{1973} + a_2 \cdot F_3^{1978} + a_3 \cdot {}_aD_3^{1978} + a_4 \cdot {}_\delta D_3^{1979}.$$

The ordered pair $(E_3^{1978}, {}_aw_3^{1978})$ may be used to determine that $a_1 = 0$, as the migration assumption results in a zero exposure for this pair. Similarly, $(E_3^{1978}, {}_aD_3^{1978})$ may be used to determine that $a_3 = 1$, a result which follows from the imposition of the Balducci hypothesis. The pair $(E_3^{1978}, {}_\delta w_3^{1979})$ is credited with only nine months' exposure because the unusual observation period necessitates our adjusting the assumption on δ-migration, placing it on June 30, 1979. This pair then leads us to conclude that $a_2 = \tfrac{3}{4}$. Finally, $(E_3^{1978}, {}_\delta D_3^{1979})$ must be credited with a full year's exposure due to the Balducci handling of deaths, producing $a_4 = \tfrac{1}{4}$. Thus,

$$\left. E_3 \right]_3^4 = \tfrac{3}{4} \cdot F_3^{1978} + {}_aD_3^{1978} + \tfrac{1}{4} \cdot {}_\delta D_3^{1979},$$

producing

$$E_3 = 7515$$

and

$$q_3 = \tfrac{30}{7515}.$$

The student should be cognizant that the exhaustive treatment accorded to the solution of Example 5-7 was intended to underline the fact that even unusual problems may be handled with great flexibility without necessitating memorization of formulas. In fact, it is recommended that complex problems, such as this one, be approached with great dependence on basic principles and the method of undetermined coefficients rather than with a collection of memorized formulas which may often be found inapplicable.

FORMULAS BASED UPON UNIFORM DEATHS

Every valuation schedule exposure formula thus far considered has been based upon the Balducci hypothesis. However, a set of quite accurate and useful formulas may also be derived based upon the assumption of a uniform distribution of deaths over the unit age interval under consideration. An analysis of such formulas will uncover a striking similarity between the results arising from the two different mortality assumptions. In fact, perhaps the single most widely used of all exposure formulas is based upon the assumption of uniform deaths. Yet we shall see that it differs in only a minor way from a formula developed earlier in this chapter.

Derivation of these new formulas is achieved through techniques which are quite unlike those used under the Balducci hypothesis. The two methods with which we are most familiar, that is, the netting of potential and cancelled exposure and the method of undetermined coefficients, are technically invalid under the assumption of uniform deaths. Each of these methods relies heavily upon the treatment of deaths dictated by the Balducci hypothesis. But as this is the only factor prohibiting application of our earlier methods for the new derivations, it will not be surprising to find that the old and new sets of formulas vary *only* in the treatment of the death terms.

Due to the fact that formulas based upon a uniform distribution of deaths usually are founded either upon an assumption of no migration or of migration only at year-end or on birthdays, we shall not be concerned here with the general migration assumptions which were treated exhaustively in connection with the formulas based upon the Balducci hypothesis. Further, we shall only consider the single-diagonal and double-diagonal types of "building block" formulas, as composites are easily constructed therefrom, as noted earlier for the Balducci family of formulas.

Double-Diagonal Formulas

Let us consider the standard double-diagonal situation in which the observation period is the calendar year z, deaths are grouped by age last birthday, and births are assumed to fall on July 1. Further, we shall assume

FIGURE 5-13

Calendar Year z

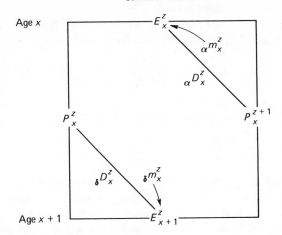

that α-migration occurs just after birthdays and that δ-migration occurs just before birthdays. In other words, all migration is assumed to fall on the birthday nearest the actual date of new entry or withdrawal.

It is obvious from Figure 5-13 that

$$\left(E_x^z + {}_{\alpha}m_x^z\right) \cdot {}_{1/2}q_x + P_x^z \cdot {}_{1/2}q_{x+(1/2)} = D_x^z. \tag{5-15}$$

Multiplying Equation (5-15) by ${}_{1/2}p_x = 1 - {}_{1/2}q_x$, we have

$$\left(E_x^z + {}_{\alpha}m_x^z\right) \cdot {}_{1/2}p_x \cdot {}_{1/2}q_x + P_x^z \cdot {}_{1/2}q_{x+(1/2)} \cdot {}_{1/2}p_x = D_x^z \cdot \left(1 - {}_{1/2}q_x\right). \tag{5-16}$$

Again, from Figure 5-13, we have

$$\left(E_x^z + {}_{\alpha}m_x^z\right) \cdot {}_{1/2}p_x = P_x^{z+1}. \tag{5-17}$$

Substituting Equation (5-17) and

$${}_{1/2}p_x \cdot {}_{1/2}q_{x+(1/2)} = q_x - {}_{1/2}q_x$$

into Equation (5-16), we obtain

$$P_x^{z+1} \cdot {}_{1/2}q_x + P_x^z \cdot \left(q_x - {}_{1/2}q_x\right) = D_x^z \cdot \left(1 - {}_{1/2}q_x\right). \tag{5-18}$$

Finally, imposing the uniform distribution of deaths assumption, specifically that

$${}_{1/2}q_x = \tfrac{1}{2} \cdot q_x,$$

we have

$$q_x = \frac{D_x^z}{\tfrac{1}{2} \cdot \left(P_x^z + P_x^{z+1}\right) + \tfrac{1}{2} \cdot D_x^z}. \tag{5-19}$$

Formula (5-19), the widely utilized formula alluded to earlier, has often been used by demographers in the construction of mortality tables based upon census data and vital statistics records.

It will be recalled that the analogous formula, with the same migration assumptions but based upon the Balducci hypothesis, was

$$q_x = \frac{D_x^z}{\frac{1}{2} \cdot (P_x^z + P_x^{z+1}) + {}_\alpha D_x^z}.$$

Due to the fact that the separation of D_x^z into its α- and δ-components is not practical, generally requiring more effort than would be justified, it is often assumed in demographic calculations that

$$\tfrac{1}{2} \cdot D_x^z = {}_\alpha D_x^z,$$

clearly a reasonable assumption. When such an approximation is valid, as is usually the case for ages other than the extremely young and extremely old, it is evident that exposures calculated under the Balducci hypothesis are equivalent to those calculated under the assumption of a uniform distribution of deaths.

Similar formulas based upon birth dates other than July 1 are likewise easy to derive. For example, let us consider births on October 1 and migration on birthdays in the double-diagonal case considered above. Each step of the following derivation should be justified by the student:

$$(E_x^z + {}_\alpha m_x^z) \cdot {}_{1/4}q_x + P_x^z \cdot {}_{3/4}q_{x+(1/4)} = D_x^z,$$

$$(E_x^z + {}_\alpha m_x^z) \cdot {}_{1/4}p_x \cdot {}_{1/4}q_x + P_x^z \cdot {}_{3/4}q_{x+(1/4)} \cdot {}_{1/4}p_x = D_x^z \cdot (1 - {}_{1/4}q_x),$$

$$P_x^{z+1} \cdot {}_{1/4}q_x + P_x^z \cdot (q_x - {}_{1/4}q_x) = D_x^z \cdot (1 - {}_{1/4}q_x),$$

$$q_x(\tfrac{1}{4} \cdot P_x^{z+1} + \tfrac{3}{4} \cdot P_x^z + \tfrac{1}{4} \cdot D_x^z) = D_x^z.$$

Solving, we have the expression

$$q_x = \frac{D_x^z}{\frac{3}{4} \cdot P_x^z + \frac{1}{4} \cdot P_x^{z+1} + \frac{1}{4} \cdot D_x^z}, \tag{5-20}$$

analogous to the Balducci-based formula

$$q_x = \frac{D_x^z}{\frac{3}{4} \cdot P_x^z + \frac{1}{4} \cdot P_x^{z+1} + {}_\alpha D_x^z}.$$

Again, it is evident that the two differ only in their handling of the death term. Further, since the α-period is, in this special case, only one-fourth of a calendar year, the approximation

$${}_\alpha D_x^z = \tfrac{1}{4} \cdot D_x^z$$

is easily justified. Such an approximation clearly makes the two formulas identical.

Single-Diagonal Formulas

The handling of single-diagonal situations under the uniform death assumption varies little from that of the double-diagonal cases already considered. One point which must not be overlooked is that the unit age interval does not necessarily run from integer to integer as in the double-diagonal formulas. For example, if $[x - \frac{1}{2}, x + \frac{1}{2}]$ is the unit age interval, the assumption of uniform distribution of deaths leads to the identity

$$_{1/2}q_{x-(1/2)} = \tfrac{1}{2} \cdot q_{x-(1/2)},$$

whereas the more familiar

$$_{1/2}q_x = \tfrac{1}{2} \cdot q_x$$

is invalid.

As an illustrative derivation of a single-diagonal formula based upon uniform deaths, let us develop the expression for $q_{x-(1/3)}$ under the assumptions of May 1 births, δ-migration on January 1, and α-migration on

FIGURE 5-14

Calendar Year z

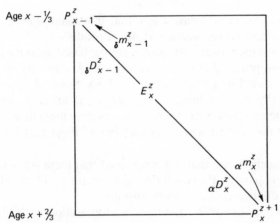

December 31. Using an observation period of the calendar year z and a grouping of deaths by calendar age, we have, from Figure 5-14,

$$(P_{x-1}^z + {}_\delta m_{x-1}^z) \cdot {}_{1/3}q_{x-(1/3)} + E_x^z \cdot {}_{2/3}q_x = D_{x\backslash}^z. \tag{5-21}$$

Multiplying by $_{1/3}p_{x-(1/3)}$ and substituting

$$(P_{x-1}^z + {}_\delta m_{x-1}^z) \cdot {}_{1/3}p_{x-(1/3)} = E_x^z,$$

we have

$$E_x^z \cdot {}_{1/3}q_{x-(1/3)} + E_x^z \cdot {}_{1/3}p_{x-(1/3)} \cdot {}_{2/3}q_x = D_{x\backslash}^z \cdot (1 - {}_{1/3}q_{x-(1/3)}). \tag{5-22}$$

Finally, since

$$_{1/3}q_{x-(1/3)} = \tfrac{1}{3} \cdot q_{x-(1/3)}$$

and

$$_{1/3}p_{x-(1/3)} \cdot {}_{2/3}q_x = q_{x-(1/3)} - {}_{1/3}q_{x-(1/3)},$$

Equation (5-22) leads to

$$q_{x-(1/3)}\left(E_x^z + \tfrac{1}{3} \cdot D_{x\backslash}^z\right) = D_{x\backslash}^z.$$

Solving,

$$q_{x-(1/3)} = \frac{D_{x\backslash}^z}{E_x^z + \tfrac{1}{3} \cdot D_{x\backslash}^z}. \qquad (5\text{-}23)$$

The formula analogous to Formula (5-23) under the Balducci hypothesis was found earlier to be

$$q_{x-(1/3)} = \frac{D_{x\backslash}^z}{E_x^z + {}_\delta D_{x-1}^z}.$$

Clearly, with the birth assumption imposed here, the approximation

$$_\delta D_{x-1}^z = \tfrac{1}{3} \cdot D_{x\backslash}^z$$

is a logical one. Again, it is easily seen that this assumption causes the two mortality assumptions to produce identical results.

The relationships between exposure formulas based upon the two common mortality assumptions should now be evident. A summary of both sets of formulas is depicted in Tables 5-6, 5-7, and 5-8. Some of these results have been specifically derived here, while additional selected derivations are included in the exercises. Several observations from these three tables should be helpful to the student when any member of these families of formulas is needed.

First, it is easily shown that if it is assumed that there is no *net* migration, i.e., $_\alpha n = {}_\alpha w$ and $_\delta n = {}_\delta w$, the two Balducci formulas are identical within each table, as are the two uniform death formulas.

Second, as implied earlier, assumption of migration on birthdays results in formulas in which the E_x^z terms are missing. Similarly, formulas based upon migration at end points of calendar years contain no P_x^z terms.

Third, the death terms in formulas located diagonally opposite each other in Tables 5-6, 5-7, and 5-8 are *complementary*. That is, if one formula has a death term represented either by α-deaths *or* δ-deaths, the diagonally opposite formula has the other. If the death term of a given formula is a numerical coefficient multiplied by *all* the deaths, the diagonally opposite formula contains a death term whose coefficient is the numerical complement of its diagonal partner. Equivalently, addition of the death terms of any two diagonally opposite formulas yields the *total* of the observed deaths.

TABLE 5-6

Double-Diagonal Formulas
Deaths by Age Last Birthday
Calendar Year z
Births m Months After January 1

	Mortality assumption	
Migration assumption	*Balducci*	*Uniform deaths*
Birthdays	$E_x\Big]_x^{x+1} = \dfrac{m}{12} \cdot P_x^z + \dfrac{12-m}{12} \cdot P_x^{z+1} + {}_\alpha D_x^z$	$E_x\Big]_x^{x+1} = \dfrac{m}{12} \cdot P_x^z + \dfrac{12-m}{12}\, P_x^{z+1} + \dfrac{12-m}{12} \cdot D_x^z$
End points of calendar year	$E_x\Big]_x^{x+1} = \dfrac{12-m}{12} \cdot E_x^z + \dfrac{m}{12} \cdot E_{x+1}^z + \dfrac{m}{12} \cdot D_x^z$	$E_x\Big]_x^{x+1} = \dfrac{12-m}{12} \cdot E_x^z + \dfrac{m}{12} \cdot E_{x+1}^z + {}_\delta D_x^z$

TABLE 5-7

Single-Diagonal Formulas
Deaths by Calendar Age
Calendar Year z
Births m Months After January 1

Mortality assumption

Migration assumption	*Balducci*	*Uniform deaths*
Birthdays	$\left. \cdot E_x \right|_{x-m/12}^{x+\frac{12-m}{12}} = \frac{m}{12}\cdot P_{x-1}^z + \frac{12-m}{12}\cdot P_x^{z+1} + \frac{12-m}{12} D_{x|}^z$	$\left. E_x \right|_{x-m/12}^{x+\frac{12-m}{12}} = \frac{m}{12}\cdot P_{x-1}^z + \frac{12-m}{12}\cdot P_x^{z+1} + {}_\alpha D_x^z$
End points of calendar year	$\left. E_x \right|_{x-m/12}^{x+\frac{12-m}{12}} = E_x^z + {}_\delta D_{x-1}^z$	$\left. E_x \right|_{x-m/12}^{x+\frac{12-m}{12}} = E_x^z + \frac{m}{12}\cdot D_{x|}^z$

TABLE 5-8

Single-Diagonal Formulas
Deaths by Age Last Birthday
Birthdays in z to Birthdays in $z+1$
Births m Months After January 1

Mortality assumption

Migration assumption	Balducci	Uniform deaths
Birthdays	$E_x\Big]_x^{x+1} = P_x^{z+1} + {}_\alpha D_x^z$	$E_x\Big]_x^{x+1} = P_x^{z+1} + \dfrac{12-m}{12}D_x^{z|z+1}$
End points of calendar year	$E_x\Big]_x^{x+1} = \dfrac{12-m}{12}\cdot E_x^z + \dfrac{m}{12}\cdot E_{x+1}^{z+1} + \dfrac{m}{12}\cdot D_x^{z|z+1}$	$E_x\Big]_x^{x+1} = \dfrac{12-m}{12}\cdot E_x^z + \dfrac{m}{12}\cdot E_{x+1}^{z+1} + {}_\delta D_x^{z+1}$

Note: $D_x^{z|z+1} = {}_\alpha D_x^z + {}_\delta D_x^{z+1}$.

Fourth, since the exposure formulas under the Balducci hypothesis are readily derived, perhaps the most efficient means of producing any desired formula based upon uniform distribution of deaths is first to determine the Balducci version with the migration assumption opposite that desired. Then, application of the third observation above produces the desired death term, with the coefficients of the census terms easily found by techniques described earlier. It is strongly recommended that the student depend on this or an equivalent technique rather than attempting to memorize by rote any of the formulas we have discussed.

EXAMPLE 5-8   Find the value of $E_{50}]_{50}^{51}$, using an observation period of the calendar year 1976, assuming June 1 births and no net migration. Obtain answers for each of the basic mortality assumptions. You are given the following observed data:

$$P_{50}^{1976} = 1000, \quad E_{51}^{1976} = 970, \quad P_{50}^{1977} = 928, \quad \text{and} \quad E_{50}^{1976} = 950.$$

SOLUTION   As there is known to be no net migration, the number of observed deaths is easily obtained, and, as indicated in Figure 5-15,

$$_aD_{50}^{1976} = 22 \quad \text{and} \quad _\delta D_{50}^{1976} = 30.$$

FIGURE 5-15

1976

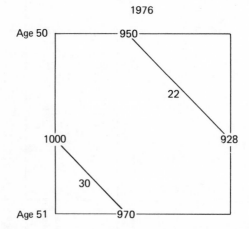

Using the Balducci hypothesis and the values of P_x^z, we have

$$E_{50}\Big]_{50}^{51} = \tfrac{5}{12} \cdot P_{50}^{1976} + \tfrac{7}{12} \cdot P_{50}^{1977} + {_aD_{50}^{1976}}$$

$$= \tfrac{5}{12} \cdot 1000 + \tfrac{7}{12} \cdot 928 + 22$$

$$= 980.$$

Using the Balducci hypothesis and the values of E_x^z, the appropriate formula is

$$E_{50}\Big]_{50}^{51} = \tfrac{7}{12} \cdot E_{50}^{1976} + \tfrac{5}{12} \cdot E_{51}^{1976} + \tfrac{5}{12} \cdot D_{50}^{1976}$$

$$= \tfrac{7}{12} \cdot 950 + \tfrac{5}{12} \cdot 970 + \tfrac{5}{12} \cdot 52$$

$$= 980.$$

As expected, these two results are equal because of the absence of net migration.

The death terms in the two Balducci-based formulas were $_xD$ and $\tfrac{5}{12} \cdot D$, respectively. Thus, in the corresponding formulas based upon uniform deaths, the death terms must be $\tfrac{7}{12} \cdot D$ and $_\delta D$, respectively. Thus, we have

$$E_{50}\Big]_{50}^{51} = \tfrac{5}{12} \cdot P_{50}^{1976} + \tfrac{7}{12} \cdot P_{50}^{1977} + \tfrac{7}{12} \cdot D_{50}^{1976}$$

$$= \tfrac{5}{12} \cdot 1000 + \tfrac{7}{12} \cdot 928 + \tfrac{7}{12} \cdot 52$$

$$= 988\tfrac{1}{3}$$

and

$$E_{50}\Big]_{50}^{51} = \tfrac{7}{12} \cdot E_{50}^{1976} + \tfrac{5}{12} \cdot E_{51}^{1976} + _\delta D_{50}^{1976}$$

$$= \tfrac{7}{12} \cdot 950 + \tfrac{5}{12} \cdot 970 + 30$$

$$= 988\tfrac{1}{3},$$

as expected.

SUMMARY

It is often desirable to conduct a study of mortality on a well-defined group of lives for whom detailed records with respect to entry and withdrawal are not readily available. In such instances, accurate records of the size of the group at periodic intervals, in conjunction with detailed data on deaths, will suffice. Exposure formulas which are based only upon periodic counts of active lives and numbers of deaths are known as valuation schedule formulas, because the primary source of the required input is generally a valuation of various aspects of the status of the group. Such valuations are usually prepared at the close of business at the end of each fiscal year, but often interim valuations are also available.

In view of the useful notation already developed in the field of demography, it has not been necessary to construct a new set of actuarial notation for use in valuation schedule formulas. The basic symbols P_x^z and E_x^z, along with a division of each year into an α-period and a δ-period for each life, represent the only demographic notation and concepts which are needed. Examples have shown that all valuation schedule formulas, though ostensibly developed with large populations and the calendar year-end valuation in mind, are easily adapted to studies more relevant to actuarial work. Insured life studies and fiscal year studies, for example, are easily effected through the use of formulas which employ notation once specifically relegated to the field of demography.

All valuation schedule formulas have been categorized according to whether a single year of observation gives rise to one or two diagonals in a two-dimensional representation of the progression of the lives through the observation period. Formal derivations of both types of formulas have been presented. It has been further observed that most terms of such formulas may be readily determined without formal derivation, merely by a careful analysis of the migration and birth assumptions being imposed. The method of undetermined coefficients was found to be quite helpful, either for complete derivations or for the determination of the coefficients of the death terms once the other coefficients have been obtained. Progress from these building block formulas, based upon single-year observation periods, to the more practical composite formulas was found to be a trivial matter of summation.

The assumption that deaths during any unit age interval are uniformly distributed gives rise to a family of formulas varying only slightly from those based upon the Balducci hypothesis. It will be recalled from Chapter Two that our original selection of the Balducci hypothesis was not based upon the criterion of accuracy but upon other considerations which were largely esthetic in nature. Thus, the uniform death formulas should be accorded the same credibility as their Balducci analogs. In fact, the formula

$$q_x^z = \frac{D_x^z}{\frac{1}{2} \cdot (P_x^z + P_x^{z+1}) + \frac{1}{2} \cdot D_x^z},$$

based upon uniform deaths, is probably the most widely used of all valuation schedule formulas. Its parallel under the Balducci hypothesis,

$$q_x^z = \frac{D_x^z}{\frac{1}{2} \cdot (P_x^z + P_x^{z+1}) + {_\alpha}D_x^z},$$

obviously varies from it only slightly but is somewhat less practical due to the necessity of separating α-deaths from δ-deaths. As shown in Tables 5-6, 5-7, and 5-8, the pairs of formulas arising from the two mortality assumptions differ only in the death terms themselves.

Having now presented valuation schedule formulas and individual record formulas in this and the preceding chapter, it remains for us to consider the intimate relationship between these seemingly dissimilar families. This investigation will be the subject of Chapter Six.

EXERCISES

1. You are conducting a mortality investigation covering experience in calendar year z, with deaths grouped by calendar age. Assume that
   (i) All births occur on July 1;
   (ii) $_\delta n$ and $_\delta w$ occur a few moments before exact age x;
   (iii) $_\alpha n$ and $_\alpha w$ occur a few moments after exact age x;
   (iv) A valuation schedule formula is to be used.
   What is the exposure associated with $q_{x-(1/2)}$?

2. In a mortality study from policy anniversaries in z to policy anniversaries in $z + 1$, deaths have been grouped by lower attained age. Assume that
   (i) Policies are issued on June 1;
   (ii) $_\alpha w$ occurs a few moments before the end of the calendar year;
   (iii) $_\delta w$ occurs a few moments after the start of the calendar year.

   If

   $$E_x = a_1 \cdot E_x^z + a_2 \cdot P_x^{z+1} + a_3 \cdot E_{x+1}^{z+1} + a_4 \cdot {}_\alpha D_x^z + a_5 \cdot {}_\delta D_x^{z+1},$$

   what information about the constants can be obtained by considering a policy included in E_x^z which terminated in $_\delta w_x^{z+1}$?

3. A mortality study, using December 31 valuation in-force schedules, ran from anniversaries in 1974 to anniversaries in 1978. Deaths have been tabulated according to insuring age on the last anniversary preceding death, and the Balducci hypothesis is used. Find an expression for q_x^l.

4. Determine the assumptions as to birth and migration upon which the the following formula is based:

   $$E_x\Big]_x^{x+1} = \tfrac{1}{6} \cdot (E_x^z + P_x^{z+1}) + \tfrac{1}{3} \cdot (P_x^z + E_{x+1}^z) + \tfrac{5}{6} \cdot {}_\alpha D_x^z + \tfrac{1}{3} \cdot {}_\delta D_x^z.$$

5. The formula

   $$E_x\Big]_x^{x+1} = a_1 \cdot P_x^z + a_2 \cdot E_x^z + a_3 \cdot P_x^{z+1} + a_4 \cdot E_{x+1}^z + a_5 \cdot {}_\delta D_x^z + a_6 \cdot {}_\alpha D_x^z$$

   is based upon November 1 births, δ-migration four months before age $x + 1$, and α-migration one month after age x. Find

   $$\sum_{t=1}^{6} a_t.$$

6. Actuaries P, Q, R, and S, upon viewing the accompanying diagram based upon July 1 births, calculated $E_x]_x^{x+1}$ to be 433, 408, 431 and 410, respectively.

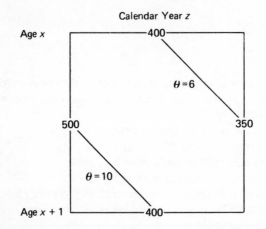

Calendar Year z

Age x ——400——

$\theta = 6$

500   350

$\theta = 10$

Age $x + 1$ ——400——

(a) State the most likely assumptions of each actuary regarding mortality and migration.
(b) What exposure would actuary T compute if he assumed α-migration on October 1, δ-migration on April 1, and the Balducci hypothesis?

7. Find D_x^z, given

$$D_{x\backslash}^z = 8, \qquad D_{x+1}^z = 3,$$

$$D_{x+1\backslash}^z = 9, \qquad {}_\delta D_{x-1}^z = 3,$$

$$D_x^{z\backslash z+1} = 9, \qquad {}_\delta D_x^{z+1} = 2 \cdot {}_\alpha D_{x+1}^z.$$

8. Based upon the following data, calculate: (a) mortality rates at half-ages, using a 1976-1977 calendar year observation period;

(b) mortality rates at integral ages, using an observation period from birthdays in 1976 to birthdays in 1978.

State your assumptions.

	Number living on December 31		
CYB	1975	1976	1977
1950	5200	5200	5000
1951	5300	5100	5100
1952	5600	5600	5400

$_\alpha D_x^z = 20$, $_\delta D_x^z = 16$ for all x, z.

9. The following values are known for a mortality study in which all of the births have been assumed to fall on July 1. The Balducci hypothesis was assumed.

z \ x	P_x^z				E_x^z		
	50	51	52	53	51	52	53
1970	500	480	450	400	510	490	460
1971	550	530	500	480	550	540	510
1972	580	560	550	520	590	560	520
1973	600	585	550	500			

$$\left. \begin{array}{l} _\alpha D_x^z = 2 \\ _\delta D_x^z = 3 \end{array} \right\} \text{ for all } x, z$$

(a) Assuming migration on birthdays, determine q_{52} using an observation period from birthdays in 1970 to birthdays in 1973.

(b) $E_{51}]_{50\frac{1}{4}}^{51\frac{1}{4}}$ was found to be 1680, with a 1970-1972 calendar year observation period. It was assumed that all migration occurred on some fixed date in each calendar year. What was that date?

(c) Using a double-diagonal method, $E_{52}]_{52}^{53}$ was found to be $1551\frac{2}{3}$, with a 1970-1972 calendar year observation period. If the α-migration was placed on October 1, where was the δ-migration placed?

10. Derive a valuation schedule exposure formula for $\mu_{x+(1/3)}$ under the following assumptions:
    (i) Births occurred on July 31;
    (ii) Deaths were tabulated by calendar age;
    (iii) The observation period was 1975, 1976, and 1977;
    (iv) Balducci mortality is assumed;
    (v) α-Migration occurred on October 1;
    (vi) δ-Migration occurred on March 1.

11. You are given values for E_{30}^{1976}, E_{31}^{1977}, P_{30}^{1977}, $_\alpha D_{30}^{1976}$, and $_\delta D_{30}^{1977}$. Assume that birthdays occur on May 15. Stating all of your assumptions, derive a valuation schedule exposure formula which will make fullest use of the given data.

12. (a) Under the assumption of uniform distribution of deaths within the unit age interval under consideration and ignoring migration, derive the single-diagonal formula for $q_{x-(1/2)}$.

    (b) Under the assumptions stated above and using the formula just derived, determine $q_{21\frac{1}{4}}$ from the following data:

    $$P_{21}^{1974} = 500, \quad _\alpha D_{22}^{1974} = 8, \quad _\delta D_{21}^{1974} = 12,$$

    $$P_{22}^{1975} = 480, \quad _\delta D_{22}^{1974} = 12, \quad _\alpha D_{22}^{1973} = 15.$$

13. The following data are available for a select study of mortality. The observation period covers the calendar years 1975–1977. Compute as many mortality rates as possible.

Cal. yr of issue	In force		Withdrawals			Deaths		
	Dec. 31	Number	1975	1976	1977	1975	1976	1977
1973	1974	1320	96	92	66	4	8	4
1972	1975	1360	94	74	72	6	6	8
1971	1977	1000	72	90	90	8	10	10

Which mortality assumption did you use, and why?

14. Determine the valuation schedule formula under the $_t q_x = t \cdot q_x$ assumption in each of the following two cases:
    (a)   (i) Deaths are tabulated by age last birthday;
         (ii) Births occur on September 1;
        (iii) Migration occurs on birthdays;
         (iv) The observation period was from birthdays in 1974 to birthdays in 1975.
    (b)   (i) Deaths are tabulated by age last birthday;
         (ii) Births occur on June 1;
        (iii) α-Migration is placed on the following December 31;
         (iv) δ-Migration is placed on the preceding January 1;
          (v) The observation period was the calendar year 1975.

15. If all births occur on September 1 and there is no net migration, calculate q_x from given data

$$E_x^z = 100, \quad E_{x+1}^z = 93, \quad P_x^z = 100, \quad \text{and} \quad P_x^{z+1} = 98$$

under each of the following assumptions:
    (a) $_{1-t}q_{x+t} = (1 - t)q_x, 0 \le t \le 1.$
    (b) $_t q_x = t \cdot q_x, 0 \le t \le 1.$

16. The accompanying diagram indicates in force and death data from a mortality study. Births are assumed to have occurred on October 1. Calculate the amount of exposure between ages 30 and 31, using double-diagonal formulas, under each of the following sets of migration and mortality assumptions:
    (a) Migration on birthdays, Balducci hypothesis.
    (b) Migration at end points of calendar years, Balducci hypothesis.
    (c) Migration on birthdays, uniform distribution of deaths.
    (d) Migration at end points of calendar years, uniform distribution of deaths.

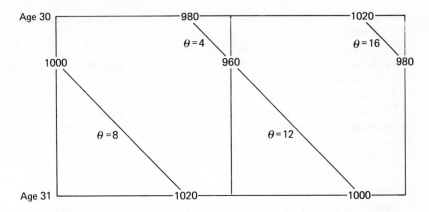

17. Using the diagram given in Exercise 16 and the same four migration-mortality assumptions, recalculate the exposure by treating the problem as three single diagonals rather than two double diagonals. By adding the three exposure amounts in each case, verify that the results found earlier were correct.

18. You are conducting a select mortality investigation covering experience in calendar year z, with deaths grouped by calendar duration. Assume that all policies are issued July 1, z and that withdrawals occur at exact duration $t = \frac{1}{4}$. Determine the correct expression for $_{1/2}q_{[x]}$.

19. Derive Formula (5-12), with the aid of a diagram, by
    (a) Beginning with the traditional "potential minus cancelled" approach and then eliminating the migration terms.
    (b) Using the method of undetermined coefficients.

20. A small life insurance company has just completed an aggregate mortality investigation of its individual policy experience. The investigation covered calendar years 1976 and 1977 and included all issues of 1975 and prior years. A sample of the data gathered for the two years is shown below:

Insuring age (x)	E_x^{1976}	E_x^{1977}	D_x^{1976}	D_x^{1977}
40	16,006	20,394	3	5
41	8,317	14,875	4	3
42	5,800	7,809	4	6

After making certain assumptions as to the distribution of anniversaries and transactions throughout the year, the actuary developed a formula for the mortality rate q_x^I in terms of E_x^z, E_{x+1}^z, and D_x^z. From this formula, q_{40}^I was determined to be .00025.

(a) Using the method of undetermined coefficients, develop the actuary's formula for q_x^l.

(b) Using the formula in (a), calculate q_{41}^l.

(c) Assuming that the insuring age is the age last birthday on the issue date, calculate q_{41}.

21. A certain community took a census of its residents as of July 1, 1975. The census data were tabulated by calendar year of birth. The community also maintains records of total deaths and deaths by cause for each calendar year. Deaths are tabulated by age last birthday on the date of death. Develop a formula for $q_{45}^{(i)}$, the absolute annual rate of mortality from cause (i) at age 45, for calendar year 1975. Define all symbols, and specify all assumptions used.

22. Values of P_x^z, E_x^z, $_aD_x^z$, and $_\delta D_x^z$ pertaining to the population of a community are available for all ages and all calendar years from the community's records. Deaths are grouped by age last birthday, and the observation period is the calendar year z. Using all of the given data, derive a formula for the exposure associated with q_x in terms of these symbols (and variations of them with respect to the superscripts and subscripts). Specify all assumptions used.

23. A pension fund has as its fiscal year the period running from September 1 to August 31. Fiscal year of birth is defined as the calendar year containing the August 31 which precedes the actual date of birth. Valuations are made as of December 31 of each year rather than as of the end of the fiscal year. The following data are available with respect to this fund:

	Fiscal year of birth			
	1944	*1945*	*1946*	*1947*
Number of members on Dec. 31,				
1974	560	600	620	510
1975	570	620	610	500
1976	610	640	660	540
1977	620	620	650	520
Number of deaths in				
Calendar year 1975	4	6	2	4
Calendar year 1976	4	8	4	8
Calendar year 1977	6	8	6	6

Using the observation period which will make maximum use of the available data,

(a) Derive an appropriate exposure formula to be used in determining mortality rates. Define all symbols, and indicate the assumptions upon which the formula is based.

(b) Compute all of the mortality rates which can be obtained from the data, and indicate the actual ages to which they apply.

24. The fiscal year of a large pension plan is divided into four quarters. New entrants and withdrawals are permitted only at the beginning of each quarter. A valuation schedule is prepared as of the beginning of each quarter, after new entrants and withdrawals. Let

$_aI_x^z, _bI_x^z, _cI_x^z, _dI_x^z$ = the number of lives covered at the beginning of each quarter in fiscal year z who were tabulated at x, where $x = z - \text{FYB}$;

$_a\theta_x^z, _b\theta_x^z, _c\theta_x^z, _d\theta_x^z$ = the deaths tabulated at age x during each quarter of fiscal year z.

To study the mortality experience under the plan, using the fiscal year as the observation period, the following exposure formulas have been proposed:

(a) $E_x = _cI_x^z + _a\theta_x^z + _b\theta_x^z$.

(b) $E_x = \frac{1}{2} \cdot \left(_aI_x^z + _aI_{x+1}^{z+1} + _a\theta_x^z + _b\theta_x^z + _c\theta_x^z + _d\theta_x^z\right)$.

(c) $E_x = \frac{1}{2} \cdot \left(_aI_{x+1}^z + _aI_{x+1}^{z+1}\right) + _c\theta_x^z + _d\theta_x^z$.

(d) $E_x = \frac{1}{4} \cdot \left(_aI_x^z + _bI_x^z + _cI_x^z + _dI_x^z\right) + \frac{3}{4} \cdot _a\theta_x^z + \frac{1}{2} \cdot _b\theta_x^z + \frac{1}{4} \cdot _c\theta_x^z$.

(e) $E_x = \frac{1}{8} \cdot \left(_aI_x^z + _aI_{x+1}^{z+1}\right) + \frac{1}{4} \cdot \left(_bI_x^z + _cI_x^z + _dI_x^z\right)$
$\qquad + \frac{7}{8} \cdot _a\theta_x^z + \frac{5}{8} \cdot _b\theta_x^z + \frac{3}{8} \cdot _c\theta_x^z + \frac{1}{8} \cdot _d\theta_x^z$.

Each of these formulas is based upon the assumption that $_{1-t}q_{x+t} = (1 - t)q_x$. Discuss the suitability of each formula for the proposed mortality study, and indicate upon what additional assumptions, if any, it is based. State which formula you would use, and justify your selection.

Counterpart Formulas

INTRODUCTION

In Chapters Four and Five, two separate families of exposure formulas were developed. Through numerous examples, we have seen how each family of formulas may be used to compute rates of mortality, with the selection of the appropriate formula generally dependent on the form of the available data. Where individual records comprise the data, we have chosen to work with individual record formulas based upon selected tabulating rules which categorize the exposed lives. Where in-force data are available, the expeditious choice of formulas has been of the valuation schedule variety for which detailed migration records are unnecessary.

Notwithstanding the visual dissimilarity of the two families of formulas, we shall see that there are no differences whatever in valuation schedule and individual record formulas when the formulas are reduced to their basic components. It is our objective in this chapter to demonstrate the true equivalence of the two families. The development of this basic equivalence will be approached through examples and accompanying diagrams which depict their close interrelationships. No new theory need be presented; it remains only to analyze carefully that which has been developed earlier.

Before proceeding further, it is necessary to state and discuss a definition, the understanding of which is essential to the development of this chapter. Two formulas, one a valuation schedule formula and the other an individual record formula, are said to be *counterparts* if they embody the same set of underlying assumptions. Counterpart formulas always produce the same set of exposures when applied to a given body of data. Although we shall see that this is true with the aid of examples in which the formulas are analyzed verbally and diagrammatically, it should be intuitively evident that two formulas based upon the same assumptions must necessarily produce identical results.

The student should guard against a careless interpretation of the definition of counterpart formulas. It does not logically follow from this definition that two formulas producing identical exposures are necessarily counterparts. For example, if an individual card formula assumes migration on birthdays and a valuation schedule formula assumes migration on August 1, the two are clearly not counterparts, even if they are based upon identical assumptions in all other respects. However, if a given group of exposed lives exhibits no *net* migration, then these two formulas *will* produce identical exposures when applied to that group. It is thus easily seen that the generation of identical exposures is not necessarily indicative that counterpart formulas are at work. If exposures are different, however, the formulas are clearly not counterparts.

Our analysis will first involve consideration of formulas whose observation periods consist of only a single year, either a calendar year or a period between successive birthdays. Subsequent expansion to longer periods of observation will be easily effected and should shed additional light upon the student's understanding of the counterpart concept. Clearly, since we may not even discuss individual record formulas unless we are dealing with the Balducci hypothesis, all ensuing analysis will be based upon the Balducci pattern of mortality; this assumption will not be specifically stated in each case.

SINGLE-DIAGONAL FORMULAS

Considering first the simplest of all possible cases, in which a single diagonal runs from corner to corner in a two-dimensional diagram, let us think of the observation period as being one fiscal year in length. Let us define g, $_am$, and $_bm$ as follows:

g = an in-force count as of a date which is k months after the initial date of the fiscal year;

$_am$ = the net migration occurring between the beginning of the fiscal year and the date at which g is determined;

$_bm$ = the net migration occurring between the date at which g is determined and the terminal date of the fiscal year.

The death terms, $_a\theta$ and $_b\theta$, are defined analogously. To simplify notation, the relationships $_am + _bm = m$ and $_a\theta + _b\theta = \theta$ are often used. It will be noted from Figure 6-1 that the in-force counts at the extremes of the diagram are simply labeled s and e, for starters and enders, respectively, without identifying subscripts. Such subscripts are unnecessary at this point,

FIGURE 6-1

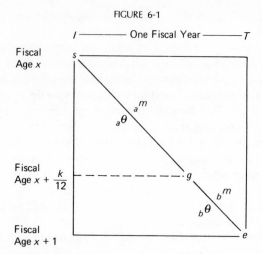

but we shall see later that they must be given careful consideration when we are dealing with more complex problems.

Before proceeding to any type of exposure formula, migration assumptions are necessary. Let us assume that all a-migration occurs m months, $(0 \leq m \leq k)$ after fiscal age x and that all b-migration occurs n months $(0 \leq n \leq 12 - k)$ prior to fiscal age $x + 1$. The individual record and valuation schedule exposure formulas are easily seen to be

$$\left. E_x \right]_x^{x+1} = s + \frac{12 - m}{12} \cdot {}_a m + \frac{n}{12} \cdot {}_b m \tag{6-1}$$

and

$$\left. E_x \right]_x^{x+1} = \frac{m}{12} \cdot s + \frac{12 - m - n}{12} \cdot g + \frac{n}{12} \cdot e + \frac{12 - m}{12} \cdot {}_a \theta + \frac{n}{12} \cdot {}_b \theta. \tag{6-2}$$

The student will recall that valuation schedule formulas in Chapter Five, of the type illustrated by Formula (6-2), were often obtained by substituting identities into individual record formulas such as Formula (6-1) in order to eliminate migration terms.

A thorough, though somewhat tedious, method of verifying that Formulas (6-1) and (6-2) are in fact counterparts is to consider every ordered pair which could possibly be encountered in Figure 6-1. Such an exercise is technically unnecessary because it is clear that either of the formulas may readily be turned into the other without the introduction of any type of approximation. However, the verification of each entry in Table 6-1 should aid the student in his understanding of the means by which the two types of formulas produce identical exposures.

TABLE 6-1

Exposure determined through

Ordered pair	*Analysis of assumptions*	*Formula (6-1)*	*Formula (6-2)*
$(s, {}_aw)$	$\dfrac{m}{12}$	$1 - \dfrac{12-m}{12}$	$\dfrac{m}{12}$
$(s, {}_a\theta)$	1	1	$\dfrac{m}{12} + \dfrac{12-m}{12}$
$(s, {}_bw)$	$1 - \dfrac{n}{12}$	$1 - \dfrac{n}{12}$	$\dfrac{m}{12} + \dfrac{12-m-n}{12}$
$(s, {}_b\theta)$	1	1	$\dfrac{m}{12} + \dfrac{12-m-n}{12} + \dfrac{n}{12}$
(s, e)	1	1	$\dfrac{m}{12} + \dfrac{12-m-n}{12} + \dfrac{n}{12}$
$({}_an, {}_aw)$	0	$\dfrac{12-m}{12} - \dfrac{12-m}{12}$	0
$({}_an, {}_a\theta)$	$1 - \dfrac{m}{12}$	$\dfrac{12-m}{12}$	$\dfrac{12-m}{12}$
$({}_an, {}_bw)$	$1 - \dfrac{m}{12} - \dfrac{n}{12}$	$\dfrac{12-m}{12} - \dfrac{n}{12}$	$\dfrac{12-m-n}{12}$
$({}_an, {}_b\theta)$	$1 - \dfrac{m}{12}$	$\dfrac{12-m}{12}$	$\dfrac{12-m-n}{12} + \dfrac{n}{12}$
$({}_an, e)$	$1 - \dfrac{m}{12}$	$\dfrac{12-m}{12}$	$\dfrac{12-m-n}{12} + \dfrac{n}{12}$
$({}_bn, {}_bw)$	0	$\dfrac{n}{12} - \dfrac{n}{12}$	0
$({}_bn, {}_b\theta)$	$\dfrac{n}{12}$	$\dfrac{n}{12}$	$\dfrac{n}{12}$
$({}_bn, e)$	$\dfrac{n}{12}$	$\dfrac{n}{12}$	$\dfrac{n}{12}$

The following widely applicable special cases of Formulas (6-1) and (6-2) are pairs of counterpart formulas:

$$E_x \Big]_x^{x+1} = s + {}_a m,$$

$$= g + {}_a \theta;$$

$$E_x \Big]_x^{x+1} = s + \tfrac{1}{2} \cdot ({}_a m + {}_b m),$$

$$= \tfrac{1}{2} \cdot s + \tfrac{1}{2} \cdot e + \tfrac{1}{2} \cdot \theta;$$

and

$$E_x \Big]_x^{x+1} = s + \tfrac{3}{4} \cdot {}_a m + \tfrac{1}{4} \cdot {}_b m,$$

$$= \tfrac{1}{4} \cdot s + \tfrac{1}{2} \cdot g + \tfrac{1}{4} \cdot e + \tfrac{3}{4} \cdot {}_a \theta + \tfrac{1}{4} \cdot {}_b \theta.$$

EXAMPLE 6-1 Suppose an organization operates with a fiscal year ending on September 30 and computes in-force data on each January 1 in addition to September 30 of each year. The data in Table 6-2 relate to those members born between April 1, 1926 and March 31, 1927. Compute a fiscal age mortality rate, with fiscal 1978 as an observation period, using two separate but realistic migration assumptions. Undertake the computations utilizing two pairs of counterpart formulas. Translate the answers to a true age basis.

TABLE 6-2

Members as of October 1, 1977	2000
Net migration October 1–December 31, 1977	60
Net migration January 1–September 30, 1978	−30
Deaths October 1–December 31, 1977	12
Deaths January 1–September 30, 1978	18

SOLUTION The fiscal year of birth has clearly been determined as the calendar year containing the September 30 *nearest* the true date of birth. This problem, then, deals with a group of lives whose FYB = 1926, and the resulting mortality rate will be $q_{51}^F \doteq q_{51}$. Figure 6-2 is helpful.

Assuming a-migration on November 15 and b-migration on May 15, the respective midpoints of the a- and b-periods, we have the counterparts

$$E_{51} = \tfrac{1}{8} \cdot s + \tfrac{1}{2} \cdot g + \tfrac{3}{8} \cdot e + \tfrac{7}{8} \cdot {}_a \theta + \tfrac{3}{8} \cdot {}_b \theta$$

$$= \tfrac{1}{8} \cdot 2000 + \tfrac{1}{2} \cdot 2048 + \tfrac{3}{8} \cdot 2000 + \tfrac{7}{8} \cdot 12 + \tfrac{3}{8} \cdot 18$$

$$= 2041 \tfrac{1}{4}$$

FIGURE 6-2

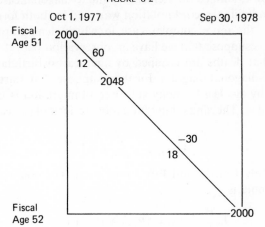

and

$$E_{51} = s + \tfrac{7}{8} \cdot {}_a m + \tfrac{3}{8} \cdot {}_b m$$

$$= 2000 + \tfrac{7}{8} \cdot 60 + \tfrac{3}{8} \cdot (-30)$$

$$= 2041\tfrac{1}{4}.$$

Assuming that all migration occurs on the *fiscal birthday* (September 30) in the calendar year of migration, we have

$$E_{51} = g + {}_a \theta$$

$$= 2048 + 12 = 2060$$

and

$$E_{51} = s + {}_a m$$

$$= 2000 + 60 = 2060.$$

The first migration assumption thus produces

$$q_{51}^F = \frac{30}{2041\tfrac{1}{4}} \doteq q_{51},$$

while the second gives

$$q_{51}^F = \frac{30}{2060} \doteq q_{51}.$$

Significantly, but not surprisingly, different migration assumptions led to different exposure values.

Having now examined the elementary single-diagonal case in which non-subscripted individual record notation was used for both formulas, we must now consider the more complex case in which demographic notation is utilized. Let us suppose that we have an observation period of the calendar year z and that deaths are grouped by age nearest birthday, producing a typical single-diagonal diagram. Further, suppose that starters and enders are grouped by age last birthday and that all migration is grouped by age nearest birthday. The single interval exposure formula is easily seen to be

$$E_x \Big]_{x-(1/2)}^{x+(1/2)} = \sum_{y=a}^{x-1} j_y + \tfrac{1}{2} \cdot m_x, \tag{6-3}$$

based upon July 1 births and July 1 migration. The counterpart valuation schedule formula is

$$E_x \Big]_{x-(1/2)}^{x+(1/2)} = \tfrac{1}{2} \cdot (P_{x-1}^z + P_x^{z+1}) + \tfrac{1}{2} \cdot D_{x\backslash}^z. \tag{6-4}$$

FIGURE 6-3

Calendar Year z

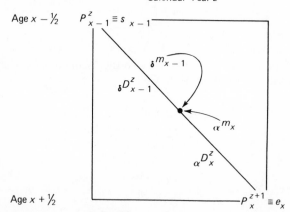

Figure 6-3 reflects the birth and migration assumptions. Note that, in Figure 6-3, the death and migration terms are subscripted in a manner consistent with the demographic requirement that all subscripts refer to age last birthday.

It now remains to demonstrate that Formulas (6-3) and (6-4), purported to be counterparts, are indeed equivalent. To facilitate this demonstration, it has been indicated in Figure 6-3 that the symbols P_{x-1}^z and P_x^{z+1} represent starters and enders and, because starters and enders are grouped by age last birthday, are equivalent to s_{x-1} and e_x, respectively. Likewise, the quantities $_\delta m_{x-1} + _\alpha m_x$ and $_\delta D_{x-1}^z + _\alpha D_x^z$ are seen to be equivalent to m_x and θ_x in individual record notation, as migration and deaths are grouped by age nearest birthday. Figure 6-4, merely a vertical extension of

FIGURE 6-4

Calendar Year z

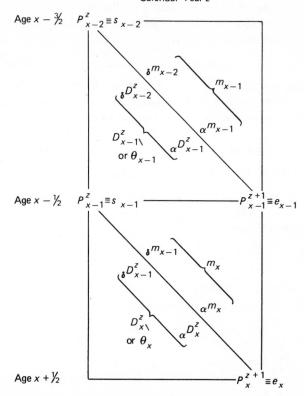

Figure 6-3, indicates this combination of two demographically subscripted terms into single terms subscripted consistently with the individual record tabulating rules.

Now, examining Formula (6-3) and considering the starter decks first, we see from the term $\sum_{y=a}^{x-1} j_y$ that all starter decks subscripted $x - 1$ or less appear with a unit coefficient. The fact that we may safely ignore all but the s_{x-1} term is most easily seen from Figure 6-4. The P_{x-2}^z group, equivalent to s_{x-2}, appears in the individual record formula and is correctly credited with a full unit of potential exposure for the unit interval defined by θ_x. However, the ultimate disposition of this deck is depicted in Figure 6-4. Before any such starter reaches the unit age interval $[x - \frac{1}{2}, x + \frac{1}{2}]$, several possibilities exist. He may withdraw, by virtue of being a member of m_{x-1}, or he may die, as represented by θ_{x-1}. Should neither of these eventualities occur, he must become a member of the P_{x-1}^{z+1} group or, equivalently, become a member of the e_{x-1} deck. The key to this analysis is the realization that a starter tabulated at age $x - 2$ *must* leave the mortality study at tabulated age $x - 1$. Thus, $\sum\limits_{y=a}^{x-1} j_y$ includes such a starter *twice*, once when he enters, with a coefficient of $+1$, and once when he exits, with a coefficient of -1. The same conclusion holds for every starter whose tabulated subscript is $x - 2$ or less.

The other decks included in $\sum\limits_{y=a}^{x-1} j_y$ lend themselves to similar analysis. The new entrants subscripted $x - 1$ or less are likewise seen to leave the observed group in another deck subscripted $x - 1$ or less, and, if not, must be enders subscripted $x - 1$ or less. In summary, it might be stated that the e_{x-1}, e_{x-2}, ... decks act to "dispose of" any lives remaining on their respective diagonals prior to their entry into the unit age interval $[x - \frac{1}{2}, x + \frac{1}{2}]$. Thus, the only remaining deck in $\sum\limits_{y=a}^{x-1} j_y$ is s_{x-1}, as it is the only deck subscripted $x - 1$ or less which appears on a diagonal running through the unit age interval $[x - \frac{1}{2}, x + \frac{1}{2}]$ in the year of observation. Thus, Formula (6-3) has become

$$E_x \Big]_{x-(1/2)}^{x+(1/2)} = s_{x-1} + \tfrac{1}{2} \cdot (n - w)_x .$$

But $(n - w)_x$ is clearly equivalent to $P_x^{z+1} + D_{x\backslash}^z - P_{x-1}^z$, and since it has been established that $s_{x-1} \equiv P_{x-1}^z$, we have

$$E_x \Big]_{x-(1/2)}^{x+(1/2)} = \tfrac{1}{2} \cdot (P_{x-1}^z + P_x^{z+1}) + \tfrac{1}{2} \cdot D_{x\backslash}^z ,$$

or Formula (6-4). Several summarizing observations must be emphasized in connection with the transformation of Formula (6-3) into Formula (6-4).

First, the only deck(s) in the $\sum\limits_{y=a}^{x-1} j_y$ term which must be retained are those which are on a diagonal which contains lives exposed during the period of observation and within the unit age interval in question. All decks falling on "higher" diagonals algebraically net out to zero.

Second, a potential notational inconsistency has already surfaced in the process of the transformation. Consider the $_\delta m_{x-1}$ term in Figures 6-3 and 6-4. When dealing with demographic notation, we have considered the $x - 1$ subscript to represent age *last* birthday, as defined in Chapter Five. Yet in the individual record formula, we have included this migration in the m_x deck, where x refers to age *nearest* birthday. Obviously, the same general comments may be made with respect to the $_\delta D_{x-1}^z$ term. Rather than violate the well-defined notation associated with two different families of formulas, let us agree that, within the context of individual record formulas, categories will be subscripted in a manner consistent with the appropriate tabulating rules. For this reason, in the analysis of the $\sum\limits_{y=a}^{x-1} j_y$ term of Formula (6-3), an individual record formula, the migration which would be represented by $_\delta m_{x-1}$ in demographic notation was treated as part of m_x, as the individual record formula was based upon tabulation of migration by age nearest birthday. Similarly, where valuation schedule formulas are used, we shall adopt the "age last birthday" interpretation of the subscript.

As a result of this notational problem, the student must always proceed with caution when categories in individual record formulas are not tabulated by age last birthday, insuring age last anniversary, last fiscal age, or curtate duration. For example, if we were told that $n_{25} = 100$, we would need additional clarifying information for this fact to be meaningful. If the demographic convention has been followed, the 100 new entrants would be assumed to have come under observation between ages 25 and 26. However, if migration is tabulated by age nearest birthday as in the previous example and the subscripts determined in a manner consistent with this rule, the 100 lives fall on the single diagonal running between ages $24\frac{1}{2}$ and $25\frac{1}{2}$. Thus the 25 subscript is not truly meaningful if there is any uncertainty as to the notation being utilized.

Third, in the process of the transformation, it was noted that $s_{x-1} \equiv P_{x-1}^z$ and $e_x \equiv P_x^{z+1}$, among other similar relationships. The student must guard against the assumption that such equivalences hold in every instance. For example, if starters had been tabulated by age *next* birthday, the P_{x-1}^z lives would have been represented by s_x in individual record notation.

If, in the preceding demonstration, starters and enders had been tabulated by age *next* birthday, the valuation schedule formula would have remained unchanged, but the individual record formula would have been

$$E_x \Big]_{x-(1/2)}^{x+(1/2)} = \sum_{y=a}^{x-1} j_y + (s - e)_x + \tfrac{1}{2} \cdot (n - w)_x, \qquad (6\text{-}5)$$

ultimately reducing to

$$E_x \Big]_{x-(1/2)}^{x+(1/2)} = s_x + \tfrac{1}{2} \cdot (n - w)_x. \qquad (6\text{-}6)$$

The quantity $\sum_{y=a}^{x-1} j_y - e_x$ from Formula (6-5) would then be equal to zero, as it represents the lives which entered and left the observed group before reaching age $x - \frac{1}{2}$. It is thus clear that the mere existence of a category subscripted x does not guarantee its appearance in the simplified version of the individual record formula. In this case, the e_x deck falls on the diagonal above that which actually is the "single diagonal" of the problem, and it therefore does not appear in Formula (6-6).

A final single-diagonal application, illustrated in Example 6-2, indicates that anniversary-to-anniversary select studies may be handled with the theory already developed with no additional complications. Of primary importance in Example 6-2 is the extreme caution required with respect to notational considerations which result from the demographic mandate that all subscripts refer to age last birthday (or duration last anniversary) regardless of the individual record tabulating rules.

EXAMPLE 6-2   A select mortality study of policies with issue age 40, measuring experience from policy anniversaries in 1976 to policy anniversaries in 1977, is based upon the following tabulating rules:

$$\theta_t : t = \text{Policy year of death},$$

$$s_t : t = 1976 - \text{CYI},$$

$$w_t : t = \text{CYW} - \text{CYI},$$

$$e_t : t = 1977 - \text{CYI}.$$

Develop the counterpart individual record and valuation schedule exposure formulas under a reasonable withdrawal assumption, and show that they are equivalent.

SOLUTION   This problem is best visualized through the use of two closely related diagrams, one reflecting proper demographic notation and the other incorporating notation consistent with the given individual record tabulating rules. In both diagrams, the components of the subscripts which indicate the issue age have been ignored for the sake of simplicity, as all lives in both diagrams were issued insurance protection at age 40. For example, the symbols E_{t-1} and $_\alpha D_{t-1}$ might be more precisely written as $E_{[40]+t-1}$ and $_\alpha D_{[40]+t-1}$. Differences in the subscripts of the death and withdrawal terms in Figures 6-5 and 6-6 arise from the adherence to demographic and individual record notation, respectively. Further, each diagram is based upon an assumption of July 1 issues.

FIGURE 6-5

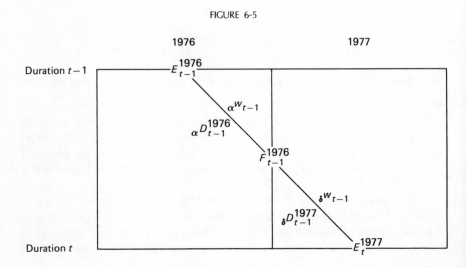

FIGURE 6-6

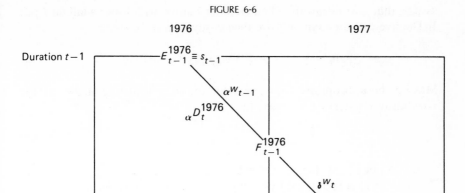

The differences in the subscripts on the deaths in the two diagrams are easily explained. Figure 6-5, based upon demographic notation which insists upon "last anniversary" subscripts for all categories, properly affixes subscripts of $t - 1$ to all deaths. In Figure 6-6, since deaths are tabulated by policy year of death, or next duration, they are properly subscripted t.

The withdrawal subscripts require a bit more analysis. In Figure 6-5, no notational problem exists, as again the "last anniversary" subscripts prevail. However, the calendar duration tabulating rule for withdrawals necessitates the subdivision of the individual record withdrawal category into two components, as follows:

$$_\alpha w_t : t = \text{CYW} - \text{CYI},$$

$$_\delta w_t : t = \text{CYW} - \text{CYI}.$$

The subscripts assigned to the two types of withdrawals in Figure 6-6 must necessarily be different, as all withdrawals arise from policies with the same calendar year of issue $(1977 - t)$, while the two types of withdrawals actually occur in adjacent calendar years. The fact that the labeling of withdrawal terms in Figure 6-6 has been done properly may now be seen by noting that the quantity $\text{CYW} - \text{CYI}$ is

$$1976 - (1977 - t) = t - 1$$

and

$$1977 - (1977 - t) = t$$

for the withdrawals on the upper and lower halves of the diagonal, respectively.

Derivation of the individual record exposure formula now awaits only the selection of an assumption as to the occurrence of withdrawals. Let us assume that α-withdrawals fall on October 1 and δ-withdrawals fall on April 1. The five category symbols are then easily seen to be

$$\theta_t \Big]_{t-1}^{t}, \quad s_t^t, \quad _{\alpha}w_t^{t+(1/4)}, \quad _{\delta}w_t^{t-(1/4)}, \quad \text{and} \quad e_t^t.$$

Making the appropriate adjustment for the inconvenient f-factor for the α-withdrawal category, we have, for $t \geq 1$,

$$E_t \Big]_{t-1}^{t} = n + \sum_{y=0}^{t-1} j_y - \tfrac{1}{4} \cdot {_{\delta}w_t} + \tfrac{1}{4} \cdot {_{\alpha}w_{t-1}}. \tag{6-7}$$

Development of the counterpart valuation schedule formula from Formula (6-7) is facilitated by noting the following equivalences:

$$E_{t-1}^{1976} \equiv s_{t-1}$$

and

$$E_t^{1977} \equiv e_t.$$

Further, we conclude from Figure 6-6 that, for $t > 1$,

$$\sum_{y=0}^{t-1} j_y = s_{t-1} - {_{\alpha}w_{t-1}},$$

as all of the other terms in the summation fall on diagonals above that under consideration. The n term of Formula (6-7), placed by definition at exact duration zero, falls on the diagonal which runs through the unit age interval during the observation period only if $t = 1$; in this case, n and s_0 are essentially interchangeable. We have earlier indicated a preference for the use of n where a choice exists, as starters at exact duration zero are properly denoted as new entrants.

Formula (6-7) thus becomes

$$E_t \Big]_{t-1}^{t} = s_{t-1} - \tfrac{1}{4} \cdot {_{\delta}w_t} - \tfrac{3}{4} \cdot {_{\alpha}w_{t-1}} \qquad (t > 1)$$

$$= n - \tfrac{1}{4} \cdot {_{\delta}w_1} - \tfrac{3}{4} \cdot {_{\alpha}w_0} \qquad (t = 1). \tag{6-8}$$

Substituting

$$_{\alpha}w_{t-1} = E_{t-1}^{1976} - {_{\alpha}D_t^{1976}} - F_{t-1}^{1976}$$

and

$$_{\delta}w_t = F_{t-1}^{1976} - {_{\delta}D_t^{1977}} - E_t^{1977},$$

we have

$$E_t \Big]_{t-1}^{t} = \tfrac{1}{4} \cdot E_{t-1}^{1976} + \tfrac{1}{2} \cdot F_{t-1}^{1976} + \tfrac{1}{4} \cdot E_t^{1977}$$

$$+ \tfrac{1}{4} \cdot {_{\delta}D_t^{1977}} + \tfrac{3}{4} \cdot {_{\alpha}D_t^{1976}} \qquad (t > 1), \tag{6-9}$$

in which deaths are still subscripted as in Figure 6-6. In dealing with the special case in which $t = 1$, the only adjustment to Formula (6-9) would be the substitution of n for E_0^{1976}. Finally, rewriting Formula (6-9) in demographically correct notation, we have

$$E_t \Big]_{t-1}^{t} = \tfrac{1}{4} \cdot E_{t-1}^{1976} + \tfrac{1}{2} \cdot F_{t-1}^{1976} + \tfrac{1}{4} \cdot E_t^{1977}$$

$$+ \tfrac{1}{4} \cdot {}_{\delta}D_{t-1}^{1977} + \tfrac{3}{4} \cdot {}_{\alpha}D_{t-1}^{1976},$$

a valuation schedule formula which is clearly correct, as it could have been written directly from Figure 6-5 once withdrawal assumptions had been imposed.

DOUBLE-DIAGONAL FORMULAS

In our consideration of single-diagonal counterpart formulas, it was possible to illustrate, as in Figure 6-1, pairs of formulas based solely upon the individual record symbols, s, n, w, e, and θ, because the lives represented by the extremes of each single diagonal were clearly the starters and enders for the period of observation. With a double-diagonal diagram, complications arise. The number of lives at the center of the top and bottom of the typical unit square are neither starters nor enders and, in fact, cannot be generally represented by a single individual record symbol. For this reason, we shall begin our analysis of counterpart formulas for double-diagonal diagrams by considering a simple case, necessarily using demographic notation for the valuation schedule formula.

Let us suppose that deaths are tabulated by age last birthday in a mortality study whose observation period is the calendar year z. Migration is also grouped by age last birthday, while starters and enders are tabulated by the following rules:

$$s_x : x = z - 1 - \text{CYB}$$

and

$$e_x : x = z - \text{CYB}.$$

It is required to develop counterpart formulas based upon the assumptions of July 1 births, α-migration on October 1, and δ-migration on April 1.

The entire problem may be illustrated with a single diagram, as notational inconsistencies do not develop due to the tabulation of both migration and deaths by age last birthday. Referring to Figure 6-7 and recalling the migration assumptions imposed, the valuation schedule formula is easily seen to be

$$\left. E_x \right]_x^{x+1} = \tfrac{1}{4} \cdot (P_x^z + E_{x+1}^z + E_x^z + P_x^{z+1})$$

$$+ \tfrac{1}{4} \cdot {}_\delta D_x^z + \tfrac{3}{4} \cdot {}_\alpha D_x^z. \tag{6-10}$$

In obtaining the individual record counterpart, we must first write the category symbols and superscripts

$$\left. \theta_x \right]_x^{x+1}, \quad s_x^{x+(1/2)}, \quad {}_\alpha m_x^{x+(1/4)}, \quad {}_\delta m_x^{x+(3/4)}, \quad \text{and} \quad e_x^{x+(1/2)},$$

with the migration superscripts easily seen by observing the placement of migration in Figure 6-7. The individual record formula thus becomes

$$\left. E_x \right]_x^{x+1} = \sum_{y=a}^{x-1} j_y + \tfrac{1}{2} \cdot s_x + \tfrac{3}{4} \cdot {}_\alpha m_x + \tfrac{1}{4} \cdot {}_\delta m_x - \tfrac{1}{2} \cdot e_x. \tag{6-11}$$

It now remains to demonstrate that Equations (6-10) and (6-11) are counterparts.

Beginning with Formula (6-11), we must first examine the term $\sum_{y=a}^{x-1} j_y$ in order to retain only those terms which actually produce exposure within the unit square represented by Figure 6-7. This task will be simplified by the construction of Figure 6-8, merely a vertical extension of Figure 6-7, which includes the unit interval from $x - 1$ to x and which indicates the individual record equivalents of the P symbols. Based upon earlier discussions, it should be clear that the ender terms tabulated at ages $x - 1$ and

FIGURE 6-7

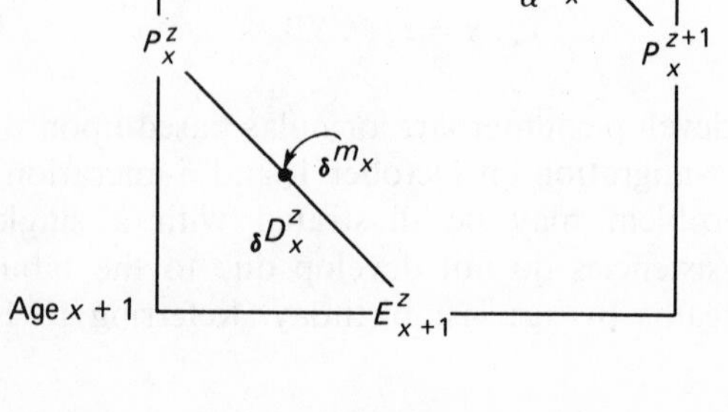

Calendar Year z

FIGURE 6-8

Calendar Year z

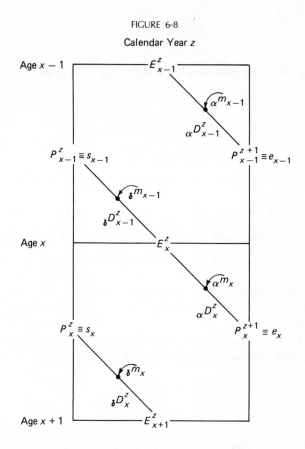

less serve to remove from observation all lives which fall on the top diagonal shown in Figure 6-8 or on any higher diagonal not pictured. Thus the $\sum_{y=a}^{x-1} j_y$ term becomes

$$s_{x-1} + {}_\delta m_{x-1} - {}_\delta D^z_{x-1}.$$

Formula (6-11) is now seen to be

$$E_x\Big]_x^{x+1} = s_{x-1} + {}_\delta m_{x-1} - {}_\delta D^z_{x-1} + \tfrac{1}{2} \cdot s_x + \tfrac{3}{4} \cdot {}_\alpha m_x$$

$$+ \tfrac{1}{4} \cdot {}_\delta m_x - \tfrac{1}{2} \cdot e_x.$$

It is evident from Figure 6-8 that

$$s_{x-1} + {}_\delta m_{x-1} - {}_\delta D^z_{x-1} = E^z_x,$$

$$E^z_x + {}_\alpha m_x - {}_\alpha D^z_x = P^{z+1}_x,$$

and

$$P_x^z + {}_\delta m_x - {}_\delta D_x^z = E_{x+1}^z.$$

By making these substitutions and replacing individual record symbols with their respective equivalents, we finally have

$$\left. E_x \right]_x^{x+1} = E_x^z + \tfrac{1}{2} \cdot P_x^z + \tfrac{3}{4} \cdot (P_x^{z+1} + {}_aD_x^z - E_x^z)$$

$$+ \tfrac{1}{4} \cdot (E_{x+1}^z + {}_\delta D_x^z - P_x^z) - \tfrac{1}{2} \cdot P_x^{z+1}$$

$$= \tfrac{1}{4} \cdot (P_x^z + E_{x+1}^z + E_x^z + P_x^{z+1}) + \tfrac{3}{4} \cdot {}_aD_x^z + \tfrac{1}{4} \cdot {}_\delta D_x^z,$$

the valuation schedule counterpart represented by Equation (6-10). Note that in this particular case the $\sum_{y=a}^{x-1} j_y$ term proved to be identical to E_x^z. This will not always occur in double-diagonal situations, as will be seen shortly.

Let us now reconsider the preceding problem with only the minor change that migration is assumed to occur on birthdays *nearest* the actual date of migration. Since the tabulating rule for migration remains unchanged, Figure 6-8 may be used with the single adjustment in mind. The individual record category symbols are now

$$\left. \theta_x \right]_x^{x+1}, \quad s_x^{x+(1/2)}, \quad {}_am_x^x, \quad {}_\delta m_x^{x+1}, \quad \text{and} \quad e_x^{x+(1/2)},$$

producing

$$\left. E_x \right]_x^{x+1} = \sum_{y=a}^{x-1} j_y + \tfrac{1}{2} \cdot s_x + {}_am_x - \tfrac{1}{2} \cdot e_x.$$

Upon performing the same substitutions used earlier, we have

$$\left. E_x \right]_x^{x+1} = s_{x-1} + {}_\delta m_{x-1} - {}_\delta D_{x-1}^z + \tfrac{1}{2} \cdot s_x + {}_am_x - \tfrac{1}{2} \cdot e_x$$

$$= E_x^z + \tfrac{1}{2} \cdot P_x^z + {}_aD_x^z - E_x^z + P_x^{z+1} - \tfrac{1}{2} \cdot P_x^{z+1}$$

$$= \tfrac{1}{2} \cdot (P_x^z + P_x^{z+1}) + {}_aD_x^z,$$

the familiar double-diagonal formula.

The student should verify that a third migration assumption, placing migration at the nearest end point of the calendar year, produces the following counterparts:

$$\left. E_x \right]_x^{x+1} = \sum_{y=a}^{x-1} j_y + \tfrac{1}{2} \cdot s_x + \tfrac{1}{2} \cdot {}_am_x + \tfrac{1}{2} \cdot {}_\delta m_x - \tfrac{1}{2} \cdot e_x$$

and

$$E_x \Big]_x^{x+1} = \tfrac{1}{2} \cdot E_x^z + \tfrac{1}{2} \cdot E_{x+1}^z + \tfrac{1}{2} \cdot D_x^z.$$

Extra care must be accorded the analysis of counterpart formulas in a double-diagonal setting when migration is tabulated other than by age last birthday. Example 6-3 illustrates a much more general situation than those previously considered.

EXAMPLE 6-3   It is required to compute exposure values for a mortality study in which deaths are tabulated by age last birthday and in which the observation period is the calendar year 1976. Births are assumed to occur on September 1, α-migration on November 1, and δ-migration on May 1.

Derive counterpart formulas for E_x. Test the accuracy of both formulas with the following data:

$$P_x^{1976} = 100, \quad P_x^{1977} = 110, \quad E_x^{1976} = 120, \quad E_{x+1}^{1976} = 98,$$
$$_\alpha D_x^{1976} = 2, \quad \text{and} \quad _\delta D_x^{1976} = 4.$$

SOLUTION   To derive the individual record formula, tabulating rules must be determined. Let us use the following:

$$\theta_x : x = \text{Age last birthday at death},$$
$$s_x : x = 1975 - \text{CYB},$$
$$_\alpha m_x : x = \text{CYM} - \text{CYB},$$
$$_\delta m_x : x = \text{CYM} - \text{CYB},$$
$$e_x : x = 1976 - \text{CYB}.$$

It should be noted that, while notational difficulties would be minimized by choosing to tabulate migration by age last birthday, the calendar age rule has been chosen in order to illustrate further the differences between individual record and demographic subscripts. The chosen tabulating rules, in conjunction with the September 1 birth assumption, produce the following symbols:

$$\theta_x \Big]_x^{x+1}, \quad s_x^{x+(1/3)}, \quad _\alpha m_x^{x+(1/6)}, \quad _\delta m_x^{x-(1/3)}, \quad \text{and} \quad e_x^{x+(1/3)}.$$

The individual record exposure formula is thus

$$E_x \Big]_x^{x+1} = \sum_{y=a}^{x-1} j_y + \tfrac{2}{3} \cdot s_x + \tfrac{5}{6} \cdot {}_\alpha m_x + {}_\delta m_x$$
$$+ \tfrac{1}{3} \cdot {}_\delta m_{x+1} - \tfrac{2}{3} \cdot e_x.$$

FIGURE 6-9

1976

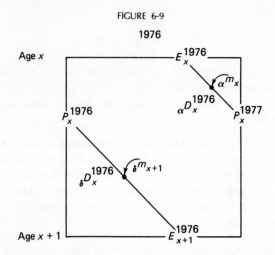

The desired valuation schedule formula is easily determined from Figure 6-9 in which migration is subscripted in a manner consistent with the individual record tabulating rules. Coefficients in the following formula should be verified by the student:

$$E_x \Big]_x^{x+1} = \tfrac{1}{3} \cdot (P_x^{1976} + E_{x+1}^{1976}) + \tfrac{1}{6} \cdot (E_x^{1976} + P_x^{1977})$$

$$+ \tfrac{5}{6} \cdot {}_\alpha D_x^{1976} + \tfrac{1}{3} \cdot {}_\delta D_x^{1976}.$$

The latter formula, the easier of the two from which to calculate the exposure, gives

$$E_x \Big]_x^{x+1} = \tfrac{1}{3} \cdot (100 + 98) + \tfrac{1}{6} \cdot (120 + 110)$$

$$+ \tfrac{5}{6} \cdot 2 + \tfrac{1}{3} \cdot 4$$

$$= 107\tfrac{1}{3}.$$

In applying the individual record formula, it must first be realized that, through techniques discussed earlier,

$$\sum_{y=a}^{x-1} j_y + {}_\delta m_x = E_x^{1976} = 120,$$

$$s_x \equiv P_x^{1976} = 100,$$

$$e_x \equiv P_x^{1977} = 110,$$

$${}_\alpha m_x = P_x^{1977} + {}_\alpha D_x^{1976} - E_x^{1976} = -8,$$

and

$$_\delta m_{x+1} = E_{x+1}^{1976} + {}_\delta D_x^{1976} - P_x^{1976} = 2.$$

Plugging these substitutions into the individual record formula produces

$$E_x \Big]_x^{x+1} = 120 + \tfrac{2}{3} \cdot (100 - 110) + \tfrac{5}{6} \cdot (-8) + \tfrac{1}{3} \cdot 2$$

$$= 107\tfrac{1}{3},$$

as before.

It is extremely important to note that it would have been ambiguous for Example 6-3, as stated, to give migration data without being specific as to the interpretation of subscripts. Had we chosen to tabulate migration by age last birthday, a perfectly logical and valid choice, the two units of δ-migration would have been denoted as $_\delta m_x$ rather than $_\delta m_{x+1}$. Thus a statement in the example that $_\delta m_{x+1} = 2$ would not have been a meaningful one unless the accompanying tabulating rule had been specified. The key conclusion to this discussion is that it *does not matter* whether the δ-migration necessary for the exposure calculation in Example 6-3 is subscripted x, $x + 1$, or even $x - 1$ or some other age. If we have the in-force and death data available in a diagram such as Figure 6-9, the exposure values are available regardless of the subscripts used to represent the various migration components. Where such subscripts are either given or desired, they are meaningful only in the presence of a defining tabulating rule. This fact is further illustrated by the following example.

EXAMPLE 6-4   Develop, if possible, a unique counterpart formula for the following:

$$E_x \Big]_x^{x+1} = \tfrac{2}{3} \cdot P_x^z + \tfrac{1}{3} \cdot P_x^{z+1} + {}_\alpha D_x^z.$$

SOLUTION   The given formula is clearly of the double-diagonal variety, as its two in-force components arise from two different years of birth. The given coefficients imply that the assumed average birth date is September 1 and that migration is assumed to have occurred on birthdays. Figure 6-10 results, with the subscripts of the migration terms deliberately omitted.

An individual record counterpart of the given formula may not be uniquely written, as the subscripts of the migration terms are not uniquely known. In addition, though we know that the starters for the study are represented by P_x^z, this in-force quantity would be labeled s_{x-1}, s_x, or s_{x+1}, for example, under the three tabulating rules

$$s_x : x = z - 2 - \text{CYB}.$$

$$s_x : x = z - 1 - \text{CYB},$$

and

$$s_x : x = z - \text{CYB}.$$

These three rules produce superscripts for the s_x deck of $x + \frac{4}{3}$, $x + \frac{1}{3}$, and $x - \frac{2}{3}$, respectively. Since our birth assumption indicates that the true age of the P_x^z lives is $x + \frac{1}{3}$, only with the middle tabulating rule above will the proper subscript for the starters be x.

FIGURE 6-10

Calendar Year z

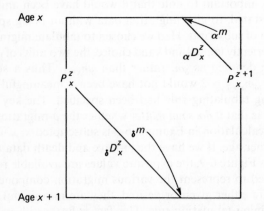

If, however, we are willing to assume that all *individual record* categories are tabulated by age last birthday (or last anniversary, last duration, or last fiscal age, as the case may be) unless stated to the contrary, a unique counterpart does arise. The category symbols then become

$$\theta_x \Big]_x^{x+1}, \quad s_x^{x+(1/3)}, \quad {}_\alpha m_x^x, \quad {}_\delta m_x^{x+1}, \quad \text{and} \quad e_x^{x+(1/3)},$$

producing the formula

$$E_x \Big]_x^{x+1} = \sum_{y=a}^{x-1} j_y + \frac{2}{3} \cdot s_x + {}_\alpha m_x - \frac{2}{3} \cdot e_x.$$

In the writing of counterpart formulas, the assumption just described has traditionally been used, but it has not always been articulated. Let us agree to follow this convention while continuing to be cognizant that, in its absence, a problem such as that posed in Example 6-4 cannot be uniquely solved.

EXAMPLE 6-5   Develop a counterpart formula for

$$E_t \Big]_t^{t+1} = n + \sum_{y=0}^{t-1} j_y + \frac{1}{3} \cdot s_t - \frac{1}{3} \cdot {}_\alpha w_t - \frac{1}{3} \cdot {}_\delta w_t - \frac{1}{3} \cdot e_t.$$

SOLUTION   Based upon the above-mentioned convention, we shall assume
that all subscripts in the given select exposure formula refer to duration
last anniversary. This assumption gives rise to Figure 6-11, in which migration

FIGURE 6-11

Calendar Year z

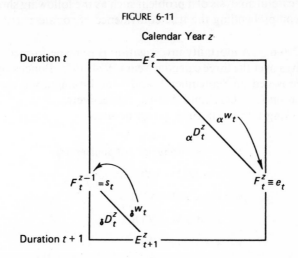

is placed at the end points of calendar year z and issues are placed on May 1.
These conclusions are evident from a consideration of the category symbols
upon which the given formula is clearly based,

$$\theta_t \Big]_t^{t+1}, \quad s_t^{t+(2/3)}, \quad {}_\alpha w_t^{t+(2/3)}, \quad {}_\delta w_t^{t+(2/3)}, \quad \text{and} \quad e_t^{t+(2/3)}.$$

Finally, aided by Figure 6-11, we may readily determine that the
counterpart is

$$E_t \Big]_t^{t+1} = \tfrac{2}{3} \cdot E_t^z + \tfrac{1}{3} \cdot E_{t+1}^z + \tfrac{1}{3} \cdot \left({}_\alpha D_t^z + {}_\delta D_t^z \right)$$

$$= \tfrac{2}{3} \cdot E_t^z + \tfrac{1}{3} \cdot E_{t+1}^z + \tfrac{1}{3} \cdot D_t^z.$$

Note that no indication of the period of observation was stated in
Example 6-5. The solution proceeded, however, as if the observation period
had been the single calendar year z. Had the study been performed over a
period consisting of several calendar years, the correct counterpart would
have simply been a summation of the one actually obtained. For example,
for an observation period of the four calendar years 1975–1978, the correct
answer to Example 6-5 would have been

$$E_t \Big]_t^{t+1} = \sum_{z=1975}^{1978} \left(\tfrac{2}{3} \cdot E_t^z + \tfrac{1}{3} \cdot E_{t+1}^z + \tfrac{1}{3} \cdot D_t^z \right).$$

COMPOSITE FORMULAS

Demonstration that two exposure formulas are indeed counterparts involves no new techniques when the observation period is several years in length. However, a careful analysis of a problem such as the following should aid the student in comprehending the true equivalence of counterpart formulas.

EXAMPLE 6-6* A mortality investigation is to be performed on a group of insured lives over the three calendar years 1973–1975. Policies are assumed to have been issued on September 1, and α- and δ-migration are treated as having fallen on October 1 and April 1, respectively.

The following tabulating rules are to be used:

$$\theta_x : x = \text{Insuring age last anniversary,}$$

$$s_x : x = 1972 - \text{VYB,}$$

$$_\alpha m_x : x = \text{CYM} - \text{VYB,}$$

$$_\delta m_x : x = \text{CYM} - \text{VYB,}$$

$$e_x : x = 1975 - \text{VYB.}$$

The following facts are given:

$$F_{32}^{1972} = 1000, \qquad E_{32}^{1973} = 1040, \qquad _\alpha D_{32}^z = 5, \left.\begin{array}{c} \\ \\ \end{array}\right\} \text{ for all } z.$$

$$F_{32}^{1973} = 1040, \qquad E_{32}^{1974} = 1100, \qquad _\delta D_{32}^z = 15,$$

$$F_{32}^{1974} = 1100, \qquad E_{32}^{1975} = 1200,$$

$$F_{32}^{1975} = 1220, \qquad E_{33}^{1973} = 1020,$$

$$E_{33}^{1974} = 1030,$$

$$E_{33}^{1975} = 1080,$$

(a) Develop counterpart formulas for E_x.
(b) Calculate E_{32}, using each formula independently.
(c) Demonstrate that the basic assumptions and each of the formulas produce equivalent contributions to E_{32} for each of the following ordered pairs:

(i) $\left(_\alpha n_{32}^{1973}, _\delta w_{33}^{1974}\right)$.
(ii) $\left(_\alpha n_{31}^{1973}, _\delta w_{33}^{1975}\right)$.
(iii) $\left(s_{30}, e_{33}\right)$.

---

* The student may recall that this example appeared earlier as Example 5-6. At that time a less detailed solution was presented, using only the valuation schedule formula approach.

SOLUTION

(a) The individual record formula is constructed from the following category symbols:

$$\left.\theta_x\right]_x^{x+1}, \quad s_x^{x+(1/3)}, \quad {}_\alpha m_x^{x+(1/12)}, \quad {}_\delta m_x^{x-(5/12)}, \quad \text{and} \quad e_x^{x+(1/3)}.$$

Accordingly,

$$\left.E_x\right]_x^{x+1} = \sum_{y=a}^{x-1} j_y + \tfrac{2}{3} \cdot s_x + \tfrac{11}{12} \cdot {}_\alpha m_x + {}_\delta m_x$$
$$+ \tfrac{5}{12} \cdot {}_\delta m_{x+1} - \tfrac{2}{3} \cdot e_x.$$

The following valuation schedule formula is easily determined with the aid of Figure 6-12, which is based upon the single year of observation z:

$$\left.E_x\right]_x^{x+1} = \tfrac{1}{4} \cdot F_x^{z-1} + \tfrac{5}{12} \cdot E_{x+1}^z + \tfrac{1}{12} \cdot E_x^z + \tfrac{1}{4} \cdot F_x^z$$
$$+ \tfrac{11}{12} \cdot {}_\alpha D_x^z + \tfrac{5}{12} \cdot {}_\delta D_x^z.$$

FIGURE 6-12

Calendar Year z

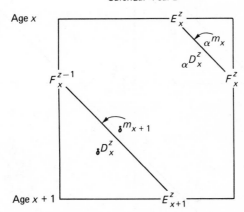

The correct formula for the given observation period is therefore

$$\left.E_x\right]_x^{x+1} = \sum_{z=1973}^{1975} (\tfrac{1}{4} \cdot F_x^{z-1} + \tfrac{5}{12} \cdot E_{x+1}^z + \tfrac{1}{12} \cdot E_x^z + \tfrac{1}{4} \cdot F_x^z$$
$$+ \tfrac{11}{12} \cdot {}_\alpha D_x^z + \tfrac{5}{12} \cdot {}_\delta D_x^z).$$

(b) The calculation of E_{32} from the two formulas is aided by the examination of a detailed diagram (Figure 6-13) which contains data for the

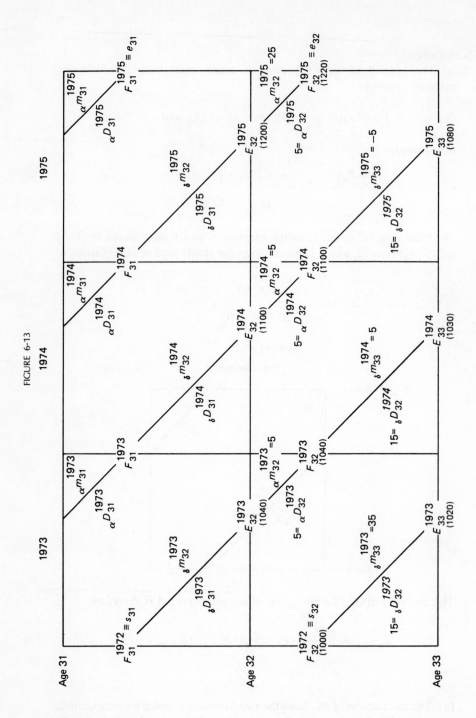

FIGURE 6-13

complete observation period. For the purpose of comparing the formulas and demonstrating their equivalence, Figure 6-13 has been vertically extended to include the age interval above that under investigation. The student should note that many entries in Figure 6-13 are represented in both demographic and individual record notation, e.g., $F_{31}^{1972} \equiv s_{31}$. The migration terms are written in a manner consistent with the individual record tabulating rules and are superscripted with the calendar year in which migration occurred. Numerical values for migration between insuring ages 32 and 33 are obtained from the given data. The value of E_{32} from the valuation schedule formula, the input for which is easily obtained from Figure 6-13, is found as follows:

$$E_{32} \Big]_{32}^{33} = \tfrac{1}{4} \cdot (1000 + 1040 + 1100) + \tfrac{5}{12} \cdot (1020 + 1030 + 1080)$$

$$+ \tfrac{1}{12} \cdot (1040 + 1100 + 1200) + \tfrac{1}{4} \cdot (1040 + 1100 + 1220)$$

$$+ \tfrac{11}{12} \cdot (5 + 5 + 5) + \tfrac{5}{12} \cdot (15 + 15 + 15)$$

$$= 3240.$$

In applying the individual record formula, the following equivalences should first be verified by the student:

$$\sum_{y=a}^{31} j_y + {}_{\delta}m_{32} = \sum_{y=a}^{31} j_y + {}_{\delta}m_{32}^{1973} + {}_{\delta}m_{32}^{1974} + {}_{\delta}m_{32}^{1975}$$

$$= 1040 + 1100 + 1200 = 3340,$$

$$s_{32} = 1000, \qquad e_{32} = 1220,$$

$${}_{a}m_{32} = {}_{a}m_{32}^{1973} + {}_{a}m_{32}^{1974} + {}_{a}m_{32}^{1975} = 5 + 5 + 25 = 35,$$

$${}_{\delta}m_{33} = {}_{\delta}m_{33}^{1973} + {}_{\delta}m_{33}^{1974} + {}_{\delta}m_{33}^{1975} = 35 + 5 - 5 = 35.$$

Thus,

$$E_{32} \Big]_{32}^{33} = \sum_{y=a}^{31} j_y + {}_{\delta}m_{32} + \tfrac{2}{3} \cdot s_{32} + \tfrac{11}{12} \cdot {}_{a}m_{32} + \tfrac{5}{12} \cdot {}_{\delta}m_{33} - \tfrac{2}{3} \cdot e_{32}$$

$$= 3340 + \tfrac{2}{3} \cdot 1000 + \tfrac{11}{12} \cdot 35 + \tfrac{5}{12} \cdot 35 - \tfrac{2}{3} \cdot 1220$$

$$= 3240,$$

as before.

(c) Let us now consider the exposure contribution to E_{32} for the designated ordered pairs indicated by each of the formulas and by reference to the assumptions underlying both formulas. The basic technique is to locate the ordered pair on the 2×3 diagram (Figure 6-13), analyze migration assumptions, and search for all terms in the two formulas in which the policy is included.

(i) $({}_{x}n_{32}^{1973}, {}_{\delta}w_{33}^{1974})$. *Assumptions:* Exposed from 10-1-73 until 4-1-74, producing six months' exposure. *Individual record:* $\frac{11}{12} - \frac{5}{12} = \frac{1}{2}$. *Valuation schedule:* F_{32}^{1973} appears twice, with coefficient of $\frac{1}{4}$, totaling $\frac{1}{2}$.

(ii) $({}_{x}n_{31}^{1973}, {}_{\delta}w_{33}^{1975})$. *Assumptions:* Exposed from 9-1-74 until 4-1-75, producing seven months' exposure. *Individual record:* $1 - \frac{5}{12} = \frac{7}{12}$. *Valuation schedule:* Included in E_{32}^{1974} and in F_{32}^{1974} (appears twice), producing a total contribution to $E_{32}]_{32}^{33}$ of $\frac{1}{12} + \frac{1}{4} + \frac{1}{4} = \frac{7}{12}$.

(iii) (s_{30}, e_{33}). *Assumptions:* Exposed from 9-1-74 until 9-1-75, producing a full unit of exposure. *Individual record:* 1 (from $\sum\limits_{y=a}^{31} j_y$; e_{33} does not appear). *Valuation schedule:* Included in E_{32}^{1974} $(\frac{1}{12})$, F_{32}^{1974} $(\frac{1}{4} + \frac{1}{4})$, and E_{33}^{1975} $(\frac{5}{12})$, totaling $\frac{12}{12} = 1$.

The student with a complete understanding of all aspects of the lengthy but comprehensive Example 6-6 has clearly mastered the interrelationships between counterpart formulas. If such mastery remains unattained, the student should choose additional ordered pairs to analyze, making sure that entry and exit fall on the same diagonal.

A FINAL ILLUSTRATION

The foregoing discussion on the subject of counterpart formulas has been one of largely academic interest. In the practical application of the theory of table construction, the necessity to demonstrate equivalence of individual record and valuation schedule formulas does not arise. Rather, the actuary must analyze the nature of the available data and determine which of the two major types of formulas is the more feasible. Yet, it must always be remembered that, regardless of the form of the data, both options remain open even though one is usually clearly preferable. Example 6-7, more easily solved with a valuation schedule formula, illustrates the use of the counterpart individual record formula as well. It further underlines the fact, observed earlier in this text, that the Balducci hypothesis should be assumed to apply to the decrement under consideration rather than automatically to the decrement of death.

EXAMPLE 6-7   You have been asked to analyze employee turnover for a large industrial concern. The information in Tables 6-3 and 6-4 is available. There were 4000 employees hired in 1973 and 4200 hired in 1974.

Calculate rates of termination, independently, from counterpart formulas. Indicate all assumptions used.

TABLE 6-3

Number of employees in service
on December 31

Completed years of service	1972	1973	1974
0	3800	3700	4000
1	3600	3600	3600
2	3300	3500	3500
3	3100	3200	3300

TABLE 6-4

Terminations,
other than by death,
in calendar year

Calendar year of hire (CYH)	1973	1974
1974	—	120
1973	110	100
1972	90	90
1971	70	80
1970	60	—

SOLUTION   Reasonable assumptions which should and will be adopted, in the absence of any indications to the contrary, are

(a) Hirings occurred on July 1, on the average;

(b) Deaths occurred on July 1, on the average;

(c) *Terminations* occurred in a manner consistent with the Balducci hypothesis.

Clearly, the optimum period of observation is the two calendar years 1973 and 1974.

Figure 6-14 incorporates the given data and, while not absolutely necessary for the solution, is helpful in applying each of the formulas to be derived. Terminations are placed below each diagonal, consistent with the fact that this is a study of terminations. Deaths, found by algebraic manipulation of in-force and termination data, are placed above the diagonals, as they have the same status generally accorded to migration.

It is important to note that termination and death figures are not available by α- and δ-breakdowns. Therefore, it is theoretically preferable to treat unit intervals as running from half-duration to half-duration, so that we may deal

FIGURE 6-14

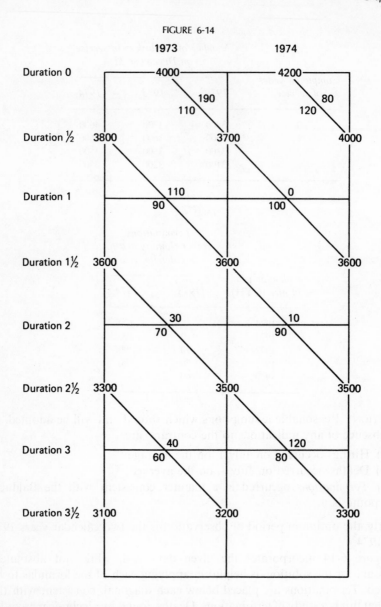

with single-diagonal exposure formulas (in which half of the total terminations are required) rather than with double-diagonal formulas (in which the α-terminations would be required).

The valuation schedule formulas thus become

$$E_t\bigg|_{t-(1/2)}^{t+(1/2)} = \tfrac{1}{2} \cdot \sum_{z=1973}^{1974} (F_{t-1}^{z-1} + F_t^z + w_{t\backslash}^z) \quad (t > 0)$$

and

$$E_0 \Big]_0^{1/2} = \tfrac{1}{2} \cdot \sum_{z=1973}^{1974} (n^z + F_0^z + w_{0\setminus}^z),$$

where n^z represents issues of year z and $w_{0\setminus}^z$ represents those terminations in year z arising from issues of the same year. Plugging in the data from the above diagram, we have

$$E_0 \Big]_0^{1/2} = \tfrac{1}{2} \cdot (4000 + 4200 + 3700 + 4000 + 110 + 120) = 8065,$$

$$E_1 \Big]_{1/2}^{1\frac{1}{2}} = \tfrac{1}{2} \cdot (3800 + 3600 + 3700 + 3600 + 90 + 100) = 7445,$$

$$E_2 \Big]_{1\frac{1}{2}}^{2\frac{1}{2}} = \tfrac{1}{2} \cdot (3600 + 3500 + 3600 + 3500 + 70 + 90) = 7180,$$

and

$$E_3 \Big]_{2\frac{1}{2}}^{3\frac{1}{2}} = \tfrac{1}{2} \cdot (3300 + 3200 + 3500 + 3300 + 60 + 80) = 6720.$$

The required termination rates are now seen to be

$$_{1/2}q_0^w = \tfrac{230}{8065}, \quad q_{1/2}^w = \tfrac{190}{7445}, \quad q_{1\frac{1}{2}}^w = \tfrac{160}{7180}, \quad \text{and} \quad q_{2\frac{1}{2}}^w = \tfrac{140}{6720}.$$

The tabulating rules and category symbols for the individual record formula are

$$w_t : t = \text{CYW} - \text{CYH}, \qquad w_t \Big]_{t-(1/2)}^{t+(1/2)};$$

$$s_t : t = 1972 - \text{CYH}, \qquad s_t^{t+(1/2)};$$

$$\theta_t : t = \text{CYD} - \text{CYH}, \qquad \theta_t^t;$$

$$e_t : t = 1974 - \text{CYH}, \qquad e_t^{t+(1/2)}.$$

The formula is now easily seen to be

$$E_t \Big]_{t-(1/2)}^{t+(1/2)} = n + \sum_{y=0}^{t-1} j_y - \tfrac{1}{2} \cdot \theta_t.$$

The entries in Table 6-5, obtained directly from Figure 6-14, should be verified by the student, keeping in mind that $n = 8200$. The values of E_t, identical to those computed from the valuation schedule counterpart, may now be used to calculate termination rates. However, at this point, equivalence of the two sets of rates is obvious.

TABLE 6-5

t	s_t	θ_t	e_t	w_t	j_t	$\sum_{y=0}^{t-1} j_y$	f_t	E_t
0	3800	270	4000	230	-700	0	-135	8065
1	3600	110	3600	190	-300	-700	-55	7445
2	3300	40	3500	160	-400	-1000	-20	7180
3	3100	160	3300	140	-500	-1400	-80	6720

It is now incumbent upon the student to determine which of these two methods is preferable. Objectively, the degree of difficulty and the time required by the two seem quite comparable. In the absence of the diagram (Figure 6-14), however, the valuation schedule formula could probably have been applied with less chance for careless error because of the absence of specifically stated death data.

SUMMARY

In theory, every exposure calculation problem can be approached by either of two techniques, both producing identical results. These techniques involve the use of two formulas which are counterparts, one being of the individual record variety and the other in valuation schedule form. Practical considerations, generally based upon the form in which data are available, often make one technique more efficient, but not more accurate, than the other. Of primary importance is the logical fact that two formulas which embody identical assumptions must produce identical exposures, even though the formulas might appear quite different at first glance.

The demonstration that two counterpart formulas are truly equivalent is largely an academic exercise. The actuary performing a mortality study will generate exposures using only one formula, and its counterpart will be of little or no practical importance. Yet a total appreciation of the overall theory of mortality table construction cannot exist in the absence of a clear understanding of both the conceptual and notational inter-relationships of pairs of counterpart formulas.

Two observations must be made with respect to the potential notational problems arising when counterpart formulas are analyzed. Each of these observations relates to the traditional necessity of having subscripts denote age last birthday in formulas which depend on demographic symbols. The fact that subscripts often do not refer to age last birthday when the actuarially oriented individual record formulas are used may give rise to confusion unless certain guidelines are carefully imposed.

First, and most importantly, the subscripts of death terms in valuation schedule formulas always refer to age last birthday, or, in other contexts, to duration last anniversary, last insuring age, or last fiscal age. In individual card formulas, such subscripts are determined only after reference to the tabulating rules chosen for the study. Thus, D_{40}^{1977}, when used in conjunction with demographic notation such as E_{40}^{1977} or P_{40}^{1977}, refers to deaths during 1977 between ages 40 and 41. However, D_{40}^{1977}, when used in conjunction with individual record symbols such as s_{40} or e_{40}, is technically an undefined quantity unless the tabulating rule for deaths is specified. A similar remark could be made with respect to migration symbols.

Second, the convention has been somewhat reluctantly adopted that whenever an individual record formula is stated and its counterpart desired, or vice versa, we shall assume that the individual record subscripts refer to last age or duration unless there is information to the contrary. As mentioned earlier, this approach has been used in the past, but it has engendered some confusion. Of course, it is both preferable and more instructive to define individual record subscripts fully so that no ambiguity is possible.

In Chapter Six we have introduced little, if any, new theory; the chapter was designed solely to consolidate the ideas of Chapters Four and Five. The exercises which follow afford the student ample opportunity to test his understanding through the manipulation and transformation of given formulas into their counterparts. Where migration symbols are given in these exercises, it should be understood that the subscripts of such terms represent the tabulated age consistent with the individual record tabulating rules.

EXERCISES

1. Write the counterparts of each of the following:

    (a) $E_x \Big]_x^{x+1} = \frac{1}{6} \cdot P_x^z + \frac{1}{12} \cdot E_{x+1}^z + \frac{5}{12} \cdot P_x^{z+1} + \frac{4}{12} \cdot E_x^z$

    $\qquad + a \cdot {}_aD_x^z + b \cdot {}_\delta D_x^z.$

    (b) $E_x \Big]_x^{x+1} = \sum\limits_{y=a}^{x-1} j_y + (n-w)_x + \frac{5}{12} \cdot (s-e)_x.$

2. For each of the following exposure formulas, state the assumptions made with respect to migration. Then write individual record tabulating rules and the counterpart formula.

    (a) $E_x \Big]_{x-(5/12)}^{x+(7/12)} = \sum\limits_{z=1976}^{1977} \left(\frac{2}{3} \cdot P_{x-1}^z + \frac{1}{3} \cdot P_x^{z+1} + \frac{1}{3} \cdot D_{x\backslash}^z \right)$

(b) $E_x \Big]_x^{x+1} = \sum_{z=1975}^{1976} [\frac{1}{4} \cdot (E_x^z + P_x^z) + \frac{1}{6} \cdot P_x^{z+1} + \frac{1}{3} \cdot E_{x+1}^z$

$\qquad\qquad + \frac{3}{4} \cdot {}_\alpha D_x^z + \frac{1}{3} \cdot {}_\delta D_x^z]$.

3. Write the counterpart of each of the following, stating the assumptions underlying each:

(a) $s + \frac{5}{12} \cdot (n - w)$.

(b) $s + \frac{5}{12} \cdot ({}_\alpha n - {}_\alpha w)$.

(c) $\frac{1}{6} \cdot s + \frac{2}{3} \cdot g + \frac{1}{6} \cdot e + \frac{5}{6} \cdot {}_\alpha\theta + \frac{1}{6} \cdot {}_b\theta$.

Check to see that each of your answers agrees with the underlying assumptions for the cases $({}_\alpha n, {}_b w)$ and $({}_b n, {}_b\theta)$.

4. Write the counterpart formula for each of the following:

(a) $\displaystyle\sum_{z=1974}^{1977} [\frac{1}{2} \cdot (F_x^{z-1} + F_x^z) + {}_\alpha D_x^z]$.

(b) $\displaystyle\sum_{z=1974}^{1977} (F_x^z + {}_\alpha D_x^z)$.

5. The following exposure formula is given:

$$E_x \Big]_x^{x+1} = \sum_{z=1975}^{z=1977} (\frac{1}{3} \cdot E_x^z + \frac{1}{2} \cdot P_x^{z+1} + \frac{1}{6} \cdot E_{x+1}^{z+1}$$

$$\qquad\qquad + \frac{2}{3} \cdot {}_\alpha D_x^z + \frac{1}{6} \cdot {}_\delta D_x^{z+1}).$$

(a) Write the counterpart formula, tabulating all migration by age last birthday and assuming all births on July 1.

(b) Using each formula, determine the correct amount of exposure between x and $x + 1$ to be attributed to each of the following cases:

(i) $(E_{x-1}^{1975}, {}_\delta w_x^{1977})$.

(ii) $({}_\alpha n_{x-2}^{1975}, E_{x+1}^{1978})$.

(iii) $(s_{x-1}, {}_\alpha D_x^{1976})$.

(iv) $({}_\delta n_{x-1}^{1976}, {}_\alpha w_x^{1976})$.

6. A mortality study has the calendar years 1975–1976 as its observation period. Births are assumed to occur on September 1, and α-migration and δ-migration are assumed to occur on November 1 and May 1, respectively. The following tabulating rules are used:

$$\theta_x : x = \text{CYD} - \text{CYB},$$

$$s_x : x = 1975 - \text{CYB},$$

$${}_\alpha m_x : x = \text{CYM} - \text{CYB},$$

$${}_\delta m_x : x = \text{Age last birthday},$$

$$e_x : x = 1976 - \text{CYB}.$$

(a) Stating your assumptions, determine the valuation schedule exposure formula for the determination of E_{40}. Develop the counterpart individual card formula as well.

(b) By using the following data, find the value of E_{40}, using each of your formulas independently (some of the data are obviously irrelevant):

$$P_{38}^{1975} = 1000, \qquad E_{39}^{1975} = 1010,$$

$$P_{39}^{1975} = 900, \qquad E_{40}^{1975} = 900,$$

$$P_{39}^{1976} = 1000, \qquad E_{40}^{1976} = 1010,$$

$$P_{40}^{1976} = 870,$$

$$P_{40}^{1977} = 1000,$$

$$_{\delta}m_{38}^{1975} = 20, \qquad _{\delta}m_{39}^{1975} = 10,$$

$$_{\alpha}m_{38}^{1975} = 15, \qquad _{\delta}m_{39}^{1976} = 30,$$

$$_{\alpha}m_{39}^{1975} = -6, \qquad _{\alpha}m_{39}^{1976} = 15,$$

$$_{\alpha}m_{40}^{1975} = -20, \qquad _{\alpha}m_{40}^{1976} = -5.$$

7. A mortality study is being conducted under the following conditions:
   (i) Births occur on May 1.
   (ii) The observation period is the three calendar years 1976–1978.
   (iii) α-Migration occurs on nearest October 1.
   (iv) δ-Migration occurs on nearest January 1.
   (v) Balducci mortality is assumed.
   (vi) Deaths are tabulated by calendar age.
   (vii) Migration is tabulated by calendar age.
   (a) Write the tabulating rules and the appropriate individual record exposure formula for finding E_{51}.
   (b) Derive a valuation schedule exposure formula for E_{51}.
   (c) Using each of your formulas, calculate the numerical value of E_{51} and the corresponding q, given

$$P_{50}^{1976} = 800, \qquad E_{51}^{1976} = 806, \qquad P_{51}^{1977} = 794,$$

$$P_{50}^{1977} = 850, \qquad E_{51}^{1977} = 865, \qquad P_{51}^{1978} = 862,$$

$$P_{50}^{1978} = 900, \qquad E_{51}^{1978} = 905, \qquad P_{51}^{1979} = 900,$$

$$_{\alpha}D_{51}^{1976} = 9, \qquad _{\delta}D_{50}^{1976} = 4,$$

$$_{\alpha}D_{51}^{1977} = 12, \qquad _{\delta}D_{50}^{1977} = 3,$$

$$_{\alpha}D_{51}^{1978} = 10, \qquad _{\delta}D_{50}^{1978} = 5.$$

8. A mortality study of insured lives is based upon the following:
   (i) The observation period is the two calendar years 1976–1977.
   (ii) Deaths are tabulated by insuring age last anniversary.
   (iii) Withdrawals are tabulated by calendar insuring age.
   (iv) α-Withdrawals are assumed on October 31.
   (v) δ Withdrawals are assumed on April 30.
   (vi) Balducci mortality is assumed.
   (vii) August 1 is the average issue date for each calendar year.
   (viii) Starters and enders are tabulated by last insuring age.
   (a) Write the tabulating rules and the resulting individual record exposure formula.
   (b) Write the counterpart valuation schedule formula.
   (c) Show that your formulas produce the same value for E_{20}, using some or all of the following data:

$$s_{18} = 160, \quad {}_\delta D_{19}^{1976} = 4, \quad {}_\alpha D_{20}^{1976} = 4,$$
$$s_{19} = 90, \quad {}_\delta D_{19}^{1977} = 8, \quad {}_\alpha D_{20}^{1977} = 6,$$
$$s_{20} = 80, \quad {}_\delta D_{20}^{1976} = 3,$$
$$ {}_\delta D_{20}^{1977} = 5,$$

$$ {}_\delta m_{20}^{1976} = 14, \quad {}_\alpha m_{20}^{1976} = 24,$$
$$ {}_\delta m_{20}^{1977} = -12, \quad {}_\alpha m_{20}^{1977} = 6,$$
$$ {}_\delta m_{21}^{1976} = 23,$$
$$ {}_\delta m_{21}^{1977} = 15, \quad P_{19}^{1977} = 220.$$

   (d) For each of the following ordered pairs, demonstrate that your formulas produce the same amount of exposure:

$$(P_{19}^{1976}, {}_\alpha w_{20}^{1976}),$$
$$({}_\alpha n_{19}^{1976}, P_{20}^{1978}),$$
$$({}_\delta n_{20}^{1976}, E_{21}^{1977}),$$
$$(s_{18}, {}_\delta D_{19}^{1977}),$$
$$({}_\delta n_{20}^{1976}, {}_\delta D_{20}^{1976}).$$

9. A study of mortality, covering the calendar years 1976–1977, is based on the following assumptions:
   (i) Births fall on May 1.
   (ii) Deaths are tabulated by age last birthday.
   (iii) Balducci mortality is assumed.

(iv) α-Migration occurs on November 1.
(v) δ-Migration occurs on March 1.
(vi) All migration is tabulated by age last birthday.
The following data are available:

$$P_x^{1976} = 500, \qquad E_x^{1976} = 700,$$

$$P_x^{1977} = 720, \qquad E_x^{1977} = 800,$$

$$P_x^{1978} = 810, \qquad E_{x+1}^{1976} = 450,$$

$$E_{x+1}^{1977} = 700,$$

$$_\alpha D_x^{1976} = 10, \qquad _\delta D_x^{1976} = 4,$$

$$_\alpha D_x^{1977} = 12, \qquad _\delta D_x^{1977} = 8.$$

Stating all of your assumptions, determine both the individual record and valuation schedule exposure formulas. Show that each gives the same value for E_x.

10. It is desired to determine q_{30} using the two-year observation period 1977–1978. Births are assumed to occur on September 1, and α- and δ-migration are assumed to occur on October 1 and June 1, respectively. The following tabulating rules are used:

$$\theta_x : x = \text{Age last birthday at death},$$

$$s_x : x = 1976 - \text{CYB},$$

$$_\alpha m_x : x = \text{CYM} - \text{CYB},$$

$$_\delta m_x : x = \text{Age next birthday},$$

$$e_x : x = 1978 - \text{CYB}.$$

(a) Write counterpart exposure formulas for E_{30}.
(b) Use the following data with *each* of your formulas to find the value of E_{30}:

$$s_{30} = 802, \qquad\qquad E_{30}^{1977} = 1000,$$

$$e_{30} = 850, \qquad\qquad E_{30}^{1978} = 900,$$

$$E_{31}^{1977} = 850 = E_{31}^{1978}, \qquad P_{30}^{1978} = 900,$$

$$_\delta D_{30}^{1977} = 10, \qquad\qquad _\delta D_{30}^{1978} = 40,$$

$$_\alpha D_{30}^{1977} = 20, \qquad\qquad _\alpha D_{30}^{1978} = 10.$$

11. A mortality study is being made on a group of lives observed from January 1, 1975 through December 31, 1976. Deaths are tabulated by

age last birthday. The tabulating rule for starters, $s_x : x = 1974 - $ CYB, results in a category symbol of $s_x^{x+(2/3)}$. It is assumed that δ-migration occurs on February 1 and α-migration on October 1.

(a) Stating your assumptions, determine the appropriate valuation schedule exposure formula.

(b) Similarly, determine the individual record exposure formula.

(c) Using your two formulas independently, calculate E_{40}, given the following data:

$$E_{40}^{1975} = 500, \qquad {_\alpha}D_{40}^{1975} = 8,$$

$$E_{40}^{1976} = 600, \qquad {_\alpha}D_{40}^{1976} = 4,$$

$$E_{41}^{1975} = 420, \qquad {_\delta}D_{40}^{1975} = 6,$$

$$E_{41}^{1976} = 560, \qquad {_\delta}D_{40}^{1976} = 2.$$

$$P_{40}^{1975} = 400,$$

$$P_{40}^{1976} = 550,$$

$$P_{40}^{1977} = 580,$$

12. The observation period of a mortality study is the calendar years 1976 and 1977. All births are assumed to have occurred on May 15. The δ-migration is assumed to occur on the nearest January 1, while the α-migration is assumed to occur on the nearest August 15. The following tabulating rules are given:

$$\theta_x : x = \text{Age last birthday},$$

$$s_x : x = 1976 - \text{CYB},$$

$${_\delta}m_x : x = \text{CYM} - \text{CYB},$$

$${_\alpha}m_x : x = \text{Age next birthday},$$

$$e_x : x = 1977 - \text{CYB}.$$

Derive counterpart formulas for E_x. Then calculate the exposure from each formula, given the following data:

$$P_x^{1976} = 500, \qquad\qquad e_x = 615,$$

$$E_x^{1976} = 550, \qquad {_\alpha}D_x^{1976} = 10,$$

$$P_x^{1977} = 525, \qquad {_\alpha}D_x^{1977} = 15,$$

$$E_x^{1977} = 600, \qquad {_\delta}D_x^{1976} = 5,$$

$${_\delta}m_{x+1}^{1976} = 30, \qquad {_\delta}D_x^{1977} = 5.$$

$${_\delta}m_{x+1}^{1977} = 5,$$

13. The observation period of a mortality study is the calendar years 1977–1978. Deaths are tabulated by age last birthday, and all births are assumed to have occurred on September 1. Each type of migration is handled separately and tabulated by calendar age.

    (a) Write the tabulating rules and the individual record exposure formula.

    (b) Derive the appropriate valuation schedule exposure formula.

    (c) Show that both of your formulas produce the same value of E_{40}, given the following:

$$P_{37}^{1977} = 800, \qquad E_{38}^{1977} = 800, \qquad P_{38}^{1978} = 800, \qquad {}_a m_{40}^{1978} = 5,$$

$$P_{38}^{1977} = 700, \qquad E_{39}^{1977} = 700, \qquad P_{39}^{1978} = 700, \qquad {}_\delta m_{41}^{1978} = 20,$$

$$P_{39}^{1977} = 600, \qquad E_{40}^{1977} = 600, \qquad P_{40}^{1978} = 600,$$

$$P_{40}^{1977} = 500, \qquad E_{41}^{1977} = 500, \qquad {}_\delta m_{40}^{1978} = 10,$$

$$\quad {}_a D_x^z = 5 \qquad \text{(for all } x \text{ and } z\text{)},$$

$$\quad {}_\delta D_x^z = 15 \qquad \text{(for all } x \text{ and } z\text{)}.$$

14. For the following mortality study using valuation in-force data, the fiscal year of birth is defined as the calendar year containing the April 30 following the actual date of birth. Migration is assumed to occur on fiscal birthdays. The observation period is January 1, 1975 through April 30, 1977.

    (a) Derive an individual record formula for the exposures, compatible with the data available. Calculate the exposures.

    (b) Derive the counterpart valuation schedule formula for the exposures, compatible with the data available. Calculate the exposures.

FYB	In force Jan. 1, 1975	In force April 30, 1977
1946	1600	1300
1947	1650	1300
1948	1700	1248

FYB	Migration in			Deaths in		
	1975	1976	1977	1975	1976	1977
1946	−75	−100	?	60	45	9
1947	−80	−120	?	60	60	5
1948	−90	−160	?	70	60	12

15. In a pension fund mortality study, the actuary assigns to each member a fiscal year of birth which is equal to the calendar year containing the October 1 which follows the actual date of birth. The following data are available with respect to the pension fund:

	FYB		
	1955	*1956*	*1957*
Number of members on			
Dec. 31, 1974	1000	1050	1080
Dec. 31, 1975	1020	1060	1080
Dec. 31, 1976	1040	1070	1090
Dec. 31, 1977	1050	1080	1100
Dec. 31, 1978	1060	1090	1110
Deaths in calendar year			
1975	6	8	10
1976	7	9	11
1977	8	10	12
1978	9	11	13

Using an observation period which makes maximum use of the given data, calculate the exposures both with an individual record formula and a valuation schedule formula.

16. (a) Derive a select valuation schedule exposure formula under the following assumptions:

(i) All policies are issued on May 1.

(ii) Observation is from 1976 anniversaries to 1978 anniversaries.

(iii) Deaths are tabulated by duration last anniversary.

(iv) α-Withdrawals are on October 1; δ-withdrawals are on March 1.

(v) $_{1-t}q_{x+t} = (1 - t) \cdot q_x, 0 \leq t \leq 1$.

(vi) All withdrawals are tabulated by calendar duration.

(b) Find $q_{[x]+t}$, using your formula, from the following:

$$E_t^{1976} = 1200, \quad {}_\alpha D_t^{1976} = 6, \quad {}_\delta D_t^{1977} = 4, \quad {}_\alpha w_t^{1976} = 30,$$

$$E_t^{1977} = 1500, \quad {}_\alpha D_t^{1977} = 12, \quad {}_\delta D_t^{1978} = 6, \quad {}_\alpha w_t^{1977} = 48,$$

$$\qquad\qquad\qquad\qquad\qquad\qquad {}_\delta w_{t+1}^{1977} = 8, \quad {}_\delta w_{t+1}^{1978} = 18.$$

(c) Find $q_{[x]+t}$ using an individual record formula.

17. A mortality study is being performed on the members of a pension fund. The period of observation is January 1, 1973 to December 31, 1977. The tabulating rules are as follows:

$$s_x : x = 1973 - \text{FYB},$$

$$n_x : x = \text{CYN} - \text{FYB},$$

$$w_x : x = \text{CYW} - \text{FYB},$$

$$e_x : x = 1977 - \text{FYB},$$

$$\theta_x : x = \text{CYD} - \text{FYB}.$$

Fiscal years of birth are assigned by the rule

FYB = Calendar year containing the April 1 preceding the date of birth.

(a) Derive a valuation schedule exposure formula for this study, and write the counterpart individual record formula.

(b) Show that your two formulas produce identical exposure values for each of the following cases:

(i) $(P_{x-2}^{1973}, w_x^{1974})$,   *(iii)* (n_x^{1977}, P_x^{1978}),

(ii) $(P_{x-5}^{1973}, \theta_{x-1}^{1976})$,   *(iv)* $(n_{x-2}^{1973}, w_x^{1975})$.

CHAPTER SEVEN

Practical Aspects
of Mortality Studies

INTRODUCTION

In the first six chapters of this text we have dealt with the mathematical and theoretical considerations basic to the computation of exposure values and rates of mortality. Formulas have been derived and illustrative examples presented, but little attention has been paid to the practicalities which demand careful recognition before formulas can be efficiently applied to a body of data. Although many aspects of a mortality study involve reasoning and judgment for which no absolute guidelines may be established, it must be emphasized that only a study based upon detailed preliminary planning can truly prove to be worthwhile. Clearly, a mortality study which is technically sound may prove to be of minimal value unless its design is consistent with the underlying purpose of the study.

Some of the more important problems encountered in the design of a mortality investigation of insured lives involve the treatment of nonmedical issues, substandard business, and other portfolio elements which tend to produce heterogeneities. In addition, the actuary must decide how to handle the death of a person whose life was insured by more than one policy. Another question which must be confronted is whether the termination by death of a $1 million policy should be treated identically to that of a much smaller policy. Further, it must be resolved whether a calendar year study or an anniversary-to-anniversary study is preferable. Finally, once the study has been completed and mortality rates or ratios determined, numerous criteria should be applied to the results as measures of the validity of the procedures which were utilized. These and similar considerations form the basic content of this final chapter.

Throughout, we shall deal only with the types of mortality studies which are made on the life insurance policies of one insurer or a group of insurers. However, much of what follows is relevant to other types of studies as well. In fact, many important types of investigations for which the theory of table construction is essential involve considerations similar to those to be discussed in this chapter.

A mortality study which is of primary interest to many actuaries is that which is conducted annually by the Society of Actuaries through its Committee on Mortality Under Ordinary Insurances and Annuities. Data for this study are contributed each year by approximately 20 of the largest life insurers in the United States and Canada. So that the student of the theory of table construction might gain added insights into the practicalities of a large, comprehensive, highly professional study, the Society has graciously agreed to the inclusion of the Instructions for the submission of data for the 1975–1976 study as an appendix to this text. Appendices to the Instructions themselves are not included due to limited space and to the fact that they basically include only coding procedures and other detail which would not be of real value to the student.

The fundamental concepts of this chapter have been taken from Chapter Five of *Measurement of Mortality* by Harry Gershenson. The author is grateful to the Society of Actuaries for the permission to draw heavily from this earlier work.

SOURCES OF DATA

Several of the files maintained by life insurers are useful in the securing of the basic data upon which a study of policyholder mortality may be based. In some cases these files are created with little or no consideration given to the possibility of their use in the gathering of mortality statistics. In most instances, however, the files contain data in a form which clearly anticipates the needs of those persons who are responsible for the evaluation of the company's mortality experience.

The *application file* contains the original application for insurance as well as any evidence of insurability which may have accompanied the application. Questions which might subsequently arise concerning the original risk can be answered through referral to this application file. In some instances, policy changes subsequent to issue are reflected in the application file as well.

The *policy master file*, or in-force file, contains data on all policies currently in force and is used by the insurer primarily for such routine purposes as billing, dividend payment, and reserve valuation. This file generally contains such information as whether the policy was medically or nonmedically issued and whether it was issued at a standard or sub-standard rate, facts which would be of obvious interest to the actuary conducting a mortality study. Since the policy master file usually does not include data on terminated policies, its use as the sole source of data for mortality studies is generally only feasible when a valuation schedule study, of the type described in Chapter Five, is to be implemented. If, however, transactions subsequent to policy issue are included, this file could be a major source of information for individual record studies as well.

The *transaction file* contains data on policies which have been terminated, showing the same detail for such policies as the policy master file shows for those still in force. A combination of these two files provides all data needed for a mortality investigation, regardless of the type of formula being used.

Of major importance is the *death claim file*, ostensibly created for such purposes as showing claim distribution by state and calculating the reserve for death claims incurred but not paid. However, this file also serves as a source for the determination of the exact date of a death, its cause, and the amount of the claim which results.

PERIOD OF OBSERVATION

One of the first decisions to be made in the design of a mortality study involves the selection of the period of observation which will produce the most meaningful and useful results. Two basic questions arise, the first dealing with the actual length of the observation period and the second involving the nature of the period, that is, whether it should cover an integral number of calendar years, an anniversary-to-anniversary period, or perhaps some combination of the two.

An observation period which is too long has the shortcoming that it may include experience during periods in which significantly differing conditions affecting mortality were prevalent. For example, an observation period covering the decade of the 1940's would combine years of total war with those of relative peace. A mortality study over any decade of the first half of this century would necessarily combine data before and after significant strides had been made in several fields of medical endeavor, such as the near-elimination of deaths from childhood diseases and polio. Perhaps the simplest general guide that can be imposed in the selection of an observation period is that the period should not be so long that it includes out-of-date influences which would be inappropriate in the short-term prediction of mortality. On the other hand, periods which are of short duration may not generate a sufficient volume of data to produce statistically significant results. Many recent investigations have been performed over a five-year period, and, while there is nothing intuitive which makes a period of this exact length ideal, it does seem to meet the criterion of being neither too short nor too long. The student should be aware, however, that the maintenance of relatively homogeneous conditions with regard to medical and sociological changes could permit the safe use of longer periods. Similarly, significant medical breakthroughs in the areas of heart disease and cancer or a serious economic depression would make longer periods of observation inappropriate as a basis for predicting future experience.

Calendar year mortality studies, while introducing no particular problems from a mathematical or theoretical viewpoint, possess certain practical disadvantages. A standard assumption, often used in this text, is that issues of any calendar year have an average issue date of July 1. To the extent that this assumption is invalid, due perhaps to agency incentive programs or the continual increase in new business issued during the year, distortions can occur when the July 1 assumption is retained. A little reflection will reveal that this problem is not a factor when anniversary-to-anniversary studies are used. Distortions due to lags in reporting issues, deaths, and other terminations may also weaken the validity of calendar year studies. Yet, certain advantages exist as well. A practical one is that more data are available from an *n*-year calendar year study than from an *n*-year anniversary-to-anniversary study. For example, the calendar years 1974–1978, inclusive, produce five years' experience, while the period from anniversaries in 1974 to anniversaries in 1978 is only four years in length. In addition, since most aspects of an insurer's experience are measured on a calendar year basis, notably the financial experience reflected by the calendar year annual statement, it may seem preferable for mortality results to be determined on the same basis.

The advantages and disadvantages of an anniversary-to-anniversary study are essentially the converses of those given for calendar year studies. The preponderance of present-day mortality studies, notably including those of the Society of Actuaries, are of the anniversary-to-anniversary variety. The fact that many of these investigations are of the continuing type partially negates the disadvantage that not as much data is available as from calendar year studies.

UNIT OF INVESTIGATION

Without giving careful consideration to the matter, it would probably be assumed by most students that the individual life is the basic unit in the typical study of mortality. However, this is generally not the case. Instead, the unit of investigation is usually policies, amounts of insurance, or an entity known as selection units. All have their own advantages and disadvantages, often arising from considerations of convenience rather than from considerations of accuracy.

It is not unusual for a person to purchase several policies with the same

company at different stages of life. Additional purchases may occur when
the need for insurance protection increases or when financial considerations
make the purchase of supplemental insurance feasible. A mortality study
based solely upon individual *lives* demands that such an individual be
counted only once regardless of the number of policies purchased. To effect
such a study, all cases of multiple policies on a single life must be identified,
a task which is not generally easy to accomplish. When data from different
companies are to be combined, as in the continuing mortality investigation
of the Society of Actuaries, the problem of identifying lives with more than
one policy is obviously compounded further. Therefore, while investigation
by lives may well produce the theoretically most accurate results, it is not
popular largely because of the difficulties inherent in identifying duplications
of insurance on a single life.

The use of the individual *policy* as the unit of investigation eliminates
the main weakness of investigation by lives. Distortions are clearly introduced, however, as the death of a person insured by five policies creates
five deaths in the numerator of the resulting mortality rate. Presumably,
persons with multiple policies do not exhibit noticeably better or poorer
mortality patterns than those with only a single policy. As long as this
may reasonably be assumed, the distortion created by the use of policies
as the basic unit is not significant. Further, if the study includes quite
large amounts of data, errors arising due to multiple policies tend to be
insignificant. Extreme caution is advisable when the data are relatively
sparse, either for the total investigation or for that cell in which the
death occurs. One expedient which may prove helpful in such circumstances
is the calculation of the number of policies per death for each cell. In the
final smoothing of the observed rates, the actuary may then give less
credence to those cells whose results appear out of line and which exhibit
a relatively high number of policies per death.

A third possible unit of investigation, the *selection unit*, was created to
temper somewhat the disadvantages of the life and the policy methods.
A selection unit is created each time a person purchases insurance,
whether or not more than one policy is purchased at that time. Thus, a
"unit" is created at each point of "selection," and multiple selections are
treated as policies issued to different individuals. The complications arising
in the measurement of experience by lives are mitigated somewhat by the
selection unit approach, as identification of multiple issues at the same point
in time is easier than identifying them when issued at different times.
However, the problem of the length of time over which multiple policies
are exposed is a thorny one when such policies do not all terminate
simultaneously. In addition, the use of selection units does not solve the
problem of duplication when intercompany studies are conducted. However,
the attempt to identify duplications in such instances is usually omitted,
as it is felt that any error thus introduced is of a very minor magnitude.

Studies of mortality of insured lives are most commonly based upon yet a different type of unit, that of *amounts of insurance*. It is felt by many actuaries that the basic purpose of mortality investigations is not merely historical or statistical but utilitarian, that is, for use in pricing future policies to be sold to policyholders with the same general characteristics as those upon whom the investigation is based. Therefore, to the extent that policies issued for large amounts result in better or poorer mortality experience, it is widely believed that this experience should be reflected in mortality rates and, in turn, in future premium rates. Of course, complications arise when this method is employed, notably when several huge claims in a single cell distort the resulting mortality rate. The effect of such fluctuations can be somewhat muted by the elimination, in both exposure values and deaths, of any protection in a single policy in excess of some predetermined level, such as $100,000 or $250,000. Occasionally, parallel studies are performed, one by policies and the other by amounts, in order to measure the degree to which policies with large face amounts exhibit mortality patterns different from those with smaller face amounts.

Certain unique problems arise when the amount of insurance is taken as the unit of investigation. Some types of policies are such that no single amount of insurance exists. Notable among these are family income policies, in which the face amount is a function of the time remaining in the stipulated family income period, and juvenile policies, which often exhibit a sharp increase in protection upon attainment of majority by the insured. Perhaps most common among such policies is decreasing term insurance in which face amounts periodically decrease until the date of expiry. To avoid undue complications arising from insistence upon exactness, it is standard practice to carry such policies at a constant amount in the calculation of exposures. Family income policies are generally carried for the average amount of protection over the period of coverage, and nonlevel term plans are handled similarly. Juvenile policies are usually carried for the ultimate face amount, a practice which is justified by the extremely small proportion of such policies which result in death claims prior to the age at which the face amount actually reaches its ultimate size. The amount of a death claim, used as a component of the numerator of the mortality rate, is taken to be the amount for which the policy is carried in the exposures, regardless of the actual size of the death claim. The actual procedure for handling these unusual policies varies from insurer to insurer. Some even prefer to eliminate such troublesome policies from mortality investigations altogether.

When amounts of insurance form the basis of mortality studies, special care must be taken when a death claim is paid which is less than the amount anticipated by the terms of the policy. This occurs most often in cases of claims which are contested because of alleged misrepresentation. In such cases the actual payment to the beneficiary is the return of all premiums or an amount reached by compromise between the insurer and the beneficiary.

Return of premiums is also the usual payment made to beneficiaries in cases of suicide within the suicide limitation period (usually two years after issue) or in cases of war deaths when the insurer has excluded liability for such deaths by the attachment of a military exclusion rider at the original issue date of the policy. In all such cases, the amount actually treated as a death claim for the purposes of mortality investigations is that actually paid, even though the full face amount is included in the exposures.

CLASSES OF POLICIES

Since most mortality studies have as their primary objective the estimation of future mortality, it is of great importance that the classes of lives under investigation be as homogeneous as possible and, similarly, that consideration be given to the composition of future policyholder groups when mortality studies of existing policyholders are conducted. For example, if it is anticipated that nonmedical issues will comprise the bulk of the policies to be issued in the near future, an insurer should attempt to duplicate the expected mix in its mortality investigation to the closest extent practical. Several classifications of policies must be carefully considered when the composition of the lives to be included is being determined.

For obvious reasons, policies which are insured with an extra premium must be handled separately from those insured on a standard basis. To fail to do so would be to ignore the best predictor of mortality experience, that is, the characteristics of the applicant which have to do with physical health and other pertinent factors such as occupation and personal habits. Although a study of each substandard class, according to degree of severity of the impairment, would be impractical in most companies because of the paucity of data within the individual cells, modified investigations may be undertaken by the combination of the substandard cells in twos or threes. At the very least, however, separate study of standard and substandard issues is imperative.

It is a well-documented fact that women have an average life span which is several years longer than that for men. Further, the gap has shown a tendency to increase rather than to narrow in recent years. Most insurers distinguish between the sexes in setting their premium scales; such a practice suggests that mortality data should be segregated by sex prior to the calculation of mortality rates. Companies making no distinction by sex in premium scales generally find it acceptable to combine all policies regardless of sex, with the realization that a mix, by sex, of policies in the future which is unlike that of the past requires immediate attention to the techniques of the study. A similar observation may be made with respect to the experience under annuity contracts issued to males and females.

As alluded to earlier, policies issued nonmedically, that is, without the benefit of a physical examination, should be handled separately from those issued medically. Under current practice, policies are issued medically at the older ages regardless of policy size and at the younger ages when the requested amounts of insurance are substantial. Thus, in many companies, the bulk of new business is now being issued nonmedically. Though it seems somewhat paradoxical, recent experience at the lower issue ages has in some cases produced mortality rates which are higher for medically issued policies than for those issued nonmedically. Unlike the situation in the early 1960's when nonmedical policies were relatively rare and were issued only under strictly controlled conditions, many companies now combine medical and nonmedical experience in their mortality investigations. Such a decision warrants periodic intracompany studies to test the hypothesis that the difference in medical and nonmedical experience is negligible; in recent years, such a hypothesis has been widely accepted as valid.

Theoretical considerations suggest that many other policy characteristics should require special treatment, but to take such considerations to the extreme would be to subdivide the data into so many cells that many would not be statistically significant. It has been demonstrated that mortality patterns vary with plan of insurance, size of policy, and geographical distribution of business, in addition to the occupation, marital status, and amount of formal education of the policyholder. Each of these variables is generally ignored for the practical reason mentioned above, except that those lives subject to occupational hazards sufficiently severe to require a substandard rating are always studied separately.

Certain special types of policies are often eliminated from a mortality study before it begins. Those issued as term insurance conversions, those whose issue is guaranteed regardless of insurability such as pension trust policies, and those which represent the implementation of a nonforfeiture option such as extended term or reduced paid-up policies are typical examples. Joint life insurance is also usually excluded, and some insurers even eliminate term policies, the historical experience on which has been poorer than that of permanent policies. Each of these special policy types is included by some insurers under certain circumstances. Whether or not they should be included is necessarily a subjective question and falls within the category of a judgment decision rather than one which is clear-cut such as in the case of policies issued with a substandard extra premium.

INTERPRETATION OF RESULTS

The results of any research activity must always be viewed critically before being accepted as valid. This general principle clearly applies in the case of mortality investigations, as there are a number of factors which could introduce errors or distortions in the final rates. Eleven such factors which should be given consideration will be mentioned and briefly discussed. The student should attempt to supplement this list by reflecting upon the ideas and practices presented in this chapter.

1. *Reasonableness of Results.* Clearly, results which deviate from the expected should not be rejected out of hand. However, such surprising findings should be carefully analyzed in an attempt to arrive at a rational explanation.

2. *Sufficiency of Data.* Statistical fluctuations are most severe when the volume of data is small. In the final section of this chapter we shall present techniques which will be helpful in determining the degree of confidence which is justified by a given amount of data.

3. *Homogeneity of Input Data.* The importance of maintaining homogeneous cells in mortality studies had already been observed. However, cells which have an unknown degree of homogeneity may not prove valueless if the mix of future policyholders is similar to that of the past, although combination of such data with those from other insurers must be avoided.

4. *Stability of Conditions.* There is an inherent danger in using the mortality experience of one insurer for rate making by another insurer even though the underwriting philosophies of the two are similar. Differences in policyholder distribution by age, sex, type of insurance, or even occupation obviously permit findings which differ significantly from those which would result from an entirely different policyholder mix.

5. *Maturity of Input Data.* It is theoretically desirable that the distribution of data by policy duration approximate that which would ultimately result from observing a closed block of business until all policies terminate. Often, however, increasing levels of new business give undue weight in mortality statistics to the earlier durations. This distortion may have the effect of producing aggregate mortality rates which unduly reflect the favorable effects of selection.

6. *Unit of Investigation.* It has been observed earlier that calculated mortality rates will vary somewhat depending on whether lives, policies, selection units, or amounts are used as the basic measuring unit. In particular, studies by amounts of insurance may vary radically from those based upon other units. The consequences of using results from a study by lives in calculating premium rates for policies of varying size are potentially serious.

7. *Underwriting Philosophy.* Common sense indicates that liberal underwriting standards tend to generate poorer mortality experience than standards which are restrictive. Therefore, intercompany studies are not feasible unless the underwriting philosophies of the contributors are reasonably similar.

8. *Policyholder Antiselection.* The possibility that prospective policy-holders may in some way seek an advantage over the insurer is quite real. This antiselection is often reflected in poorer risks applying for cheaper plans of insurance. The tendency of such lives to seek to purchase unusually large amounts of insurance, while undeniable, is countered by actions of the insurer to protect against such a potentially dangerous practice. Experience under the extended term option and with policies issued as a result of term conversion riders is generally conceded to be influenced by antiselection tendencies. Where antiselection is significant, the validity of mortality statistics is clearly suspect.

9. *Standard for Expected Deaths.* Many mortality investigations generate mortality ratios rather than rates. Specific attention has not been accorded mortality ratios earlier in this text because the calculation of exposures is the primary task regardless of whether ratios or rates are ultimately desired. A mortality ratio is simply the ratio of the deaths actually *observed* in a given cell to the number of deaths *expected*, the latter number determined by applying rates from a given mortality table (usually referred to as a *standard*) to the computed exposures. In the computation of mortality ratios rather than rates, the *expected deaths* to which actual deaths are compared should be determined by a modern mortality standard. To the extent that expected deaths are computed from a mortality table that does not have a slope consistent with the insurer's recent experience, the resulting mortality ratios will reveal very little about the pattern of current mortality.

10. *Length of Observation Period.* As noted earlier, observation periods which are too long tend to reflect influences which are no longer viable by the date of the study's termination. Little credence can be accorded studies which are unduly prolonged, except perhaps as a historical representation of mortality experience.

11. *Statistical Distortions.* The interpretation of mortality ratios must always be tempered by the realization that comparisons of aggregate results of two or more companies may be misleading. As illustrated in Table 7-1, two companies may exhibit identical mortality ratios, cell by

TABLE 7-1

	Company X			Company Y		
Attained age	*Expected claims*	*Actual claims*	*Ratio A/E*	*Expected claims*	*Actual claims*	*Ratio A/E*
35–45	$1,000,000	$ 500,000	50%	$1,500,000	$ 750,000	50%
45–55	$2,000,000	$1,300,000	65%	$1,500,000	$ 975,000	65%
Totals	$3,000,000	$1,800,000	60%	$3,000,000	$1,725,000	57.5%

cell, while their overall ratios may differ. This simplified but realistic example shows that the two hypothetical companies have overall mortality ratios of 60% and 57.5%, respectively, although the cell-by-cell analysis reveals that no differences in actual-to-expected mortality exist. This apparent paradox is explained by the differences in the policy mix by age groups in the two companies.

CONFIDENCE INTERVALS

Even though many millions of life-years of exposure may be contributed to a mortality study, a measurable amount of statistical error will persist. The lives involved in the study represent only a sample of the population which is under investigation. It is therefore of significant importance that the actuary be able to quantify the degree of confidence which can be placed in the resulting rates or ratios. Such analysis is possible through the application of elementary statistical theory.

A study producing mortality rates or ratios usually is of such magnitude that the assumption that they are normally distributed is considered to be realistic. We shall consider rates or ratios to be normally distributed if there are at least 35 observed deaths within a given cell. If fewer than 35 deaths are observed, a Poisson distribution is usually assumed. Let us consider the case in which mortality rates are obtained for cells in which more than 35 deaths are observed.

The following derivation of the standard deviation for the distribution of q_x is based upon the assumption of a binomial distribution. The student will recall that the variance of a binomial sample proportion of successes with n trials and with p and q the respective probabilities of success and failure is pq/n. Assuming that $p = 1$, generally a reasonably close approximation, and treating the observed exposure E_x as the number of trials, we have

$$\text{VAR}(q_x) \doteq \frac{q_x}{E_x}$$

$$\doteq \frac{(q_x)^2}{\theta_x}.$$

Finally, the desired standard deviation, σ, approximately equals

$$\frac{q_x}{\sqrt{\theta_x}}.$$

Thus, for example, a 95% confidence interval for the true value of q_x would be approximately

$$\left(q_x - \frac{2 \cdot q_x}{\sqrt{\theta_x}}, \; q_x + \frac{2 \cdot q_x}{\sqrt{\theta_x}}\right).$$

Similarly, the true value of q_x would be expected to fall in the interval

$$\left(q_x - \frac{(\frac{2}{3})q_x}{\sqrt{\theta_x}},\ q_x + \frac{(\frac{2}{3})q_x}{\sqrt{\theta_x}}\right)$$

about half of the time. Reference to a table detailing the areas under certain portions of the normal curve produces bounds on any other confidence intervals which may be desired.

When dealing with the calculation of mortality ratios, the mathematical procedure for obtaining confidence limits is quite similar. The standard deviation of the distribution of mortality ratios (M.R.), approximately

$$\frac{\text{M.R.}}{\sqrt{\theta_x}},$$

should be verified by the student, using a technique similar to that used with the mortality rate. Confidence intervals are found similarly, again based upon the assumption of having more than 35 observed deaths in the cell for which the ratio is determined.

EXAMPLE 7-1   The number of units of exposure for a given age cell is found to be 10,000. A standard table, upon which mortality ratios are to be based, indicates a mortality rate for that cell of .030. The number of observed deaths for the cell is 225. Determine a 95% confidence interval for the true mortality ratio and the true mortality rate.

SOLUTION   The "expected deaths" from the standard table are easily seen to number 300 (10,000 × .030). The resulting estimate of the mortality ratio is thus 225/300 = .75. The estimated standard deviation for the distribution is $.75/\sqrt{225} = .05$. The 95% confidence interval is that interval, centered about the observed ratio, which contains two standard deviations on either side of this ratio. Thus, we have

$$(.65, .85)$$

as the desired interval.

The observed mortality rate for the cell in question is (225/10,000), or .0225. The associated standard deviation is $.0225/\sqrt{225} = .0015$. The resulting 95% confidence interval is thus

$$(.0195, .0255).$$

It is significant to note that the two answers obtained are consistent. That is, the extremes of each confidence interval indicate a range of between 195 and 255 deaths. This is easily verified, as a mortality ratio of .65 corresponds to 195 deaths, as does a mortality rate of .0195. Similarly, a mortality ratio of .85 and a mortality rate of .0255 both correspond to 255 deaths.

In cases in which fewer than 35 deaths are observed within a given cell, the nonsymmetric Poisson distribution is generally taken as the basis for the determination of confidence limits. However, the complexity involved in producing such limits exceeds that involved in the simpler case in which the normal distribution is assumed. In addition, the width of typical confidence intervals is relatively great. For example, with 15 observed deaths and an observed mortality ratio of 150%, a 95% Poisson confidence interval has lower and upper limits of 84% and 248%, respectively. Due to the fact that most mortality investigations are extensive, permitting use of the normal distribution, no further consideration will be given here to theory or examples arising from the Poisson assumption.

SUMMARY

Any scientific investigation, in order to qualify as a work of distinction and quality, must embody both the theoretical and the practical. Mortality studies are no exception. In fact, this generalization seems especially applicable to such studies.

Mortality investigations demand great care in the areas of preliminary planning, mechanical execution, and ultimate evaluation. Each of these aspects has been given consideration at various stages of this final chapter. Yet the actuary must be ever-cognizant of the subjectivity of most of the decisions which are required. Seldom will the planning or evaluation stages of the study be routine; often the actuary must depend on his developed skills and powers of reasoning to a much greater extent than on his technical background. The considerations which have been enumerated in this chapter should be treated as general guidelines rather than as an exhaustive list of practical aspects essential to every mortality investigation.

EXERCISES

1. As compared to an anniversary-to-anniversary observation period, which, if any, of the following statements is (are) true with respect to a calendar year observation period for a study of mortality among a company's insured lives?
   (i) The effects of seasonal fluctuations in the volume of issues are less severe.
   (ii) The exposure formulas are not so elaborate.
   (iii) The results are more closely related to the other aspects of the company's financial experience.
2. Which, if any, of the following statements is (are) true when *amounts* are the unit of investigation for a study of mortality among insured lives?

   (i) The results are usually more heavily influenced by antiselection than is the case when policies are the unit of investigation.

  (ii) Sometimes only a portion of the amount insured for a given person is included in the study.

 (iii) There are usually more pronounced accidental fluctuations resulting from deaths of certain insured persons than is the case when lives are the unit.

3. Which, if any, of the following statements is (are) true when *selection units* are the unit of investigation for a study of mortality among insured lives?

   (i) Sometimes only a portion of the unit for a given insured person is included in the study.

  (ii) The results are usually more heavily influenced by antiselection than is the case when policies are the unit.

 (iii) There are usually more pronounced accidental fluctuations resulting from deaths of certain insured persons than is the case when lives are the unit.

4. Which, if any, of the following statements is (are) true with respect to the need for homogeneity of mortality data which are to be graduated?

   (i) In the interest of homogeneity, the mortality rates of standard and substandard issues are usually studied separately.

  (ii) The data should not contain irregularities which are substantially the result of any nonhomogeneity in their composition.

 (iii) The various classes of risk included in the data should all have the same basic mortality pattern.

5. A select and ultimate mortality study with a three-year select period was conducted, combining all the ordinary business of your company for a recent observation period. For a typical age x, you find that $q_{[x]}$, $q_{[x-1]+1}$, and $q_{[x-2]+2}$ are all higher than q_x. Comment upon the validity of each of the following explanations proposed by an actuarial student:

  (a) There has been a marked increase in recent years in the proportion of business issued with only nonmedical evidence.

  (b) There has been a marked increase in recent years in the proportion of business resulting from term conversions.

  (c) There has been a marked increase in recent years in the proportion of business issued to females.

6. Discuss the advantages and disadvantages of an observation period from January 1, 1970 through December 31, 1975 for a study of mortality of standard ordinary issues of a large insurer. Consider the *length, timing,* and *type* of the period in your answer.

7. As the actuary of Company A, you have completed a mortality study of your company's individual life insurance policies. The study covered the

year 1974, and the ratio of actual to expected mortality was 110%, based on the 1965–1970 Select and Ultimate Basic Tables. Company B is similar to your company in age, assets, product mix, and annual sales volume. Company B has reported a 1974 mortality ratio for its individual life insurance policies of 90%, based upon the same tables. The president of your company has asked you if these ratios are a valid indication of the relative mortality experienced by the two companies. Outline your reply.

8. Comment briefly upon at least 11 factors which must be considered in the critical evaluation of a mortality investigation.

9. What is the approximate probability that the *true* mortality rate differs from the calculated rate q_x by more than the quantity

$$\sqrt{\frac{q_x(1 - q_x)}{E_x}}?$$

10. The lower limit of the 50% confidence interval for an observed mortality ratio is $\frac{56}{45}$. Find the number of observed deaths if 50,000 units of exposure were contributed and the standard table mortality rate was 3 deaths per 1000.

11. A medium-sized company has been conducting a periodic mortality investigation of experience under its standard ordinary policies. A study is made every three years based upon the experience of the preceding calendar year. Results are obtained by policy year for quinquennial issue age groups and for males and females separately. The unit of investigation is selection units. The study makes use of specially prepared and maintained punched card records which show selection unit code, name, date of birth, date of issue, sex, plan, amount of insurance, and date and type of termination. What are the advantages and disadvantages of this program? What changes could be considered, and what are the advantages and disadvantages of such changes?

12. Verify that the standard deviation of a mortality ratio, M.R., is approximately equal to

$$\frac{\text{M.R.}}{\sqrt{\theta_x}}$$

using a reasonable set of assumptions.

Instructions for Annual Study of Mortality Under Standard Ordinary Issues Experience Between 1975 and 1976 Anniversaries*

This year the Committee's annual study of mortality on standard ordinary insurance covers the experience between 1975 and 1976 policy anniversaries. The study is to be carried out on a 15 year select and ultimate basis, by amounts of insurance, in accordance with the following instructions.

I. GENERAL INSTRUCTIONS

A. The data to be submitted will consist of four parts:

1. Recent medical issues (policy years 1–15) on a select basis.
2. Recent non-medical issues (policy years 1–15) on a select basis.
3. Recent paramedical issues (policy years 1–15) on a select basis.
4. Policy years 16 and later, on an ultimate basis. Companies which are able to do so are requested to subdivide this portion of the data in the manner described in Section II.B below.

Age is defined as the age at issue for the select contribution, and the age on the 1975 anniversary for the ultimate contribution. If your company has changed to the age last birthday basis, please indicate in your letter of transmittal which years of issue are on this basis.

B. The following classes of policies should be excluded. If it is not feasible to do so, please inform the Committee in the letter of transmittal accompanying your company's contribution which of them are included. In addition, if the maximum mortality rating permitted for standard insurance in your company varies with age, please state the mortality rating applicable to different ages.

---

* Society of Actuaries, Committee on Mortality Under Ordinary Insurance and Annuities, Boston (March 18, 1977).

1. Policies not subject to the company's usual underwriting standards, e.g.:
   a. group conversions;
   b. term conversions and renewals, unless handled in accordance with C4 below;
   c. family policy conversions on dependents;
   d. policies issued as a result of exercise of an option under a guaranteed insurability rider;
   e. policies issued on a "guaranteed issue" basis (such as certain pension trust business);
   f. policies subject to a simplified underwriting or issued up to a mortality limit higher than is customarily used by the company for standard ordinary insurance.
2. **Substandard policies.**
3. Policies in force under extended term insurance or reduced paid-up provisions.
4. Experience on wives and children insured under family policies.
5. Joint Life policies.
6. Reinsurance assumed.
7. Policies issued in Canada (if possible).

Reinsurance ceded should be included.

C. The recommended practice for certain policies is indicated below. Please describe any variations from this recommended practice in the letter of transmittal.

1. Suicide during the exclusion period:
Include in exposures for full amount and in claims for amount paid.
2. Compromised claims:
Same as 1.
3. Limited benefits under aviation exclusion clause:
Same as 1.
4. Term conversions and renewals:
Consider as issued on issue date of original term policy. If unable to treat in this manner, these policies should be excluded.
5. Policies for increasing or decreasing amounts; e.g., family income policies:
The amounts appearing in exposures and claims must be consistent. An equivalent level amount may be used in both cases.
6. Policies with graded death benefits issued to juveniles:
Include for full face amount in both exposures and claims.

D. Delayed Claims. Any deaths in policy years 1–15 which occurred prior to the 1975 anniversary, but owing to delay in reporting were not included in prior contributions, should be included this year at the correct issue age and policy year of death. The issue year should be adjusted so that the issue year plus policy year of death equals 1976. The policy year of death should be calculated on the basis of the actual date of death rather than on the date on which death was reported.

Similarly, any delayed claims in policy years 16 and later should be included at the correct attained age, i.e., the attained age nearest birthday at the policy anniversary preceding death.

II. INSTRUCTIONS FOR COMPLETION OF SUMMARY CARDS FOR EXPOSURES, ACTUAL CLAIMS, AND EXPECTED CLAIMS

A. Select mortality (policy years 1–15). A separate set of summary cards should be submitted for (1) medical issues, (2) non-medical issues and (3) paramedical issues. The data for each of these classes should include the exposures and actual claims by amounts of insurance on issues of 1961 through 1975, observed between 1975 and 1976 anniversaries.

The data should be reported in the following issue age groups:

0	20–24	50–54
1	25–29	55–59
2–4	30–34	60–64
5–9	35–39	65–69
10–14	40–44	70–74
15–19	45–49	75 and over

Companies which are in a position to submit their experience separately for male and female lives are requested to do so. If your company is unable to subdivide the data by sex, the combined data should be reported; in that case it is also requested that you furnish the Committee with figures showing the proportions (by amounts of insurance) of males and females in the standard issues of 1975 for each age group at issue, separately for medical and non-medical issues. These proportions may be based on the business issued in 1975 or on the exposures in 1975–1976 on 1975 issues, or they may be obtained by any other method which assures reasonably reliable results.

Companies which split their contribution by sex should calculate expected deaths on the 1965–1970 Male Select Basic Table for males and on the 1965–1970 Female Select Basic Table for females. Companies which do not split their contribution by sex should calculate expected deaths on the

1965–1970 Male and Female Combined Select Basic Table. (The 1965–1970 Tables are published in the 1973 Reports, p. 199 for age nearest birthday, or the 1974 Reports, p. 57 for age last birthday).

IBM card form 718668, to be completed in accordance with the instructions in Appendix A, should be used for transmitting the data. Check totals should be furnished as described in Appendix A. If readily available, it is requested that you report on the summary punch cards the number of policies terminated by death for each age group at issue and policy year duration combination entering into your company's contribution to this study.

If your company changed its non-medical rules during 1975, please advise the Committee and describe the changes.

B. Ultimate mortality (policy years 16 and later). This year's contribution should cover exposures and actual claims by amounts of insurance on issues of 1960 and earlier, observed between 1975 and 1976 policy anniversaries. Data should be reported for attained ages 15 through 100, on an individual attained age basis.

Companies which are in a position to submit their experience separately for male and female lives are requested to do so. Companies unable to subdivide their contribution by sex should report the combined data.

If possible, the data should be divided into the experience on

a. Premium-paying policies, and
b. Policies fully paid-up by their terms.

If you cannot furnish data on this basis, your contribution should be submitted without the split between premium-paying and fully paid-up policies.

Companies which are in a position to do so are also requested to subdivide their data on premium-paying business (or all their ultimate data if not split between premium-paying and fully paid-up) into (1) medical issues and (2) non-medical issues. If your company is unable to subdivide the data in this manner, the combined data should be reported as in the past.

Companies which split their contribution by sex should calculate expected deaths on the 1965–1970 Male Ultimate Basic Table for males and on the 1965–1970 Female Ultimate Basic Table for females. Companies which do not split their contribution by sex should calculate expected deaths on the 1965–1970 Male and Female Combined Ultimate Basic Table. (The 1965–1970 Tables are published in the 1973 Reports, p. 199 for age nearest birthday, or the 1974 Reports, p. 57 for age last birthday).

Data should be transmitted on IBM card form 718668, completed in accordance with the instructions in Appendix A, with check totals. If readily available, it is requested that you report on the summary punch cards the number of policies terminated by death for each attained age.

III. INSTRUCTIONS FOR COMPLETION OF WAR
DEATH SUMMARY CARDS

To complete the Committee's record of claims paid as a result of the Vietnam war, you are requested to furnish summary punch cards (using IBM card form 718668) for the number of policies and amounts of insurance paid as death claims due to the operations of war. This should be done for each age group at issue and policy year duration combination entering into your company's contribution to the experience between 1975 and 1976 anniversaries in (1) the Recent Medical Issues Study, (2) the Recent Non-medical Issues Study, (3) the Recent Paramedical Issue Study, and (4) for each attained age entering into your company's contribution to the experience between 1975 and 1976 anniversaries in the Study of Ultimate Mortality. These cards are to be coded in accordance with the instructions in Appendix A, except that (1) columns 20–31 (Exposed) and 54–63 (Expected Deaths) are not to be punched, (2) the number of policies and amounts of insurance paid as a result of war deaths are to be punched in columns 32–46, and (3) X is to be punched in column 76. The experience control numbers punched in columns 78–80 should be those of the respective studies in which the war deaths are included.

The war deaths to be reported are identified by the 1970 Committee Code 99. In coding for war deaths some companies may refer to the Report of Casualty form furnished by the various Armed Forces. Item 2 of this form has two boxes to indicate whether death arose in "battle" or in "non-battle." In addition to all "battle" deaths, it should be noted that many (but not all) "non-battle" deaths should be coded 99. For example, a death arising after battle, but due to burns received in battle, may be coded by the Government as a "non-battle" death. In cases like this, a review of the comments given in Item 2 is necessary to determine the full facts and whether death was due to the operations of war and hence a code 99.

Questions may arise with regard to the coding of military service deaths outside of the combat area which may nevertheless be attributable to the Vietnam operation. For example, a plane on the way to Vietnam may crash far outside the Vietnam area or a death in Japan may be the result of activity for the benefit of the Vietnam engagement. Such deaths should be treated as due to the operations of war, and coded 99.

Military service deaths which cannot be tied in with the Vietnam engagement should not be treated as due to operations of war. For example, the Committee's Code 89 would apply to a death resulting from a plane crash in Germany. Deaths occurring in the United States and Canada, not tied in with the Vietnam engagement, should also be assumed as not due to war.

Due to the relatively low death rate from disease among troops in Vietnam, no deaths from disease should be considered as war deaths.

Cases will no doubt arise which will be difficult to classify; the Committee would like to depend on the judgment of the individual companies on the coding of such cases, but will be receptive to questions covering specific situations.

IV. INSTRUCTIONS FOR COMPLETION OF CAUSE OF DEATH SUMMARY CARDS

Cause of death data for the death claims during policy year 1975–1976 are requested separately for (1) medical issues in policy years 1–15, (2) non-medical issues in policy years 1–15, (3) paramedical issues in policy years 1–15, and (4) issues in policy years 16 and later, subdivided as explained below. Data should be reported in the issue age, duration, and attained age groups defined in Appendix B.

Companies which can furnish cause of death data separately for male and female lives are requested to do so, even if they are unable to furnish summaries for exposures, actual claims and expected claims subdivided by sex. Except for this, the subdivision of the deaths for compilation by cause of death should correspond to the subdivision of the exposures. If the ultimate mortality experience is not subdivided into premium-paying policies and policies fully paid-up by their terms, or if ultimate premium-paying policies are not subdivided into medical and non-medical issues, these subdivisions should not be made for the cause of death data.

The data should be transmitted on IBM card form 718668, completed in accordance with the instructions in Appendix B. Check totals should be furnished as described in Appendix B; these totals should agree with the corresponding totals reported with the summary cards referred to in II above.

V. INSTRUCTIONS FOR COMPLETION OF INDIVIDUAL DEATH CLAIM CARDS FOR CLAIMS OF $100,000 AND OVER

In order to aid the Committee in analyzing the study results, companies are requested to submit data for any death claims where the amount reported under one policy, or the total amount reported for several policies issued at the same time on one individual, is $100,000 or more. An individual death claim card should be prepared for each such claim, using IBM card form 725178, in accordance with the instructions in Appendix C. The classification of these claims should correspond to the subdivision of the exposures. Any delayed claims should be reported at the ages and durations described in Section I.D.

A listing of these claim cards, if any, should be included with your company's contribution. If no such claims occurred, please indicate this in the letter of transmittal.

All columns of the summary cards which are part of a field should be punched; if any such column would otherwise be blank, a zero should be punched. The only blanks in the cards should be those columns which are not part of any field.

The work of the Committee would be simplified greatly if each company *reviewed* its contribution *carefully* before submitting it, making sure that all fields in the transmittal cards are punched *according to the specifications* given in the Appendices. The XX (numeric) punches are one example where care is needed. Also, please be sure that the transmittal cards balance with the check totals requested in Appendices A and B. In the past the check totals and transmittal cards have not balanced. This can occur if the contributing company uses a set of work cards to establish the check totals and a punch is omitted in reproducing transmittal cards from the work cards. Please make every effort to prevent this from occurring.

Answers

CHAPTER ONE

1. $\frac{18}{203}$
2. $\frac{1}{97}$
3. $\frac{2}{39}$
4. Balducci
6. $\frac{1}{133}$

7. $\dfrac{q_x}{1 - q_x}$

8. $\frac{1}{26}$
9. $746\frac{2}{3}$
10. $_{1/2|1/2}q_x$
11. $\frac{19}{27}$
12. (a) $1 - e^{-.004}$
    (b) $1 - e^{-.001}$
    (c) $1 - e^{-.0005}$
13. $\frac{3}{8}$
14. $\frac{1}{19}$
15. $\frac{1}{98}$
16. (a) .015
    (b) $\frac{3}{199}$
    (c) $\frac{1}{33}$
17. $\frac{1}{1999}$

18. $\dfrac{k}{1 - 4k}$

19. (a) 12
    (b) 11.95

20. (a) $\frac{4}{197}$
    (b) $\frac{4}{205}$
    (c) .0199
21. (a) Uniform deaths (UDD)
    (b) Balducci: $\frac{1}{13}$
       UDD: $\frac{2}{25}$
    (c) $[x - \frac{1}{4}, x + \frac{3}{4}]$
22. (a) $\frac{6}{98}$
    (b) $\frac{20}{341}$
23. (a) $\frac{1}{97}$, $\frac{43}{1067}$
    (c) $_{1/4}q_{35\frac{1}{4}} < {}_{1/4}q_{36\frac{1}{4}} < {}_{1/4}q_{36\frac{1}{4}} = {}_{1/4}q_{36}$
24. (a) $\frac{97}{99}$
    (b) $\frac{95}{97}$
    (c) $\frac{937}{958}$
    (d) $\frac{979}{1000}$
25. (a) 4620
    (b) 5040
26. $\frac{1}{3}$
27. $\frac{1}{12}(q_x)^3$

CHAPTER TWO

4. $\frac{1}{4}$
5. $\frac{17}{30}$
6. $\frac{1}{70}$
7. (a) March 31, 1975
    (b) March 31, 1976
    (c) March 31, 1976
8. (a) .020000
    (b) .020004˙
    (c) .020002
9. (a) 23, 45, 61, 12, and 53 months
    (b) 23, 39, 55, 6, and 53 months
10. μ_{x+k}
11. 12, 8, 12, 1, 7, and 0 months
12. $10\frac{1}{2}$, 6, and $6\frac{1}{2}$ months
13. (a) $\frac{3}{4}$, 0
    (b) 1, 0
    (c) 1, 0
    (d) 1, 1
14. $\frac{1}{4}$
15. 918

16. A: $1, \frac{1}{2}$
    B: $1, 1$
    C: $\frac{1}{3}, \frac{1}{6}$
    D: $\frac{2}{3}, 0$
    E: $\frac{1}{3}, 0$
17. A: $1, \frac{1}{2}$
    B: $1, 1$
    C: $\frac{1}{3}, 0$
    D: $\frac{2}{3}, \frac{1}{3}$
    E: $\frac{1}{3}, 0$

CHAPTER THREE

1. (a) 27, 26, 25, 26, 26
   (b) 27, 26, 25, 26, 27
   (c) 27, 25, 25, 26, 26
2. $x - \frac{1}{12}$
3. Births April 1
4. Births September 1, starting date January 1, 1975;
   Births August 1, starting date December 1, 1974
5. Births September 1, migration September 1;
   Births July 1, migration July 1
6. (a) $\theta_x\Big]_{x-(1/2)}^{x+(1/2)}$;   (b) $\theta_x\Big]_{x-(5/12)}^{x+(7/12)}$;   (c) $\theta_x\Big]_{x-(11/12)}^{x+(1/12)}$;   (d) $\theta_x\Big]_{x-(1/6)}^{x+(5/6)}$;

   (e) $\theta_x\Big]_{x-1}^{x}$

7. (a) $\theta_x\Big]_{x-(1/3)}^{x+(2/3)}$;   (b) $\theta_x\Big]_{x-(1/4)}^{x+(3/4)}$;   (c) $\theta_x\Big]_{x-(3/4)}^{x+(1/4)}$;   (d) $\theta_x\Big]_{x}^{x+1}$;

   (e) $\theta_x\Big]_{x-1}^{x}$

8. (a) $s_x^{x-(1/12)}$;   (b) $s_x^{x-(1/3)}$;   (c) $s_x^{x+(1/2)}$;   (d) $s_x^{x-(5/6)}$;   (e) $s_x^{x+3\frac{1}{3}}$;
   (f) s_x^{x};   (g) s_x^{x-1}
9. (a) $s_x^{x+(1/4)}$;   (b) s_x^{x};   (c) $s_x^{x+(5/6)}$;   (d) $s_x^{x-(1/2)}$;   (e) $s_x^{x+3\frac{2}{3}}$;
   (f) s_x^{x};   (g) s_x^{x-1}
10. $\theta_x\Big]_{x-(11/24)}^{x+(13/24)}$; $s_x^{x+(17/24)}$; $w_x^{x+(1/24)}$ (assumed on July 1); $e_x^{x+(17/24)}$
11. $\theta_x\Big]_{x+(5/12)}^{x+(17/12)}$; $s_x^{x-(1/6)}$; $n_x^{x+(1/12)}$; $w_x^{x-(11/12)}$; $e_x^{x+(7/6)}$ (births on July 1;
    migration on nearest August 1)

25. $q_{[40]} = \dfrac{10}{12{,}472}$; $q_{[40]+1} = \dfrac{10}{10{,}362}$; $q_{[40]+2} = \dfrac{10}{8362}$; $q_{[40]+3} = \dfrac{10}{6672}$;

$q_{[40]+4} = \dfrac{10}{4992}$; $q_{[40]+5} = \dfrac{10}{3422}$; $q_{[40]+6} = \dfrac{10}{2162}$; $q_{[40]+7} = \dfrac{10}{912}$;

$q_{[40]+8} = \dfrac{2}{2}$

26. (a) F_9
   (b) n
   (c) f_0
   (d) E_8

27. $E_x = \displaystyle\sum_{y=a}^{x-1} j_y - \tfrac{1}{6} \cdot s_{x-1} - e_x - \tfrac{1}{6} \cdot e_{x+1} + n_x + \tfrac{1}{2} \cdot n_{x+1} - \tfrac{1}{6} \cdot w_x$ (assume issues on July 1 and uniform withdrawals)

28. (a) $E_t = \displaystyle\sum_{y=a}^{t-1} j_y + \tfrac{1}{2} \cdot (s_t - w_t - e_t)$

   (b) $q_{[x]+(1/2)} = \dfrac{20}{512}$; $q_{[x]+(3/2)} = \dfrac{13}{1513}$; $q_{[x]+(5/2)} = \dfrac{15}{2459}$;

$q_{[x]+(7/2)} = \dfrac{12}{2405\frac{1}{2}}$; $q_{[x]+(9/2)} = \dfrac{20}{1402\frac{1}{2}}$; $q_{[x]+(11/2)} = \dfrac{10}{445}$

   (c) $\dfrac{20}{1392\frac{1}{2}}$

29. $q_{[x]} = \dfrac{5}{2600}$; $q_{[x]+1} = \dfrac{6}{1950}$; $q_{[x]+2} = \dfrac{7}{1550}$; $q_{[x]+3} = \dfrac{5}{1250}$; $q_{[x]+4} = \dfrac{4}{550}$

30. $q_{[45]} = \dfrac{1}{13}$; $q_{[45]+1} = \dfrac{0}{12}$; $q_{[45]+2} = \dfrac{0}{13}$; $q_{[45]+3} = \dfrac{1}{15}$; $q_{[45]+4} = \dfrac{0}{11}$;

$q_{[45]+5} = \dfrac{1}{6}$; $q_{[45]+6} = \dfrac{1}{6}$; $q_{[45]+7} = \dfrac{0}{3}$; $q_{[45]+8} = \dfrac{0}{1}$

31. (a) $E_t = \displaystyle\sum_{y=0}^{t-1} j_y + \tfrac{1}{2} \cdot s_t + n_t - w_t - \tfrac{1}{2} \cdot e_t$;

   Based on
$$s_t : t = 1969 - \text{CYI},$$
$$n_t : t = \text{CYN} - \text{CYI} \qquad (\text{conversions}),$$
$$w_t : t = \text{CYW} - \text{CYI},$$
$$e_t : t = 1976 - \text{CYI},$$
$$\theta_t : t = \text{Curtate duration at death.}$$

   (b) $[35]$: $E_3 = E_4 = \tfrac{1}{2}$; $E_0 = E_1 = E_2 = E_5 = 0$;
$[45]$: $E_1 = E_3 = \tfrac{1}{2}$; $E_2 = 2$; $E_0 = E_4 = 0$

32. 1
33. $q_{x-(1/4)}$
34. (a) The definition of "fiscal year of event"
    (b) The terminal date of the fiscal year under which the organization is operating
35. $x - \frac{1}{4}$
36. $x - \frac{7}{6}$
37. FYB: Calendar year containing the September 30 following birth;
    FYD: Calendar year containing the September 30 preceding death
38. (a) $q_{x-(3/2)}$, approximately
    (b) $q_{x-(5/4)}$
39. (a) Definition of fiscal year of event; average birthday within any calendar year; choice of T
    (b) Numerous possibilities, e.g., FYD = Calendar year containing the August 31 preceding death, births on July 1
40. (a) Definition of fiscal year of birth; choice of T
    (b) Most reasonable choice: FYB = Calendar year containing the April 30 following birth
41. (a) FYB: calendar year containing the June 1 following birth
    (b) $\theta_x : x =$ Calendar year containing the June 1 preceding death $-$ FYB;
    $s_x : x = 1972 - $ FYB;
    $n_x : x =$ Calendar year containing the June 1 preceding entry $-$ FYB;
    $w_x : x =$ Calendar year containing the June 1 following withdrawal $-$ FYB;
    $e_x : x = 1977 - $ FYB;

    $$\theta_x \Big]_x^{x+1}, \quad s_x^{x-(1/4)}, \quad n_x^{x+(1/2)}, \quad w_x^{x-(1/2)}, \quad \text{and} \quad e_x^{x+(3/4)}.$$

    Note: "Convenient" f-factors are not possible to obtain.

    (c) $\dfrac{\theta_x}{E_x} = q_x^F \doteq q_{x+(1/2)}$

    (d) $E_x = \displaystyle\sum_{y=a}^{x-1} j_y + s_x + \frac{1}{4} \cdot s_{x+1} + \frac{1}{2} \cdot n_x - w_x - \frac{1}{2} \cdot w_{x+1} - \frac{1}{4} \cdot e_x$

42. $x - 2\frac{1}{2}$
43. (a) 1954; 1955

    (b) $E_x = \displaystyle\sum_{y=a}^{x-1} j_y + \frac{1}{2}(n_x - w_x)$

    (c) 18 months
    (d) 17 months

CHAPTER FIVE

1. $\frac{1}{2}(P_{x-1}^z + P_x^{z+1} + D_{x\backslash}^z)$

2. $a_1 + a_2 = \frac{7}{12}$

3. $\dfrac{\displaystyle\sum_{z=1974}^{1977} D_x^{z\backslash z+1}}{\displaystyle\sum_{z=1974}^{1977} (F_x^z + {}_\alpha D_x^z)}$

4. Births on September 1; α-migration on November 1; δ-migration on May 1.

5. $\frac{9}{4}$

6. (a) P: Uniform deaths; migration on birthdays;
   Q: Balducci; migration at end points of calendar year;
   R: Balducci; migration on birthdays;
   S: Uniform deaths; migration at end points of calendar year
   (b) $419\frac{1}{2}$

7. 12

8. (a) $q_{23\frac{1}{2}} = \dfrac{36}{5618}$; $q_{24\frac{1}{2}} = \dfrac{72}{10,736}$; $q_{25\frac{1}{2}} = \dfrac{72}{10,336}$; $q_{26\frac{1}{2}} = \dfrac{36}{5118}$;

   (b) $q_{24} = \dfrac{36}{5620}$; $q_{25} = \dfrac{72}{10,540}$; $q_{26} = \dfrac{72}{10,340}$; $q_{27} = \dfrac{36}{5020}$

   Assumptions: Births and migration July 1; Balducci

9. (a) $\frac{15}{1606}$
   (b) March 1
   (c) March 1

10. $\displaystyle\sum_{z=1975}^{1977} (\frac{1}{6} \cdot P_{x-1}^z + \frac{7}{12} \cdot E_x^z + \frac{1}{4} \cdot P_x^{z+1} + \frac{3}{4} \cdot {}_\delta D_{x-1}^z + \frac{1}{6} \cdot {}_\alpha D_x^z)$

11. $E_{30}\Big|_{30}^{31} = \frac{5}{16} \cdot E_{30}^{1976} + \frac{1}{2} \cdot P_{30}^{1977} + \frac{3}{16} \cdot E_{31}^{1977} + \frac{11}{16} \cdot {}_\alpha D_{30}^{1976}$
    $\qquad\qquad + \frac{3}{16} \cdot {}_\delta D_{30}^{1977}$;

    Assumptions: α-Migration halfway between May 15 and December 31;
    δ-Migration halfway between January 1 and May 15;
    Balducci

12. (a) $q_{x-(1/2)} = \dfrac{D_{x\backslash}^z}{\frac{1}{2}(P_{x-1}^z + P_x^{z+1}) + {}_\alpha D_x^z}$

    (b) $q_{21\frac{1}{2}} = \frac{20}{498}$

13. $q_{[x]+(3/2)} = \frac{4}{1272}$; $q_{[x]+(5/2)} = \frac{14}{2587}$; $q_{[x]+(7/2)} = \frac{18}{3654}$; $q_{[x]+(9/2)} = \frac{18}{2399}$;

$q_{[x]+(11/2)} = \frac{10}{1055}$;

The Balducci hypothesis was assumed because α- and δ-breakdowns of deaths were not available.

14. (a) $E_x \Big]_x^{x+1} = P_x^{1975} + \frac{1}{3} \cdot D_x^{1974\backslash1975}$

    (b) $E_x \Big]_x^{x+1} = \frac{7}{12} \cdot E_x^{1975} + \frac{5}{12} \cdot E_{x+1}^{1975} + {}_\delta D_x^{1975}$

15. (a) $q_x = \dfrac{9}{101\frac{1}{3}}$

    (b) $q_x = \dfrac{9}{102\frac{1}{3}}$

16. (a) 1975
    (b) 2045
    (c) 1965
    (d) 2035

18. $_{1/2}q_{[x]} = \dfrac{{}_\alpha D_{[x]}^z}{n_{[x]}^z - \frac{1}{2} \cdot {}_\alpha w_{[x]}^z}$

20. (a) $E_x \Big]_x^{x+1} = \frac{2}{3} \cdot E_x^z + \frac{1}{3} \cdot E_{x+1}^z + \frac{1}{3} \cdot D_x^z$;

    (b) $q_{41}^l = .00035$

    (c) $q_{41} \doteq \frac{1}{2}(q_{40\frac{1}{2}} + q_{41\frac{1}{2}}) = \frac{1}{2}(q_{40}^l + q_{41}^l) = .0003$

21. $q_{45}^{(i)} = \dfrac{{}^{(i)}D_{45}^{1975}}{\frac{1}{2}(E_{45}^{1975} + E_{46}^{1975} + {}^{(i)}D_{45}^{1975})}$;

    Assumptions: Birthdays on July 1; no net migration; Balducci hypothesis; deaths due to causes other than (i) treated as withdrawals and placed at end points of 1975

22. $\dfrac{{}_\alpha D_x^z + {}_\delta D_x^z}{\frac{1}{4}(P_x^z + E_x^z + P_x^{z+1} + E_{x+1}^z) + \frac{3}{4} \cdot {}_\alpha D_x^z + \frac{1}{4} \cdot {}_\delta D_x^z}$;

    Assumptions: Births on July 1; α-migration on October 1; δ-migration on April 1; Balducci

23. (a) $E_x \Big]_{x-(2/3)}^{x+(1/3)} = \sum_{z=1975}^{1977} \frac{1}{2}(F_{x-1}^{z-1} + F_x^z + D_x^z\backslash)$;

    Assumptions: Migration on July 1; Balducci

(b) $q^F_{27\mathfrak{z}} = \tfrac{4}{507} \div q_{26\frac{5}{6}}; \ q^F_{28\mathfrak{z}} = \tfrac{10}{1140} \div q_{27\frac{5}{6}}; \ q^F_{29\mathfrak{z}} = \tfrac{16}{1783} \div q_{28\frac{5}{6}};$

$q^F_{30\mathfrak{z}} = \tfrac{18}{1859} \div q_{29\frac{5}{6}}; \ q^F_{31\mathfrak{z}} = \tfrac{12}{1226} \div q_{30\frac{5}{6}}; \ q^F_{32\mathfrak{z}} = \tfrac{6}{618} \div q_{31\frac{5}{6}}$

24. **Only Formula (d) is consistent with the migration assumptions necessitated by the statement of the problem.**

CHAPTER SIX

1. (a) $E_x \Big]^{x+1}_x = \sum\limits_{y=a}^{x-1} j_y + \tfrac{1}{4} \cdot s_x + \tfrac{2}{3} \cdot {}_am_x + \tfrac{1}{12} \cdot {}_\delta m_x - \tfrac{1}{4} \cdot e_x$

(b) $E_x \Big]^{x+1}_x = \tfrac{5}{12} \cdot P^z_x + \tfrac{7}{12} \cdot P^{z+1}_x + {}_aD^z_x$

2. (a) Migration on September 1; births on June 1;

$\theta_x : x = \text{CYD} - \text{CYB}; \qquad \theta_x \Big]^{x+(7/12)}_{x-(5/12)}$

$s_x : x = 1975 - \text{CYB}; \qquad s^{x+(7/12)}_x;$

$m_x : x = \text{CYM} - \text{CYB}; \qquad m^{x+(1/4)}_x;$

$e_x : x = 1977 - \text{CYB}; \qquad e^{x+(7/12)}_x$

(Note: Tabulation of migration by age last birthday is awkward because of the nature of the migration assumption).

(b) α-Migration on November 1; δ-migration on April 1; births on August 1;

$\theta_x : x = \text{Age last birthday}; \qquad \theta_x \Big]^{x+1}_x;$

$s_x : x = 1974 - \text{CYB}; \qquad s^{x+(5/12)}_x;$

${}_am_x : x = \text{Age last birthday}; \qquad {}_am^{x+(1/4)}_x;$

${}_\delta m_x : x = \text{Age last birthday}; \qquad {}_\delta m^{x+(2/3)}_x;$

$e_x : x = 1976 - \text{CYB}; \qquad e^{x+(5/12)}_x$

3. (a) Migration seven months after beginning of observation period;

$E = \tfrac{7}{12} \cdot s + \tfrac{5}{12} \cdot e + \tfrac{5}{12} \cdot \theta$

(b) a-Migration seven months after beginning of observation period; b-migration at end of unit age interval;

$E = \tfrac{7}{12} \cdot s + \tfrac{5}{12} \cdot g + \tfrac{5}{12} \cdot {}_a\theta$

(c) a-Migration two months after beginning of observation period; b-migration two months before end of observation period;

$E = s + \tfrac{5}{6} \cdot {}_am + \tfrac{1}{6} \cdot {}_bm$

4. (a) $E_x\Big]_x^{x+1} = \sum_{y=a}^{x-1} j_y + \frac{1}{2} \cdot s_x + {}_a m_x - \frac{1}{2} \cdot e_x$

   (b) $E_x\Big]_x^{x+1} = \sum_{y=a}^{x-1} j_y + s_x + {}_a m_x - e_x$

5. (a) $E_x\Big]_x^{x+1} = \sum_{y=a}^{x-1} j_y + s_x + \frac{2}{3} \cdot {}_a m_x + \frac{1}{6} \cdot {}_\delta m_x - e_x$

   (b) (i) 10 months
       (ii) 12 months
       (iii) 12 months
       (iv) 4 months

6. (a) $E_{40}\Big]_{39\frac{1}{2}}^{40\frac{1}{2}} = \sum_{z=1975}^{1976} \left(\frac{1}{3} \cdot P_{39}^z + \frac{1}{2} \cdot E_{40}^z + \frac{1}{6} \cdot P_{40}^{z+1} \right.$

$$+ \frac{2}{3} \cdot {}_\delta D_{39}^z + \frac{1}{6} \cdot {}_a D_{40}^z \Big)$$

$$= \sum_{y=a}^{39} j_y + s_{40} + \frac{1}{6} \cdot {}_a m_{40} - \frac{1}{3} \cdot {}_\delta m_{39}$$

   (b) $E_{40} = 1922\frac{1}{2}$

7. (a) $\theta_x : x = \text{CYD} - \text{CYB};$ $\theta_x\Big]_{x-(1/3)}^{x+(2/3)};$

   $s_x : x = 1975 - \text{CYB};$ $s_x^{x+(2/3)};$

   ${}_a m_x : x = \text{CYM} - \text{CYB};$ ${}_a m_x^{x+(5/12)};$

   ${}_\delta m_x : x = \text{CYM} - \text{CYB};$ ${}_\delta m_x^{x-(1/3)};$

   $e_x : x = 1978 - \text{CYB};$ $e_x^{x+(2/3)}$

   (b) $\sum_{z=1976}^{1978} \left(\frac{3}{4} \cdot E_{51}^z + \frac{1}{4} \cdot P_{51}^{z+1} + {}_\delta D_{51}^z + \frac{1}{4} \cdot {}_a D_{51}^z \right)$

   (c) $E_{51} = 2590\frac{3}{4}$

8. (a) $\overset{\bullet}{\theta}_x : x = \text{Insuring age last anniversary};$ $\theta_x\Big]_x^{x+1};$

   $s_x : x = 1975 - \text{VYB};$ $s_x^{x+(5/12)};$

   ${}_a m_x : x = \text{CYM} - \text{VYB};$ ${}_a m_x^{x+(1/4)};$

   ${}_\delta m_x : x = \text{CYM} - \text{VYB};$ ${}_\delta m_x^{x-(1/4)};$

   $e_x : x = 1977 - \text{VYB};$ $e_x^{x+(5/12)};$

   $E_x\Big]_x^{x+1} = \sum_{y=a}^{x-1} j_y + \frac{7}{12} \cdot (s_x - e_x) + \frac{3}{4} \cdot {}_a m_x + {}_\delta m_x + \frac{1}{4} \cdot {}_\delta m_{x+1}$

Note: Since data are not available separately for new entrants (issues) and withdrawals, both types of migration must be handled similarly rather than consistently with the August 1 issue assumption.

(b) $\left. E_x \right]_x^{x+1} = \sum\limits_{z=1976}^{1977} (\frac{1}{3} \cdot F_x^{z-1} + \frac{1}{4} \cdot E_{x+1}^z + \frac{1}{4} \cdot E_x^z + \frac{1}{6} \cdot F_x^z$

$\qquad\qquad + \frac{3}{4} \cdot {}_aD_x^z + \frac{1}{4} \cdot {}_\delta D_x^z)$

(c) $E_{20} = 262$

(d) $\frac{1}{4}$; $\frac{5}{12}$; 1; 0; impossible (the ordered pair cannot exist)

9. $\left. E_x \right]_x^{x+1} = \sum\limits_{y=a}^{x-1} j_y + \frac{1}{3} \cdot s_x + \frac{1}{2} \cdot {}_am_x + \frac{1}{6} \cdot {}_\delta m_x - \frac{1}{3} \cdot e_x$

$\qquad = \sum\limits_{z=1976}^{1977} (\frac{1}{2} \cdot E_x^z + \frac{1}{6} \cdot P_x^{z+1} + \frac{1}{6} \cdot P_x^z + \frac{1}{6} \cdot E_{x+1}^z$

$\qquad\qquad + \frac{1}{6} \cdot {}_\delta D_x^z + \frac{1}{2} \cdot {}_a D_x^z)$

$\qquad = 1413$

10. $\left. E_{30} \right]_{30}^{31} = \sum\limits_{y=a}^{29} j_y + \frac{2}{3} \cdot s_{30} + \frac{11}{12} \cdot {}_a m_{30} + {}_\delta m_{30} + \frac{1}{4} \cdot {}_\delta m_{31}$

$\qquad\qquad - \frac{2}{3} \cdot e_{30}$

$\qquad = \sum\limits_{z=1977}^{1978} (\frac{5}{12} \cdot P_{30}^z + \frac{3}{12} \cdot E_{31}^z + \frac{1}{12} \cdot E_{30}^z + \frac{3}{12} \cdot P_{30}^z$

$\qquad\qquad + \frac{11}{12} \cdot {}_a D_{30}^z + \frac{3}{12} \cdot {}_\delta D_{30}^z)$

$\qquad = 1770$

11. $\left. E_x \right]_x^{x+1} = \sum\limits_{1975}^{1976} (\frac{5}{12} \cdot E_x^z + \frac{3}{12} \cdot P_x^{z+1} + \frac{1}{12} \cdot P_x^z + \frac{3}{12} \cdot E_{x+1}^z$

$\qquad\qquad + \frac{3}{12} \cdot {}_\delta D_x^z + \frac{7}{12} \cdot {}_a D_x^z)$

$\qquad = \sum\limits_{y=a}^{x-1} j_y + \frac{1}{3} \cdot s_x + \frac{7}{12} \cdot {}_a m_x + \frac{1}{4} \cdot {}_\delta m_x - \frac{1}{3} \cdot e_x$

$\qquad = 1074$

12. $\left. E_x \right]_x^{x+1} = \sum\limits_{z=1976}^{1977} (\frac{1}{4} \cdot E_x^z + \frac{3}{8} \cdot P_x^{z+1} + \frac{3}{8} \cdot E_{x+1}^z + \frac{3}{4} \cdot {}_a D_x^z$

$\qquad\qquad + \frac{3}{8} \cdot {}_\delta D_x^z)$

$\qquad = \sum\limits_{y=a}^{x-1} j_y + s_x + \frac{3}{8} \cdot s_{x+1} - \frac{3}{8} \cdot e_x + {}_\delta m_x + \frac{3}{8} \cdot {}_\delta m_{x+1}$

$\qquad\qquad + {}_a m_{x+1} + \frac{3}{4} \cdot {}_\delta m_{x+1}$

$\qquad = 1131\frac{1}{4}$

13. (a) $\theta_x : x = $ Age last birthday at death;

   $s_x : x = 1976 - $ CYB;

   $_a m_x : x = $ **CYB** (Assumed on Nov. 1);

   $_\delta m_x : x = $ **CYB** (Assumed on May 1);

   $e_x : x = 1978 - $ CYB;

$$E_x = \sum_{y=a}^{x-1} j_y + \tfrac{2}{3} \cdot s_x + \tfrac{5}{6} \cdot _a m_x + _\delta m_x + \tfrac{1}{3} \cdot _\delta m_{x+1} - \tfrac{2}{3} \cdot e_x$$

(b) $E_x \Big]_x^{x+1} = \sum_{z=1976}^{1977} (\tfrac{1}{3} \cdot P_x^z + \tfrac{1}{3} \cdot E_{x+1}^z + \tfrac{1}{6} \cdot P_x^{z+1} + \tfrac{1}{6} \cdot E_x^z$

$\qquad\qquad + \tfrac{5}{6} \cdot _a D_x^z + \tfrac{1}{3} \cdot _\delta D_x^z)$

(c) $E_{40} = 1185$

14. (a) $E_x \Big]_{x-(1/3)}^{x+(2/3)} = \sum_{y=a}^{x-1} j_y + \tfrac{2}{3}(m_x - e_x);$

   $E_{27} = 1640; \; E_{28} = 3030; \; E_{29} = 3428; \; E_{30} = 1845; \; E_{31} = 446$

(b) $E_{27} = \tfrac{1}{3}(1700) + \tfrac{2}{3}(1540) + \tfrac{2}{3}(70) = 1640;$

   $E_{28} = \tfrac{1}{3}(1650 + 1540) + \tfrac{2}{3}(1510 + 1320) + \tfrac{2}{3}(120) = 3030;$

   $E_{29} = \tfrac{1}{3}(1600 + 1510 + 1320) + \tfrac{2}{3}(1465 + 1330) + \tfrac{2}{3}(132) = 3428;$

   $E_{30} = \tfrac{1}{3}(1465 + 1330) + \tfrac{2}{3}(1320) + \tfrac{2}{3}(45 + 5) = 1845;$

   $E_{31} = \tfrac{1}{3}(1320) + \tfrac{2}{3}(9) = 446;$

15. $E_{18} = 1085; \; E_{19} = 2149\tfrac{1}{2}; \; E_{20} = 3183\tfrac{1}{2}; \; E_{21} = 3225; \; E_{22} = 2139\tfrac{1}{2};$
   $E_{23} = 1059\tfrac{1}{2}$

16. (a) $E_t \Big]_t^{t+1} = \sum_{z=1976}^{1977} (\tfrac{5}{12} \cdot E_t^z + \tfrac{5}{12} \cdot P_t^{z+\frac{1}{6}} + \tfrac{7}{12} \cdot E_{t+1}^z + \tfrac{7}{12} \cdot _a D_t^z + \tfrac{1}{6} \cdot$

   $_\delta D^{z+1})$

(b) $q_{[x]+t} = \dfrac{28}{2650\tfrac{1}{6}}$

17. (a) $E_x \Big]_{x-(1/4)}^{x+(3/4)} = \tfrac{1}{2} \cdot \sum_{z=1973}^{1977} (P_{x-1}^z + P_x^{z+1} + D_{x\backslash}^z)$

   $\qquad\qquad = \sum_{y=a}^{x-1} j_y + s_x + \tfrac{1}{2}(n_x - w_x)$

(b) (i) $\tfrac{1}{2}$; (ii) 0; (iii) $\tfrac{1}{2}$; (iv) $\tfrac{1}{2}$

CHAPTER SEVEN

9. $\tfrac{1}{3}$

10. 196